Olivia Laing is a widely acclaimed writer and critic. Her work appears in numerous publications, including the *Guardian*, *Observer*, *New Statesman*, *Frieze* and *New York Times*. She's a Yaddo and MacDowell Fellow and was 2014 Eccles Writer in Residence at the British Library. *To the River* was shortlisted for the Royal Society of Literature Ondaatje Prize and the Dolman Travel Book of the Year. Her second book, *The Trip to Echo Spring* was shortlisted for the 2013 Costa Biography Award and the 2014 Gordon Burn Prize, and *The Lonely City* has been shortlisted for the 2016 Gordon Burn Prize. She lives in Cambridge.

'A beautifully written, elegant and subtle debut'
Financial Times

'Wonderfully allusive . . .The book's subject and structure fuse pleasingly, weaving and meandering, pooling into biographical, mythical or historical backwaters'
Observer

'Without wanting to sound gushing, her writing at its sublime best reminds me of Richard Mabey's nature prose and the poetry of Alice Oswald . . . Laing seems to lack a layer of skin, rendering her susceptible to the smallest vibrations of the natural world as well as to the frailties of the human psyche' *The Times*

'Has a Sebaldian edge to it that lifts it out of memoir and biography and into something far more tantalizing and suggestive'
Guardian

'This hugely accomplished first book draws on local lore and history, a vast range of research and some soaring lyrical writing'
The Sunday Times

'Laing is a brilliant wordsmith and this is a beautifully accomplished book' *Independent*

'Brave, distinctive, and deeply intelligent . . . The book has an intense, humming, cumulative effect' *Literary Review*

'Arrestingly beautiful . . . This is an uplifting book, which not only develops into a work of considerable richness, but . . . expresses its message of hope with increasing lyricism and uncluttered simplicity' *Evening Standard*

'Olivia Laing is a new and thoughtful voice in the tradition of W.G. Sebald' Joan Bakewell, *Daily Telegraph*

'[Laing] conveys vision and sensation with great clarity and vividness . . . Of Olivia Laing's prose, we could simply say that words have a way with her and that her delight in language is at one with her absorption in the living world'
Times Literary Supplement

'A quasi-confessional meditation-cum-travelogue of immense charm, personal observation and historical fact' *Irish Times*

'A meditation, a drifting sequence of thoughts on time and change, on loss, love and meaning, on hell and happiness, geology and evolution, science and poetry' *Spectator*

'Gorgeous, lyrical . . . a gentle, wise, observant book, both sparkling and mysterious . . . Laing's writing – sometimes clear, sometimes shifting and oblique, always appropriate to the tale she's telling – is a joy' *Metro*

'A refreshing, and inspiring, real-life story . . . Relive Laing's journey and you'll be inspired to get out into nature more often'
Psychologies

'A constant delight: dreamy and lyrical, meditative and wry. . . A beautiful - and beautifully written - book, every bit as enchanting as its watery subject' *The Lady*

ALSO BY OLIVIA LAING

The Trip To Echo Spring

The Lonely City

TO THE RIVER

A Journey Beneath the Surface

OLIVIA LAING

CANONGATE

This Canons edition published by Canongate Books in 2017

First published in Great Britain in 2011 by Canongate Books Ltd,
14 High Street, Edinburgh EH1 1TE

www.canongate.co.uk

1

For permissions acknowledgements, please see page 277.

British Library Cataloguing-in-Publication Data

A catalogue record for this book is available on
request from the British Library

ISBN 978 1 78689 158 7

Typeset in Bembo by Palimpsest Book Production Ltd,
Falkirk, Stirlingshire

Printed and bound in Great Britain by Clay Ltd, St Ives plc

For my parents and my sister,
and in memory of my grandfather,
Arthur Laing

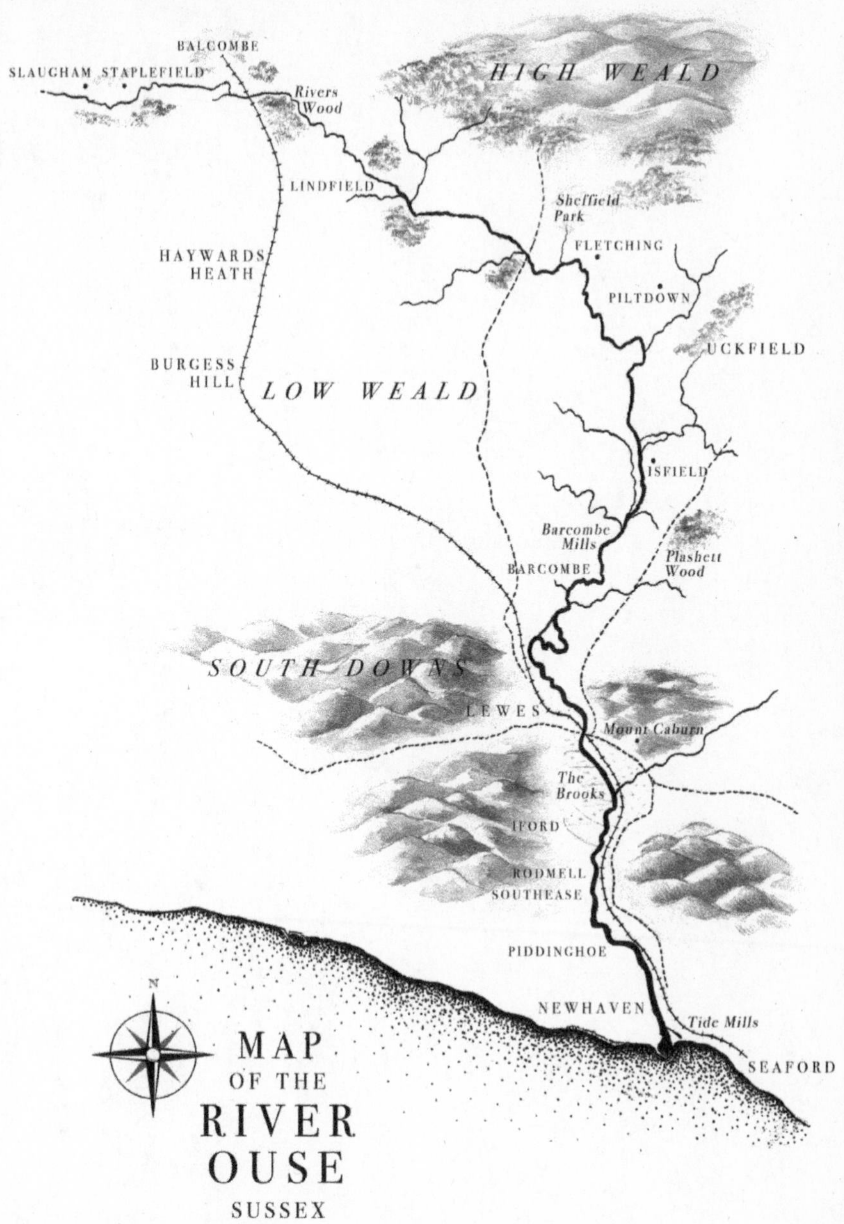
BALCOMBE
SLAUGHAM
STAPLEFIELD
HIGH WEALD
Rivers Wood
LINDFIELD
Sheffield Park
FLETCHING
HAYWARDS HEATH
PILTDOWN
UCKFIELD
BURGESS HILL
LOW WEALD
ISFIELD
Barcombe Mills
Plashett Wood
BARCOMBE
SOUTH DOWNS
LEWES
Mount Caburn
The Brooks
IFORD
RODMELL
SOUTHEASE
PIDDINGHOE
N
NEWHAVEN
Tide Mills
SEAFORD
MAP
OF THE
RIVER
OUSE
SUSSEX

All the rivers run into the sea; yet the sea is not full; unto the place from whence the rivers come, thither they return again. All things are full of labour; man cannot utter it: the eye is not satisfied with seeing, nor the ear filled with hearing. The thing that hath been, it is that which shall be; and that which is done is that which shall be done: and there is no new thing under the sun.

Ecclesiastes 1:7–9

CONTENTS

ILLUSTRATIONS

Leonard Woolf, first published alongside 'Do We Read Better Books in Wartime' in the *Picture Post*, 1944. Copyright © Felix Man and Kurt Jutton/Picture Post/Hulton Archive/Getty Images. 213

Lieutenant Ackery's Crash. Copyright © Henry Ross Alderson/climb-out.co.uk. 247

TO THE RIVER

I

CLEARING OUT

I AM HAUNTED BY WATERS. It may be that I'm too dry in myself, too English, or it may be simply that I'm susceptible to beauty, but I do not feel truly at ease on this earth unless there's a river nearby. 'When it hurts,' wrote the Polish poet Czeslaw Miłosz, 'we return to the banks of certain rivers,' and I take comfort in his words, for there's a river I've returned to over and again, in sickness and in health, in grief, in desolation and in joy.

I first came to the Ouse one June evening a decade back. I was with a boyfriend long since relinquished, and we drove from Brighton, leaving my car in the field at Barcombe Mills and walking north against the current as the last few fishermen swung their lures in hope of pike or bass. The thickening air was full of the scent of meadowsweet and if I looked closely I could make out a scurf of petals drifting idly along the bank. The river ran brimful at the edge of an open field, and as the sun dropped its smell became more noticeable: that cold green reek by which wild water betrays its presence. I stooped to dip a hand and as I did so I remembered Virginia Woolf drowned herself in the Ouse, though why or when I didn't know.

For a while I used to swim with a group of friends at Southease, near where her body was found. I'd enter the swift water in trepidation that gave way to ecstasy, tugged by a current that threatened to tumble me beneath the surface and bowl me clean to the sea. The river passed in that region through a chalk valley ridged by the Downs, and the chalk seeped into the water and turned it the milky green of sea glass, full of little shafts of imprisoned light. You couldn't see the bottom; you could barely make out your own limbs, and perhaps it was this opacity which made it seem as though the river was the bearer of secrets: that beneath its surface something lay concealed.

It wasn't morbidity that drew me to that dangerous place but rather the pleasure of abandoning myself to something vastly beyond my control. I was pulled to the Ouse as a magnet is pulled to metal, returning on summer nights and during the short winter days to repeat some walks, some swims through turning seasons until they amassed the weight of ritual. I'd come to that corner of Sussex idly and with no intention of staying long, but it seems to me now that the river cast a lure, that it caught me on the fly and held me heart-stopped there. And when things began to falter in my own life, it was the Ouse to which I turned.

⋆ ⋆ ⋆

In the spring of 2009 I became caught up in one of those minor crises that periodically afflict a life, when the scaffolding that sustains us seems destined to collapse. I lost a job by accident, and then, through sheer carelessness, I lost the man I loved. He was from Yorkshire and one of the skirmishes in our long battle concerned territory, namely where in the country we would make our home. I couldn't relinquish Sussex and nor could he quite edge himself from the hills and moors to which he had, after all, only just returned.

After Matthew left I lost the knack of sleeping. Brighton seemed unsettled and at night it was very bright. The hospital over the road had recently been abandoned and I'd look up sometimes from my work to see a gang of boys breaking windows or setting fires in the yard where ambulances once parked. At periodic intervals throughout the day I felt that I was drowning, and it was all I could do not to fling myself to the ground and wail like a child. These feelings of panic, which in more sober moments I knew were temporary and would soon pass, were somehow intensified by the loveliness of that April. The trees were flaring into life: first the chestnut with its upraised candles and then the elm and beech. Amid this wash of green the cherry began to flower and within days the streets were filled with a flush of blossom that clogged the drains and papered the windscreens of parked cars.

The shift in season was intoxicating, and it was then that the idea of walking the river locked hold of me. I wanted to *clear out*, in all senses of the phrase, and I felt somewhere deep inside me that the river was where I needed to be. I began to buy maps compulsively, though I've always been map-shy. Some I pinned to my wall; one, a geological chart of the underlying ground, was so beautiful I kept it by my bed. What I had in mind was a survey or sounding, a way of catching and logging what a little patch of England looked like one midsummer week at the beginning of the twenty-first century. That's what I told people, anyway. The truth was less easy to explain. I wanted somehow to get beneath the surface of the daily world, as a sleeper shrugs off the ordinary air and crests towards dreams.

A river passing through a landscape catches the world and gives it back redoubled: a shifting, glinting world more mysterious than the one we customarily inhabit. Rivers run through our civilisations like strings through beads, and there's hardly an age I can think of that's not associated with its own great waterway. The lands of the Middle East have dried to tinder now, but once they were fertile, fed by the fruitful Euphrates and the Tigris, from which rose flowering Sumer and Babylonia. The riches of Ancient Egypt stemmed from the Nile, which was believed to mark the causeway between life and death, and which was twinned in the heavens by the spill of stars we now call the Milky Way. The Indus Valley, the Yellow River: these are the places where civilisations began, fed by sweet waters that in their flooding enriched the land. The art of writing was independently born in these four regions and I do not think it a coincidence that the advent of the written word was nourished by river water.

There is a mystery about rivers that draws us to them, for they rise from hidden places and travel by routes that are not always tomorrow where they might be today. Unlike a lake or sea, a river has a destination and there is something about the certainty with which it travels that makes it very soothing, particularly for those who've lost faith with where they're headed.

The Ouse seemed to me then to be composed of two elements. On the one hand it was the thing itself: a river forty-two miles long that rose in a copse of oak and hazel not far from Haywards Heath, dashing in quick gills and riffles through the ancient forests of the Weald, traversing the Downs at Lewes and entering the oil-streaked Channel at Newhaven, where the ferries cross over to France. Such waterways are ten a penny in these islands. I dare say there is one that runs near you – a pretty, middling river that winds through towns and fields alike, neither pristinely wild nor reliably tame. The days of watermills and salterns may have passed, but the Ouse remains a working river after the fashion of our times, feeding a brace of reservoirs and carrying the outfall from a dozen sewage works. Sometimes, swimming at Isfield, you pass through clotted tracts of bubbles; sometimes a crop of waterweed blooms as luxuriant as an orchard with the fertiliser that's washed from the wheat.

But a river moves through time as well as space. Rivers have shaped our world; they carry with them, as Joseph Conrad had it, 'the dreams of men, the seed of commonwealths, the germs of empires'. Their presence has always lured people, and so they bear like litter the cast-off relics of the past. The Ouse is not a major waterway. It has intersected with the wider currents of history only once or twice; when Virginia Woolf drowned there in 1941 and again, centuries earlier, when the Battle of Lewes was fought upon its banks. Nonetheless, its relationship with man can be traced back thousands of years before the birth of Christ, to when Neolithic settlers first started to cut down the forests and cultivate crops by the river's edge. The ages that followed left more palpable traces: Saxon villages; a Norman castle; Tudor sewage works; Georgian embankments and sluices designed to relieve the river's tendency to overflow, though even these elaborate modifications failed to prevent the Ouse from rising up and cataclysmically flooding the town of Lewes in the early years of our own millennium.

At times, it feels as if the past is very near. On certain evenings, when the sun has dropped and the air is turning blue, when barn owls float above the meadow grass and a pared-down moon breaches the treeline, a mist will sometimes lift from the surface of the river. It is then that the strangeness of water becomes apparent. The earth hoards its treasures and what is buried there remains until it's disinterred by spade or plough, but a river is more shifty, relinquishing its possessions haphazardly and without regard to the landlocked chronology historians hold so dear. A history compiled by way of water is by its nature quick and fluid, full of submerged life and capable, as I would discover, of flooding unexpectedly into the present.

That spring I was reading Woolf obsessively, for she shared my preoccupation with water and its metaphors. Over the years

Virginia Woolf has gained a reputation as a doleful writer, a bloodless neurasthenic, or again as a spiteful, rarefied creature, the doyenne of airless Bloomsbury chat. I suspect the people who hold this view of not having read her diaries, for they are filled with humour and an infectious love for the natural world.

Virginia first came to the Ouse in 1912, renting a house set high above the marshes. She spent the first night of her marriage to Leonard Woolf there and later stayed at the house to recover from her third in a succession of serious breakdowns. In 1919, sane again, she switched to the other side of the river, buying a cold bluish cottage beneath Rodmell's church tower. It was very primitive when they first arrived, with no hot water and a dank earth closet furnished with a cane chair above a bucket. But Leonard and Virginia both loved Monks House, and its peace and isolation proved conducive to work. Much of *Mrs Dalloway*, *To the Lighthouse*, *The Waves* and *Between the Acts* was written there, along with hundreds of reviews, short stories and essays.

She was acutely sensitive to landscape, and her impressions of this chalky, watery valley pervade her work. Her solitary, often daily, excursions seem to have formed an essential part of the writing process. During the Asham breakdown, when she was banned from the over-stimulations of either walking or writing, she confided longingly to her diary:

> What wouldn't I give to be coming through Firle woods, the brain laid up in sweet lavender, so sane & cool, & ripe for the morrow's task. How I should notice everything, the phrase for it coming the moment after & fitting like a

> glove; & then on the dusty road, as I ground my pedals, so my story would begin telling itself; & then the sun would be done, & home, & some bout of poetry after dinner, half read, half lived, as if the flesh were dissolved & through it the flowers burst red & white.

'As if the flesh were dissolved' is a characteristic phrase. Woolf's metaphors for the process of writing, for entering the dream world in which she thrived, are fluid: she writes of *plunging, flooding, going under, being submerged*. This desire to enter the depths is what drew me to her, for though she eventually foundered, for a time it seemed she possessed, like some freedivers, a gift for descending beneath the surface of the world. As I sat in my hot little room I began to feel like an apprentice escape artist studying Houdini. I wanted to know how the trick was mastered, and I wanted to know how those effortless plunges turned into a vanishing act of a far more sinister sort.

Spring was giving way to summer. I'd decided to leave the city on the solstice, the hinge point of the year when light is at its peak. The superstitions about the day appealed to me: it's when the wall between worlds is said to grow thin, and it's no coincidence that Shakespeare set his topsy-turvy dream on Midsummer Eve, for on the year's briefest night magic and misrule have always held sway. England is at her most beautiful in the month of June, and in the days before I left I began to feel almost maddened by my desire to get out into the flowering fields and enter the cool, steady river.

My flat began to fill up with anxious lists. I purchased a rucksack, and a pair of lightweight trousers with blossom printed jauntily along the waist. My mother sent me a pair of sandals of unparalleled hideousness that she swore – falsely, as it turned out – were designed to prevent blisters. I spent a pleasant afternoon booking rooms in pubs along the route, including the White Hart in Lewes, where Virginia and Leonard Woolf bought Monks House at auction and then, in the excitement of the moment, had a brief and violent fight. I also bought a vast quantity of oatcakes and a large slab of cheese. I might lack variety, but I wouldn't starve.

In all this time I'd barely spoken to Matthew, and the night before I left, I did a forbidden thing. I rang him and at some point in the tangled, recriminatory conversation that followed I began to weep and found I couldn't stop. It was, though I didn't know it then, the nadir, the lowest point of that dismal spring. The next day was the solstice; after that, though the days began to shorten, something in me started to lighten and lift.

II

AT THE SOURCE

THE SWIFTS WERE THERE WHEN I woke, rising as if from deep water, rinsed clean by sleep for the first time in months. The swifts were there, and a fox in the car park of the hospital, a scrawny, mottled orange-grey fox, who sat and scratched in the sun and then slunk back into the shadows of the old incinerator. It was 21 June, the longest day of the year, the sky screened by fine cloud, the sea swaddled in mist. My pack was ready at the bottom of the bed, stuffed with neat layers of clothes and maps, the side pockets bulging with bottles of suntan lotion and water, a battered copy of *The Wild Flowers of Britain and Northern Europe* and a rusty Opinel that no longer locked.

I sang as I made the coffee. I felt almost weightless after last night's tears, as if they'd dissolved a burden that had hobbled me for months. That afternoon I planned to walk from Slaugham to where the Ouse began, in a little clay ditch that ran at the foot of a hawthorn hedge. And from there I'd take a long curve south by south-east, crossing and recrossing the stream day by day until I reached Isfield, where the path and the river ran as one through the low chalk valley that led to the sea. A week would do it, I reckoned, with plenty of time for detours on the way.

The night before, I'd spread three Ordnance Survey maps across the floor and drawn a skittering Biro line along the route I thought I'd take, patching together footpaths and lanes to get as close to the water as I could. But no matter how much I deviated from the official Ouse Way, which seemed positively hydrophobic at its start, for the first three days I'd see water only in glimpses. There are no automatic rights to roam riverbanks and much of the land the Ouse coils through is private, strung with the barbed wire and *Keep Out* signs by which England's old divisions are maintained.

I got the same train I used to catch to work, the Bedford service, which inches in and out of London, hiccuping to a halt at each of the little country stations. Haywards Heath would be the best bet, I reckoned. From there I'd take a cab to Slaugham, where I could leave my bag at the Chequers and search for the water unencumbered. I leant my head against the grubby window, drinking in the light. The line was trimmed with a ribbon of wasteground, full of the everyday plants the eye elides: brick-pink valerian, rosebay willowherb, elder, bindweed and marguerites. Outside Hassocks I caught the yellow flare of evening primrose. When it's hot, you often see a fox coiled here, a rust-spot amid the metallic glint of poppies. Today nothing stirred but the wood pigeons, clapping their wings and calling out their five syllables over and again.

The Chequers was a pretty white pub on the edge of the village green. Inside, it was deserted and stupefyingly hot. A Polish girl showed me to my room, pointing out the fire escape where I could gain access after hours. I flung my bag on the bed and went into the fields empty-handed, my pockets weighed down with maps. The air seemed to have set like jelly, quivering as I pressed against it. I climbed south between paddocks of horses, past empty, secretive gardens littered with abandoned tricycles and trampolines. By the time I reached Warninglid Lane the sun was the highest it would be all year and there were circles of sweat staining my T-shirt. As I came out from under the pines, the heat hit me smartly across the face. There was a rabbit by the verge, its guts unslung and draped across the road, the dark beads of excrement still visible beneath the puckered skin.

I'd looked at this square of the High Weald on maps for months, tracing the blue lines as they tangled through the hedges, plaiting eastward into a wavering stream. I thought I knew exactly where the water started, but I had not bargained for the summer's swift uprush of growth. At the edge of the field there was a hawthorn hedge and beside it, where I thought the stream would be, was a waist-high wall of nettles and hemlock water dropwort, its poisonous white umbels tilted to the sky. It was impossible to tell whether water was flowing or whether the ditch was dry, its moisture sucked into the drunken green. I hovered for a minute, havering. It was Sunday, hardly a car passing. Unless they were watching with binoculars from Eastlands Farm there was no one to see me slip illegally across the field to where the river was marked to start. To hell with it, I thought, and ducked beneath the fence.

The choked ditch led to a copse of hazel and stunted oak. Here the trees had shaded out the nettles and the stream could be seen, a brown whisper, hoof-stippled, that petered out at the wood's far edge. There was no spring. The water didn't bubble from the ground, rust-tinted, as I have seen it do at Balcombe, ten miles east of here. *The source* sounded a grand name for this clammy runnel, carrying the runoff from the last field before the catchment shifted towards the Adur. It was nothing more than the furthest tributary from the river's end, its longest arm, a half-arbitrary way of mapping what is a constant movement of water through air and earth and sea.

It's not always possible to plot where something starts. If I went down on my knees amid the fallen leaves, I would not find the exact spot where the Ouse began, where a trickle of rain gathered sufficient momentum to make it to the coast. This muddy, muddled birth seemed pleasingly appropriate considering the origins of the river's name. There are many Ouses in England, and consequently much debate about the meaning of the word. The source is generally supposed to be *usa*, the Celtic word for water, but I favoured the argument, this being a region of Anglo-Saxon settlement, that here it was drawn from the Saxon word *wāse*, from which derives also our word *ooze*, meaning soft mud or slime; earth so wet as to flow gently. Listen: *ooooze*. It trickles along almost silently, sucking at your shoes. An ooze is a marsh or swampy ground, and to ooze is to dribble or slither. I liked the slippery way it caught at both earth's facility for holding water and water's knack for working through soil: a flexive, doubling word. You could hear the river in it, *ooozing* up through the Weald and snaking its way down valleys to where it once formed a lethal marsh.

On Valentine's Day, before things began to go awry, Matthew gave me a map he'd made of the Ouse. He'd photocopied all the relevant OS Explorers in Huddersfield Library and then, in his obsessive way, had calculated the extent of the drainage basin, cutting the sheets along the wavering line of the watershed. Each tributary had been coloured with marker pen, orange for the Bevern, pink for the Iron River, green for the Longford and the misfit Glynde Reach. I stuck the parts together with Sellotape and for months it was tacked to my wall: 233 square miles of land the shape of a collapsed lung. By April the sun had bleached the colours away, and at some point that spring I took it down and slid it to the bottom of the papers that lined my desk.

I thought of it then, as I stood in the wood. On the map, the ditch had been coloured blue. It meant nothing in itself: a place where deer drink, a channel cleared centuries before to stop the field from flooding. A leaf drifted down and floated slowly east. I couldn't remember when it had last rained, when this water might have gathered, seeping steadily through the grasses until it trickled here. The average residence time of a single water molecule in a river this size is a matter of weeks, though this depends on currents, rains and a dozen other vagaries. If instead it infiltrates the soil, becoming groundwater, it may linger for centuries or, if it's sunk deep enough, hundreds of thousands of years. Isotope hydrology suggests that the trapped fossil water in some of the world's largest confined aquifers is over a million years old. These aquifers often underlie deserts, and it is strange to think that buried beneath the Kalahari, the Sahara and mile after mile of the arid centre of Australia are vast vaults of ancient water, stored in rock or silt. In comparison, this ditchwater at the river's head was brand new, freshly fallen from the sky. Much of it would be wicked up by the sun before it reached Slaugham Mill Pond, where it could circle with the carp for fifty years before rushing south to rejoin the sea, a thousand tonnes a minute.

The stream was barely shifting now and it was hard to believe it could change its nature so entirely. There was a stinking pond at the edge of the trees, and a tractor waiting for the morning's work. The oats had yet to ripen and everything stood very still. I could hear the faintest trickle of water pattering past roots and tiny stones, and as I waited there I remembered a stray line from a poem by Seamus Heaney, part of the vast disordered library of river literature. It was about dowsing, and it seemed to catch something of water's strangeness: 'suddenly broadcasting through a green aerial its secret stations'. It might have been the thought of fossil water that had nudged it into my mind, for I've always been fascinated by the idea that the planet contains hidden lakes and rivers as well as those that run open to the sky; the sort of concealed richness that Auden was thinking of when he wrote 'In Praise of Limestone', which ends:

Dear, I know nothing of
Either, but when I try to imagine a faultless love
Or the life to come, what I hear is the murmur
Of underground streams, what I see is a limestone landscape.

In Heaney's poem, water announces its presence with a *pluck* that jerks the forked hazel rod uncontrollably. The act seems wholly magical and so it is perhaps unsurprising that dowsing – water witching as it is known in America – has performed poorly in scientific trials, proving no better than mere chance at finding the conduits through which water passes beneath rock and soil. Be that as it may, humans by necessity must once, like all animals, have been attuned to the dark frequency by which water travels. No doubt this sensitivity has grown vestigial now, or become gummed up by car horns and the repetitive trilling of mobile phones, and yet there have been many times when, out walking in a wood, I have found myself drawn by chance or instinct to a pool or stream I didn't know existed.

I squatted beside one of the stripling oaks, crushing a fresh holly leaf into my knee. I was feeling uneasy, and the sense of trespass in the little copse had become overwhelming. The sources of rivers are often freighted with taboos, and for all their eerie beauty they do not seem, at least according to the records of mythology, wise places for humans to tarry. The seer Tiresias is said to have been blinded when he saw the goddess Athena bathing in a spring on Helikon Mountain, and his gift for prophecy came as recompense for the punishing loss of his sight.

According to the poet Callimachus the encounter happened

in midsummer – a day like today – when Athena and the nymph Khariklo, Tiresias's mother, were lying together in the creek. It was high noon, that still moment when the world is stunned by heat. Only Tiresias remained on the hill, hunting for deer with his dogs. He'd grown thirsty in the sun and he climbed down to the stream for water, not knowing it was occupied. Athena saw him pushing through the trees and she blinded him instantly, for it is forbidden to see a goddess undressed, even one who regularly bathes with your mother. *Helikon, I shall not walk on you again*, cried the nymph Khariklo. *Your price is too high: my son's eyes for a few stags*. And so Athena cleaned the boy's ears to make amends, that he could hear what the birds said, and tell it to the Boietians and to the mighty descendants of Labdakos. It was a harsh price to pay, though better, as Athena pointed out, than the fate that befell the hunter Actaeon, who was torn apart by his own dogs for seeing Artemis bathing, so that his mother had to collect his scattered bones from among the briars and brambles.

It would have to be a diminutive goddess to bathe at the Ouse's source, and yet the stream no longer seemed a benign place to be. The sense of trespass stayed with me as I looped back to Slaugham, through a private lane that led past a barn in which there hung a motionless trapeze. The path climbed up through a field of horses in medieval jousting masks and into a meadow of bent, brome and Yorkshire fog, full of bees out milling the clover. The pink and tawny grasses dipped and swayed, and above them the bees moved singly, humming as they passed until the air was full of sound.

This was better. I lay down in the sun and curled my legs beneath me. The noise was very lulling, and as my eyes began to close I remembered with the intensity of a dream an afternoon I'd once spent sprawled face down on a dirt bank in Scotland, watching bees entering and leaving a network of tiny caves that they'd cut into the earth like troglodytes. There were so many bees coming and going that the whole hillside seemed to struggle in the hot pine-scented air, agitating over and over itself. There must have been far more beneath the ground, and from each of the holes rose the sound of their wings: a distant, atonal hum, as if the soil had bedded down and was singing to itself.

Leonard Woolf used to keep bees. He had a hive at Monks House, the cottage in Rodmell that the Woolfs bought soon after the end of the First World War, and the occasion of their swarming provoked a strangely sexy entry in Virginia's diary:

> Sitting after lunch we heard them outside, & on Sunday there they were again hanging in a quivering shiny brown black purse to Mrs Thompsett's tombstone. We leapt about in the long grass of the graves, Percy all dressed up in mackintosh, & netted hat. Bees shoot whizz, like arrows of desire: fierce, sexual; weave cat's cradles in the air; each whizzing from a string; the whole air full of vibration: of beauty, of the burning arrowy desire; & speed: I still think the quivering shifting bee bag the most sexual and sensual symbol.

A few sentences later, still intoxicated by the image, she describes an ugly woman at a party, adding, 'Why bees should swarm round her, I cant say.'

It seems a very complete Woolf that emerges from this episode: sensuous, exact, perhaps herself more wasp than bee, but nonetheless as attuned to nature as she is to artifice, and keen above all to get to the bottom of things, to find the exact word to pin down a sensation or sight she's apprehended in the world. The diaries, it is true, are more shaggy, more luxuriant than the novels, and there is a stronger sense of a writer at play, practising her craft. But the polymorphous sexuality evident in this episode is entirely characteristic, and offers an appealing counter to the Virginia of the popular imagination, who might as well be made of glass.

One of the myths perpetuated about Virginia Woolf is that she was, as her name suggests, sexually unreachable: Patience on a monument, a woman constructed of alabaster and a fizzing brain. Certainly it is true that she told Leonard before the two were married, back in 1912, that she felt no physical attraction for him. But their courtship had its own charge and was, pleasingly enough, full of water, not all of it of the conventionally romantic kind. They went on a date to the *Titanic* inquest, had an initial kiss by the English Channel at Eastbourne and, on the afternoon when Virginia first declared her love, took a boat trip up the Thames at Maidenhead. A photograph taken at the time shows her looking both nervy and tough; it is a distinct improvement on the emaciated portrait in which she sits beside the poet Rupert Brooke, who looks like a plump Apollo – and also bears a distinct resemblance to Leonardo DiCaprio – in comparison to the chicken-bone girl squinting at his side.

Leonard and Virginia spent their first weekend together in Sussex, in the hills that overlook the Ouse, which passes in that region between the Downs at the base of a broad marshy valley, its final territory before the sea. Wandering through the green rolling fields, they came upon Asham, the house in which they would soon begin almost three decades of marriage. At the time of their wedding, both were in their thirties; both on the verge of completing their first novel. Leonard was Jewish, kindly, intense, his brilliance combined with a cold practicality that even then set him slightly outside the chatter of the Bloomsbury set. He had recently returned from Ceylon, where he had been working as an administrator under the auspices of the Colonial Civil Service. His father was dead, and he was afflicted despite his admirable strength of mind with a tremor of the hands that in times of stress he was helpless to control.

As for Virginia, she was an orphan. Her mother had died when she was still a child, and in 1902 her irascible father, Sir Leslie Stephen, the mountaineer and critic, was diagnosed with the bowel cancer that would kill him two years later. In the wake of each of these bereavements Virginia's mental health became unstable and she suffered the breakdowns that would, in the years after her death, come to define her. But she emerged from her madness determined to *work*; to write, and in this she was successful.

These two people, then, formed an alliance that cannot really be described as conventional. The marriage was consummated, but the sexual side never exactly took off and was soon abandoned. Virginia had a third breakdown just over a year after the wedding, and attempted suicide by overdosing on the sedative veronal before returning to a fragile equilibrium. Leonard took on at least sporadically the role of nursemaid and sometimes jailer, insisting on a programme of regular meals, early nights and limited excitements in order to keep his wife from toppling towards insanity again. But it should not be thought that Virginia was a vapid, vacant invalid, disconnected from the world in which she lived. She possessed throughout her life a glittering charm, much commented on by friends and enemies alike, as well as an acute sense of the ridiculous that made her almost incapable of self-pity.

A marriage is a private business, even for people who leave behind them such a vast litter of diaries, letters and third-party gossip. What occurs at its centre, what bonds maintain it, are not always visible, or even guessable, to the outsider's greedy eye. But the sense that arises from this residue of words is of an abiding love, comprised in equal parts of affection and intellectual stimulation. *My inviolable centre*, Virginia called Leonard, and the last words she wrote were to him alone: a testament, against all the odds, to the happiness they'd shared. The title of one of the many books about the Woolfs' liaison is *The Marriage of True Minds*, a line drawn from Sonnet 116, itself an ode to enduring love. The sentiment is accurate enough, but it is a couplet later in the poem –

Love alters not with his brief hours and weeks,
But bears it out even to the edge of doom.

– that I think may be even more appropriate, all things considered.

The bees were still passing through the meadow, drifting along their wobbling paths a few feet above my head. I rolled onto my back and spread out beneath the sun. It was so warm it felt as if my flesh were melting, and when I closed my eyes the light made a kaleidoscope on the inside of their lids. 'The bees of infinity', the filmmaker Derek Jarman once called them, 'the golden swarm . . . their pollen sacs all different yellows'. Bee-keeping was one of the activities he turned to when he was dying of AIDS, when he moved to Prospect Cottage, the little wooden house on Dungeness beach, the fifth quarter at the end of the globe. He kept them in a hive made of railway sleepers, in the garden he wrestled from the shingle, and they made honey from the woodsage in August and in January from the gorse.

In his last years, I remembered then, Jarman too went blind, when toxoplasmosis ravaged his retinas. 'Someone . . . said losing your sight must be frightening,' he wrote in his diary. 'Not so, as long as you have a safe harbour in the sea of shadows. Just inconvenient. If you woke on a dark day, had only the mind's eye with which to see your way, would you turn back?' And later: 'The day of our death is sealed up. I do not wish to die . . . yet. I would love to see my garden through several summers.' His last film, *Blue*, replicated his own sightless vision: an unchanging blue screen for seventy-nine minutes. It's the colour of the void, the saturated ultramarine of the world behind the sky. The soundtrack, a drift of memories interwoven with poetry, misquotes William Blake: 'If the doors of perception were cleansed then everything would be seen as it is.'

I stood abruptly and as I did the blood rushed to my head

and I rose amid the whirling grasses temporarily both dizzy and blind, the roar of the bees bouncing off me in a language I couldn't begin to decode, let alone to prophesy.

Back at the Chequers, I slept until the sun dropped to its final quarter, and then went to the bar, where I ate an almighty burger that fell apart when I poked it, watched over by a moustachioed dog whose owner did not move an inch the entire time I was there. But it was impossible not to go out again, into the lovely, diminishing day. The swallows were rising and falling about the church tower when I left, calling in high voices above the grave of Nelson's sister.

The path I took led to Slaugham Furnace Pond, a relic of the iron industry that once dominated this region. The idea that nature can be prised free from civilisation is, in England's over-populated south at least, absurd. The landscape hereabouts has been shaped by centuries of man's activities, as man, I suppose, has been shaped by the land. To make nails or cannons, or the dainty tweezers that even the Romans used, you needed iron, and the combination of dense woodland to fuel the charcoal fires and clay rich in ironstone ore set the Weald at the heart of the industry from before the Romans until the beginning of the Industrial Revolution.

The earliest furnace ponds were formed by damming streams with clay bays, to provide the steady outflow of water that would power the bellows of the bloomery, the furnace used to smelt iron ore. Later, after the introduction of the blast furnace, the ponds were used to drive the bellows and helve hammers in finery forges, where the raw pig iron was remelted to form the bloom that would be drawn by the hammerman into the purer bar iron. I tried to reconstruct it in my mind as I walked: the forge fires that could be seen ten miles from here, the smashing hammer blows that echoed all the way to the Downs. Now the lakes are the province of anglers, who use a language every bit as specific as that of the hammermen. *No bivvies or boilies, no keep nets. Dickie comes up trumps in furnace carp bonanza.*

The first pipistrelles were crossing Coos Lane as I reached the water. There were three cars left in the car park, along with the remnants of someone's McDonald's. It was just after sunset and everything had stilled, the sky shot faintly with rose. The reflections in the lake seemed sunk very deep. The water pleated as the carp sank and climbed, occasionally breaking the surface to shivers. Beneath them, the slow clouds made their way east. At the far side of the lake the trees were reflected in sooty green and when the fish jumped there the ripples ran in white concentric circles. On the near side, where there was only pale sky on the skin of the water, the ripples flashed dark, a trick of the light I'd never seen before. The flies were circling, and three men were fishing on the far bank, another two just north of me. Splash, and again: splash.

I hunkered down on the jetty. A plane was crossing the pinkish sky, and in the underwater world it crossed too, drawing an elongating contrail behind it. In the sky, the plane flew steadily, still gaining altitude from Gatwick. Beneath the water, though, it moved differently, the contrail whipping back and forth with the ripples so that it seemed to be swimming in sideways strokes, as a snake does. If only my vision were clear enough, I might have made out the faces at the windows far below, beneath the water's surface. I needed a goddess to clean my eyes. *If the doors of perception were cleansed, then everything would be seen as it is.*

There are sights too beautiful to swallow. They stay on the rim of the eye; it cannot contain them. I remembered something Virginia Woolf had written, about an evening 'too beautiful for one pair of eyes. Instinctively I want someone to catch my overflow of pleasure.' There was no one to turn to. Even the fishermen had fallen silent; the murmured chat about casts and catches abandoned for the day. We talk of drinking in a sight, but what of the excess that cannot be caught? So much goes by unseen. 'After an hour outside walking,' the naturalist Hannah Hinchman wrote, 'colours begin to appear much more brilliant, more saturated. Oxygen to the brain? Rods and cones sufficiently steeped?' But no matter how long I stayed outdoors, there was a world that would remain invisible to me, just at the cusp of perception, glimpsable only in fragments, as when the delphinium at dusk breathes back its unearthly, ultraviolet blue.

Deep blue, the last colour to remain before the dark. All of a sudden the sky was flooded with it. It hung for only a moment, immense and luminous, and then the night came down all at once, and closed even the west from view. I jogged home, suddenly cold, and let myself in through the fire escape, squeezing past the ironing board and the trouser press. The window was open, and just before I fell asleep voices washed up from the porch.

All right Pat, see you later, see you later Trev, nice to see you. You're not allowed on the motorway, not with them L-plates. Will you shut up a minute, I'm talking to you. Don't mind me, don't mind me, I'm a bit worried about Trevor. Trev! Trev! Me, me, me, ain't it Trevor? Aw, Irene hit me. No surprise there. Aw yeah, go on then. Trev, Trev, me, me, me, ain't it? We'll see you Christmas Eve. Ta-ra then Trev, lovely to see you. I listened to them leave, in a flurry of coughs and car engines, and then, for the night's short reach, I slept.

Next morning I set out again, after a plate of metallic tomatoes and toast spread thickly with margarine. There'd be no dithering today. I had eight miles to cover, curving south-east through the High Weald to the outskirts of Lindfield, where I'd found a room for the night. The High Weald is a strange, medieval stretch of countryside that runs from Hampshire right through to Kent. The name *weald* comes from the Old English word for woodland, and these sloping acres of entwined forest and field were once the largest wildwood in England. The Anglo-Saxons called it *Andredesleage*: a vast, knotted wilderness of oak, ash and hornbeam, alder, hazel and holly, full of wolves and wild boar. Vaguely alchemical industries grew up in the Weald: charcoal burning, iron smelting, the production of forest glass. It is astonishing what wood and earth together will yield, given a spark and a puff of air. A windowpane, say, bubbling and settling into cool green sheets, like ice on a winter's day.

The same combination of trees and clay rich in ore that made the Weald so suitable for iron also made it hard to penetrate, and in the wilder regions passage was limited to the old drovers' tracks that have lived on as deep-sunken lanes. Though deforestation was so severe in Tudor times that an act was passed banning the felling of young trees, the Weald still has the highest proportion of ancient woodland in the country. Scraps of Wealden language have also survived, and even today the river's tributaries cut through steep-sided valleys called *ghylls*, and the trees edge fields in shaggy strips known as *shaws*.

I followed a beech-lined lane into Staplefield, and then swung south, past two men from the Electricity Board sawing the lops and tops off an ash tree. In the next field a man with a dog came up as I stooped to look at a spray of yellow bells by the hedge. *Do you want to know what that is?* he asked. *What do you want, the common name or the Latin?* He stood back on his heels. *Nope, it's gone. I'll remember in a minute.* It transpired he was a gardener, though he added shamefacedly *It's forty years since I learnt all that.* He began to tell me about the cannabis that people from Brighton cultivated in the hedges hereabouts. *I picked some the other day and gave it to my wife. She's green as grass. Stoned? She couldn't walk! Thought I was trying to poison her.* He saluted me and wandered off, still trying to puzzle back the forgotten flower.

The path spilled on down a long lion-coloured meadow into a valley lined with ashes. There the river ran in riffles over the gravel beds that the sea trout need to breed. I crossed it at Hammerhill Bridge, running milky in the sun, and climbed east again into Hammerhill Copse. The land had lain open to the morning, and now it seemed to close up like a clam. There was a woman's coat hanging over the gate to the wood, the chain padlocked about it like a belt. Who drops a coat in a wood? The label had been cut out, and the pink satin lining was stippled by mould.

Hammerhill is another relic of the iron industry, and the nearby Holes Wood was where ore was once mined. The remains of the foundries are all over this region: the bell pits marked by circular depressions that fill with water come winter, the streams hiding discarded slag within their shingle beds. The local names for the layers found within a pit are lovely, shifting region by region with the lay of the land. Near Heathfield, the miner might work down through seams of *thirteen foot balls*, *greys*, *hogsheads*, *seven foot*, *pitty clouts*, *three foot pitty*, *bull* and *bottom*. Further east, in Ashburnham, there were *foxes, chevaliers* and *hazards*, each with its own character and aptitude for burning. It seemed strange to me that a cannon could be made from a lump of forge-fired rock, but perhaps it's no less strange than the history of these compacted layers of clay and shelly lime.

In the Cretaceous period, 140 million years ago, the Weald was a fragrant swamp shaded by cycads and fringed with horsetail and the ferns that still appear, black-tinged, in fossils. The Wealden Beds of sandstone and clay were deposited then as sediments of silt and sand dragged down by giant rivers that flowed from the north and west. Over time the earth's crust subsided and the sea flooded in, burying the beds under marine sand and clay that would form the layers of Lower Greensand, Gault and Upper Greensand. For the next 35 million years chalk was formed from the bodies of minute sea creatures – single-celled algae and phytoplankton – that fell at the end of their lives like rain through the warm sea, accumulating a centimetre each thousand years. At the end of the Cretaceous period, the land began to rise, and the Weald lifted again out of the water, a vast chalk dome, of which the North and South Downs are the fragmentary remains. Over time the centre was worn away, inch by inch, by rain and frost and the weathering work of water, until it was at last carved into deep clay valleys and sandstone ridges like the one on which I stood.

On the edge of Hammerhill Copse, rooks were flying in pairs above the ash trees and two swifts hunted flies in the shimmering air. It was hard to believe that the landscape had ever been other than it was now, and so it's not surprising that those infinitely slow transformations were not even guessed at by man, that late arrival, until the creaking register of geological time had almost reached the present day. Geology as a discipline was established in the late eighteenth century, and the first geologists, often clergymen, hoped that their discoveries would verify the biblical record of Genesis, which states that the world was formed out of darkness by the hand of God: a small Eden seeded by beasts; a fruited world given to God's double, man, his ersatz self, to have at his command.

Fossils are often at odds with the regions in which they're found, the stony remains of shellfish, cuttlefish and oysters abandoned many miles from the shore, and so it was generally held in the West that they were *reliquiae diluvianae*, relics left behind when the great waters that God unleashed across the world subsided, and Noah and his ark ran aground on the mountain of Ararat. This belief, gradually and categorically disproven, remains stubbornly persistent, clinging on today in the pseudo-scientific 'flood geology' of the creationists, who invoke mighty geysers and rents in the earth's tectonic plates in their bid to explain where sufficient water came from and drained to that did prevail so exceedingly upon the earth that it was sunk to the depth of fifteen cubits.

In the town where Matthew grew up they told a different story of Noah's flood, replacing the creationist piety with low English comedy. The medieval Wakefield Mystery Play has at its centre a pitched battle between Noah and his stubborn wife that culminates with an exchange of blows and insults – *ramshit! Nichol needy!* – that would make Punch and Judy blush. And when the rain stops and the ship with its cargo of paired beasts reaches land, Noah is not thrilled but horrified by the spectacle that awaits him, of a featureless earth that might never have been inhabited. 'Behold, on this green,' he cries:

. . . neither cart nor plough
Is left on the scene, neither tree nor bough,
Nor other thing,
But all is away:
Many castles, I say
Great towns of array
Flit in this flooding.

Typical Yorkshireman, I thought to myself: never bloody happy. But you don't have to believe in the testimony of Genesis to understand Noah's shock. Isn't that how the world goes, disappearing before our very eyes? The play was last performed in 1576. How many trees had survived since then, how many carts and castles and ploughs? Probably not a single oak in the whole vast Weald, though their lives make man seem puny. They had been swept up by that silent, shiftless flood which swirls perpetually across this world. In time it would obliterate everything in sight, for forms rise but briefly and collapse no matter how solid they look.

In this landscape of erasure, one plant stood out as an anomaly, a living fossil. The horsetail that choked every half-damp ditch I passed had been here when the Weald was still a tropical swamp, long before the chalky Downs were formed. If a nuclear winter ever comes to pass it's the horsetail I'll put my money on, rising stiff-fronded through the dust and rubble as it has for the last 230 million years. *Equisetum*, as it is properly known, is the living link between our own age and that of the dinosaurs. Cows trample it now, but it was growing here when the Weald was home to the iguanodon, one of the first dinosaurs to be discovered.

The earliest traces of the iguanodon were found at the beginning of the nineteenth century by the obstetrician and geologist Gideon Mantell, just over a mile from where I now stood. In this period neither the concept nor the word *dinosaur* existed and even the idea that life forms might become extinct was new and barely tolerated. Geology, as I have said, was an emerging discipline, and in the rush to find and date the layers of rock that comprised the planet's crust, a number of mysterious fossils were being unearthed and, for the first time, systematically classified. The categorisation of early mammals was fairly easy, but stranger and more ambiguous remains were also being discovered. In 1811, on the coast of Lyme Regis, the fossil-hunter Mary Anning had found the skeleton of a previously unknown marine reptile. It was named, after some considerable debate, the ichthyosaur, and over the next ten years various papers were published describing its anatomy and provenance. The discovery caused ripples of intense excitement in the scientific establishment on both sides of the Channel. What was this strange creature, which didn't look like anything so far found in the sea? How old was it? And if it really was extinct, why had God created it only to let it drop out of existence?

Like Anning, Mantell was fascinated by fossils and the secret history they seemed to encode. Originally a shoemaker's son from Lewes, he worked by necessity as a country doctor, pursuing his interest in geology between delivering the town's babies. His father had not been able to afford to send him to university, and the poverty of his background bothered him intensely. The Mantells had once been noble, and like many poor and clever children, Gideon dreamed of restoring his family name. He'd been collecting fossils since childhood; the first, an ammonite, he found just beneath the surface of one of the streams that fed the Ouse.

In the undulating landscape around Lewes Mantell carried out his earliest explorations, turning up the belemnites and bivalves that betrayed the chalk's origins on the bed of an ancient ocean. In 1816 he married, and after that he shifted his investigations north, focusing particularly on a patch of the Weald about ten miles shy of Lewes. The ground here was sandstone, and the fossils it contained were very different from the marine remains he'd become accustomed to unearthing. When his preliminary excavations at Whiteman's Green quarry revealed large bones of a kind he'd never seen before, Mantell tipped off a quarryman and was soon receiving packages of random body parts: disarticulated forms that arrived sometimes individually and sometimes as a mass embedded in rock. He worked on them by night after his doctor's rounds were finished, teasing the bones free with a chisel in the drawing room at Castle Place, the beautiful townhouse he'd bought beneath the castle.

The sheer size of the bones was baffling. Mantell thought at first they might belong to an ichthyosaur, but he was disabused of this notion when he began to notice that some of the rocks from Whiteman's Green contained traces of tropical vegetation: feathery fronds that resembled palms and tree ferns; prints of leaves that looked strangely like euphorbias, which grew in Asia and were not native to these islands. If the strata he was investigating had, as he suspected, once lain beneath a now eroded layer of chalk, then it seemed he had stumbled upon the remains of a tropical world, submerged at some unguessable period by a sea that had itself long since receded. This made the size of the bones all the more intriguing. By the early nineteenth century fossils of giant mammals were regularly being found in Europe, among them mammoths, mastodons and some sort of ancestor of the elephant. But these were always found in Tertiary rock, whereas Mantell was almost certain his bones came from a deeper and correspondingly far older layer. Ancient crocodiles had also been unearthed on the coast of France, and this had begun to seem the likeliest source for the bones when Mary Ann Mantell, Gideon's wife, stumbled across something strange.

Mantell left several written versions of this story, none of which quite tally in detail or date. What seems clear is that at some point in 1820 or 1821, his wife came across a giant tooth – perhaps more than one – on the road near Whiteman's Green, where it lay amid some stones recently hauled from the quarry. This tooth, which Mantell sometimes claimed he'd found himself, was the key to the bone puzzle, though it would take some four or five years to properly decode. More were soon found, and close inspection immediately ruled out the possibility that they'd derived from any sort of crocodile. They clearly belonged to a herbivore, being designed for grinding and much eroded by use. Even in their worn state they were huge: up to 1.4 inches long and, in Mantell's own words, 'so remarkable that the most superficial observer would have been struck with their appearance as something novel and interesting'. If they weren't from a mammal or a fish, what else could they be? The thought perplexed him, and at last, very tentatively, he began to draw the only remaining conclusion: some giant, hitherto unguessed-at member of the lizard tribe.

When I think of Mantell's work, I am reminded of a type of story common to both Greek myths and the folk tales of northern Europe, in which the hero must attempt to sort a mass of dirt and poppy seeds or separate mixed grains into their constituent parts. These labours are usually accomplished with magical help, and they occur, to give a pair of examples, in the tale of Eros and Psyche and in some of the overlapping yarns that are spun around the Russian witch Baba Yaga. I mention these myths because I think they are helpful in imagining the impossibility of the task Mantell set himself when he began to piece together from a rubble of broken and disparate bones an animal whose very existence was only just short of unimaginable.

Convincing the scientific establishment of the significance of his find was never going to be easy. Mantell was a country doctor; despite his evident brilliance he was not immediately welcomed into academic circles, and though he built up many sustaining friendships with geologists, he was also so peculiarly unlucky he sometimes felt himself quite sincerely to be cursed. In 1822 he published a book about his finds in the Weald that to his gratification was ordered four times over by the king, George IV. But despite its success, the book was not enough to get his suspicions about the giant lizard accepted. For this he needed the validation of the Geological Society, but its members rejected Mantell's thesis, suggesting politely that he must have been mistaken about the age of the rock in which the bones were found.

The next summer a friend took the tooth across the Channel to show it to the great French naturalist Georges Cuvier, but he too was dismissive, announcing that it must have derived from some sort of rhinoceros. On the verge of total despair, Mantell resolved to focus his efforts on proving the rock quarried at

Whiteman's Green was indeed from a Secondary strata, and thus considerably older than the Tertiary rock in which mammalian remains were customarily discovered.

Two things changed his fortunes. Among the mess of bones that had been hauled from Whiteman's Green were other teeth, equally large but with a tearing surface that was instantly declarative of a carnivore. Mantell wasn't the only person to have discovered such relics. The geologist William Buckland had in his possession the partial skeleton of a massive animal found near Oxford, which, as luck would have it, was unmistakably of reptilian origin. The story of the Oxford lizard is as complex in its way as that of the iguanodon, but it is sufficient for our purposes to say that in 1824 Buckland announced his discovery of megalosaurus, the first land dinosaur – though that word had still not been invented – to be officially identified. Mantell was present at this meeting of the Geological Society and, screwing up his courage, stood to announce the carnivorous teeth he'd also discovered in the Weald. Buckland agreed to visit him in Lewes, and there conceded that the teeth did belong to megalosaurus, which he thought – wrongly, as it turned out – might turn out to 'have equalled in height our largest elephant and in length fallen little short of the largest whale'.

The world was rapidly shifting towards an acceptance of Mantell's theory, and a few weeks after the meeting in which the megalosaurus was unveiled, Cuvier finally agreed that the giant herbivorous teeth were indeed reptilian in origin. Mantell was intensely gratified, and soon after came almost by chance upon the conclusive evidence he'd so long sought. Early that autumn he spent a day at the Royal College of Surgeons, searching through the Hunterian Museum's vast reserve of anatomical specimens to see if he could find a reptilian tooth that bore even a vague resemblance to his find. The work was dispiriting, and he was about to give it up when the assistant curator, Samuel Stutchbury, came ambling over for a chat. Stutchbury, it transpired, was familiar with tropical reptiles from having worked sporadically at cataloguing the specimens that slave ships sometimes deposited in Bristol, and he immediately saw a startling similarity between Mantell's tooth and that of the iguana, despite the unholy disparity in size. An iguana is about three feet long; scaling up, Mantell calculated rapidly, might make his own creature a mighty sixty feet.

In 1825, Mantell's paper on the giant lizard – now named *Iguanodon mantelli*, from the Greek for 'iguana tooth' – was read out to the Royal Society. By the end of the year, he was formally invited to become a Fellow. It was probably the happiest moment of his life, and heralded a period of unprecedented professional acclaim. Mantell began to lecture widely on the dinosaurs and their realm, bringing the lost world to life with such passion that his audiences were by all accounts spellbound.

He was still avidly collecting fossils, and in 1834 a find confirmed his earliest instincts about the iguanodon. The Maidstone slab, as it became known, was a huge lump of rock unearthed from a quarry in Kent. Embedded in it were a great variety of guddled bones, some broken and some incomplete, which Mantell instantly recognised as belonging to one or more iguanodons. This find was complete enough to allow him for the first time to make a proper guess at the creature's form, assembling what looked in his initial drawing of it something like a large reptilian dog, around thirty feet long, with a coiling tail and a spike parked on its snout. In time it became apparent to him that the forelimbs were shorter and more delicate than the hind, and could be used for plucking foliage, though in this as in much else he was contradicted by his bitter rival, the creationist Richard Owen, curator of the British Museum, who coined the word *dinosaur* and attempted to take credit for the discovery of the iguanodon.

This fortunate period in Mantell's career wasn't destined to last for long. The medical practice he established in Brighton in 1833 almost bankrupted him, and while the town council saved him temporarily by buying up the premises for use as a museum, he made such a botch of this as a financial venture that his wife Mary Ann, who had illustrated his books with her own drawings, left him, taking their four children with her. A little later Mantell's beloved daughter died, and between these two nightmarish events he became so seriously short of funds that the vast collection of fossils he'd assembled since childhood had to be sold in its entirety to the British Museum. The crowning insult came in 1841, when, living alone in Clapham, Mantell was injured in a carriage accident that permanently damaged his spine. He survived for just over a decade, still working almost daily despite the increasing pain, and died at the last in the winter of 1852, accidentally overdosing on the opium he'd begun to take liberally in the wake of his injury.

Throughout his life Gideon Mantell was afflicted by a sense of waste, for he felt himself shut out of the intellectual society he craved on account of his poverty and the heavy demands that doctoring made on his time. His diary is a melancholy litany of slights and humiliations suffered at the hands of the more educated and better born, and barely a year goes by without bursts of bitter self-recrimination at the squandering of his talents. The iguanodon acts as a counter to these thoughts, for though Mantell would go on to discover other dinosaurs and write and publish other books, it is this first find that stands as his monument. The discovery of the giant lizard shows him at his finest, summoning back from a litter of bones a world that had become buried in time, with not much more at his disposal than a chisel and a dogged refusal to be proved wrong.

There's a strange coda to Mantell's story. A persistent rumour circulates that after his death a section of his spine was stolen by Richard Owen, though how this was supposed to have been facilitated I've never seen explained. In fact, Mantell himself left a sum of money in his will to fund a post-mortem, adding that 'if any parts are worth preserving for examples of morbid changes, let them be sent to the Hunterian Collection', the same place where he had found the evidence that proved his giant tooth was reptilian in origin. The spine – which turned out to demonstrate an unusual and presumably intensely painful lateral curvature – was pickled and exhibited for almost a century in the Hunterian Museum alongside all sorts of oddities, from Roman teeth and skulls to the skeleton of the Irish giant Charles Byrne. In 1941, during the early days of the Blitz, the museum was bombed and something like 40,000 anatomical specimens were smashed to smithereens. A further rumour, repeated in almost all his biographies, is that Mantell's spine was among their number, but this is not the case. The spine survived the war intact, and was inadvertently disposed of by the museum's staff in 1970 during a clearout of the shelves, by which time much of Mantell's grand collection of fossils had been sold, lost or dispersed, an act of unmaking that this time really was contrived by the malevolent Richard Owen.

I could see Whiteman's Green from where I stood. It was one of the patches of wood that lay just to the south of the ridge. The Downs were blue behind it, and beyond them, invisible, were the low lands, the marshes that ran at sea level from Lewes to the coast. It was a wrench to imagine it as it must once have been: a tropical forest divided by a mighty and nameless river; a steamy world of tree ferns and cycads in which the English oak and ash were utterly unknown. I imagined the iguanodon passing between those flowerless forms, calling its rough music, the branches snapping beneath its feet. It was a sight that would never again be glimpsed on this earth, for it is one of the quirks of evolution that a design, once discarded, will not be repeated.

I don't know if Virginia Woolf knew of Gideon Mantell, but her last novel, completed the winter before she died, is full of visions of the primitive world he unearthed from beneath the Weald. *Between the Acts* is set in a country house on a summer's day right at the precipice of the Second World War. The narrative slips between characters, picking up stray thoughts and soliloquies as a radio picks up static. One of the women, Lucy, is reading a book called *Outline of History*, which merges two real works: G.M. Trevelyan's *History of England* and *The Outline of History* by H.G. Wells. Throughout the day images of the rich, sequestered English countryside are set in contrast to the prehistoric wilderness of the dinosaurs this book describes.

There is – initially at least – a larky comedy to these juxtapositions. One of the first comes early in the morning, when Lucy is lying in bed:

> She . . . had spent the hours between three and five thinking of rhododendron forests in Piccadilly; when the entire continent, not then, she understood, divided by a channel, was all one; populated, she understood, by elephant-bodied, seal-necked, heaving, surging, slowly writhing, and, she supposed, barking monsters; the iguanodon, the mammoth, and the mastodon, from whom presumably, she thought, jerking the window open, we descend.

Entranced by her vision, which compresses time most oddly, she fails for a moment to distinguish the maid who's entered the room bearing a tray of tea in blue china 'from the leather-covered grunting monster who was about, as the door opened, to demolish a whole tree in the green steaming undergrowth of the primeval forest'.

Between the Acts is a novel obsessed with the past, and how to make sense of it when confronted with the rupturing effect of war. Much of the narrative is concerned with describing a village play, in which England's bygone days are presented as a sort of mocking, tongue-in-cheek pastiche, a mash-up of Elizabethan poetry, Restoration comedy and Victorian triumphalism, complete with forgotten lines and interpolations by cows and rain. What is being sent up here is the official, imperial approach to history, which sees the past as a continuous pageant of coronations and battles; an approach regarded with intense suspicion by Woolf and her circle.

Despite this uneasiness, the past also proves intensely consolatory. In fact, it is startling how much the novel resembles an archaeological dig: a dig that has worked down through the cultural psyche of England, turning up the layered finds of centuries of thought. It's constructed largely from snatches of overheard or overlapping conversations, which themselves often contain fragmentary references – quotes, misquotes and allusions – to the great works of prior eras: scraps of Keats and *Lear*; orts of Racine, Swinburne and Lord Tennyson. These fragmentary relics testify to human endurance and continuity against the odds, and so too in a wider sense do Lucy's visions of the primeval past.

The novel was written on the brink of a great shift in the world, the incalculable change that followed on the heels of the Second World War. It was a change Woolf anticipated but didn't live to see. The approaching conflict appears only in glimpses, but the intensity of its threat is very strong. Sometimes the tone rises almost to despair, but *Between the Acts* is also playful and not immune to hope. It ends at night, in the timeless darkness of Lucy's visions. Violence, it is clear, will follow, but so too will love, for these are the cardinal points of experience in a world that existed long before man descended to the stage and spoke.

I left the ridge then and began to walk roughly east, descending slowly into one of the valleys through which the river flowed. Beneath me was a field of sheep and as I passed between the skinny ewes and fat, unshorn lambs, a hundred or more rooks rose out of a single oak, winging across the field and heading south-west with the wind. The noise rooks make *en masse* is staggering. What were they doing? Holding a meeting? Plotting a coup? A few swung back, the jacks of the pack, and I could hear more coughing in the trees, but they were nothing on the cacophonous crowd I'd flighted. The sheep looked up, nostrils flared. *Mayor!*, they bellowed. And again, more plaintively, *Maayor!* They followed me to the gate and watched as I went, yellow eyes slitted against the unwavering light.

It was hot now, the beginning of a heatwave that would grip the coast for a fortnight, before the summer subsided into rain. I passed up a dusty track into a farm, where I wandered bewildered between sheds that bore warnings of asbestos, unable to find the path. In an outdoor school a slouching girl was failing to get a pony over a set of trotting poles. Like an idiot I wasn't wearing any socks, and my right foot had begun to burn. *Keep hunting*, read a sign in the window of Sideneye Cottage, the words quartered white and red by the St George's flag.

The track gave way to a lane full of wild roses, sugar pink

and sugar white. They were making hay in the valley, the blue bales embossed against a suddenly fallen sky. The hedgerow here was stuffed to bursting, a botanist's sweetshop, full of St John's Wort and campion, beetroot-pink hedge woundwort, agrimony, meadowsweet and the silver-leaved tormentil that can both stem the flow of blood and dye leather red. I wanted to sink down among them and let my eyes slide shut for a while, but cars kept swooping by and the lane seemed – to my sore heel at least – to run on for ever and a week.

At last the path swung free, down a flight of wooden steps into one of the prettiest fields I've ever seen, full of rustling pink grasses hedged by elder foaming with flowers the colour of Jersey cream. I lay on my back under an oak tree and feasted, hated shoes flung off, on oatcakes, cheese and a Granny Smith, pared into slices with the rusty unlockable knife. Flies were landing on my rucksack, resting there a few seconds and then lifting clean away. Each time I closed my eyes the noise of grasshoppers switched on, as if my sight needed to be muffled before I could begin to catch what the day had to say.

I'd barely seen the Ouse all morning and now I could hear water running low under the nettles, a tributary trickling to the valley beneath. A couple of wood pigeons were entreating one another to *take two cows, Susan, take twooo cows, Susan*. Behind or above them I could hear a train passing, calling with its horn as it reached the massive viaduct that vaulted the river. The wind was sifting the leaves and the passing sun cast streaming cloud shadows across the countless grasses. There was only one more field ahead, and then the path would meet the water.

I'd had enough of waiting. I lolloped under the viaduct, hardly pausing to admire its 11 million bricks. For years I'd crossed this bridge twice daily to work, craning each time for a glimpse of the river pothering beneath. Now I was out, scot free, and I didn't have time to look up to where the trains rattled past, packed with people rebreathing air branded with discontent. At the edge of Rivers Wood, though, I slowed. The landscape had undergone one of its periodic shifts, oak giving way to alder, the high ground to the low. The trees cut out the light, discouraging the grasses. It was a gloomy place, the water stripped of its camouflage and sunk down into the clay. I walked along the bank and came to a halt by a holly bush, setting down beside a clump of wilted ransoms that released as I crushed it the pungent reek of garlic. Upriver I could hear the water running over stones, but here it came slow and grey through the sheer banks, eight feet high and vertebraed with tree roots in fantastic, impossible knots.

Later that day I would walk into Lindfield and eat chicken tikka in the village pub. I'd see a clump of orchids growing in a verge festooned with litter and I'd sleep at last in a truckle bed in a house that had been built in the last years of Henry VIII's reign, surrounded by a thousand-year-old box hedge, the oldest in Sussex. The bed was made up with sheets that had been densely hand-embroidered, white on white, and in it I passed a turbulent night, oppressed by the heat and the constant sound of a spring I could not see.

None of that mattered. As I rose I saw a deer drinking. She didn't see me as she climbed the bank; then all of a sudden she did. Her hindquarters bunched the way a horse's will, a motion I knew with my own muscles as the prelude to a buck, and then she sprang away. She moved in an oddly rigid, rocking-horse gait, bounding on stiffened legs across the track and into the darkness of the wood. She was neither rare nor extraordinary, that deer. There were thousands like her, as there were millions like me. But there she was, attending to her own path, which, for a moment, intersected mine. She was as unlikely as the iguanodon, and as imprisoned in time. It was a weave we were all caught up in. Beside me the stream was clicking east, relentless as a needle. A stitch in time, a stitch in time. Was there really more to the world than this? The details of the day – the cool still air, the sharp stink of garlic – were for a moment so precise that the great and hidden age of the earth seemed as unlikely as a dream. I ducked my head, bewildered, and followed the deer into the trees.

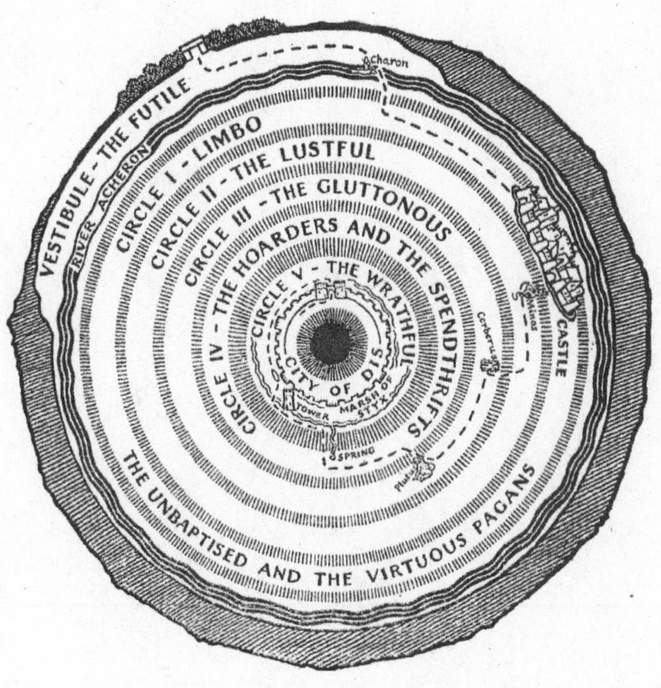

VESTIBULE - THE FUTILE
RIVER ACHERON
Charon
CIRCLE I - LIMBO
THE UNBAPTISED AND THE VIRTUOUS PAGANS
CASTLE
CIRCLE II - THE LUSTFUL
Minos
CIRCLE III - THE GLUTTONOUS
Cerberus
CIRCLE IV - THE HOARDERS AND THE SPENDTHRIFTS
Plutus
CIRCLE V - THE WRATHFUL
MARSH OF STYX
TOWER
SPRING
CITY OF DIS

III

GOING UNDER

I WAS STAYING THAT NIGHT in a house called Copyhold Hollow, which was set beneath a towering wall of beeches. The garden was bursting with flowers – peonies, columbines and overblown roses that strewed their scent through the clear dark air. I didn't sleep well, and as I lay on my truckle bed drifting in and out of dreams I thought I saw rivers I knew only from books turning like snakes through their shifting terrains. There was Eliot's strong brown god; Joyce's Liffey; the plum cake-smelling Thames of *The Wind in the Willows*; and the terrible river Alph of Coleridge's *Kubla Khan*.

Territories overlaid each other, or floated weightless, free of any known geography. The rivers riddled through worlds both real and false; they welled up in springs and fountains and gave out on great bleak estuaries and marshes. They ran through Dickens, George Eliot and the Bible, carrying bodies and babies in baskets. There was the Say and the Floss, Conrad's glittering black Congo, the swift trout courses of Hemingway and Maclean, *Huck Finn*'s Mississippi, and the Thames of *The Wasteland* and Virginia Woolf. Though they were nothing more than paper rivers, I felt almost drunk upon them, for they were the true sources of my own obsessive hydrophilia.

It was almost nine when I properly woke, and I stumbled down to breakfast in a daze, forking up sausages and gulping coffee as the house's owner talked of Berwick church and the complex intermarriages of the Bloomsbury set. It was 23 June, Midsummer Eve, the date of Shakespeare's topsy-turvy dream. The following Midsummer Day used to coincide with the solstice until, in 1752, the Julian calendar was exchanged for the Gregorian one and the two festivals drifted free. Midsummer Eve was one of those moments when the gap between worlds was said to grow thin. It was celebrated with bonfires and riotous dances, and was also the moment to pick fern seed, which conveys invisibility upon the bearer, being almost invisible itself.

I'd planned to leave before it got too hot, but by the time I'd finished the last scraps of bacon the sun was at eye-level and rising fast. There wouldn't be much river today – briefly where it crossed Sloop Lane and again in the meadows by Sheffield Park. Tomorrow, the path would join it at Vuggles Farm and that would be that, all the way down through Lewes and into the marshland of the Brooks. Today, though, I would be walking mainly in woods, the remains of the great Andredesleage that had once stretched across three counties.

The first was on the way to Lindfield, where I'd run like a maniac the night before, spooked by the shadows that gathered with the dusk. Now it was quiet and blissfully cool, opening onto a golf course still slippery with dew. The path skimmed the edge of town, crossing the high street and sidling out through the churchyard into a field of mournful cows with pointed hipbones that poked like hangers through their grubby coats. The cows were hot already, clustering in a wavering patch of shade that wouldn't last an hour.

There was no such shade on the path. I was in the full sun and the light had begun to play tricks with my eyes. Up by Hangman's Acre the grasses on either side of the track were etched so clear they glittered. Straw had been scattered on the ground, and it seemed that my vision had become impossibly sharpened; that I could count every stalk in a glance, every head of wheat, each one of the multiple and quaking grasses that bent beneath my feet. The straw was golden without being clean. The light sheered straight off it, a wave of light that didn't break but bounced straight back to the sky. At the corner of my eye the field flickered as if a hand were tweaking it, as if at any moment the whole *trompe-l'œil* might be snatched away, the painted corn on its backdrop of blue, though what that might reveal I didn't like to think.

I sat against a fencepost and smeared myself with Factor 30. There was a breeze that smelt of dust and roses licking at the hedge, and little queasy flares kept exploding in the wheat. The state was an aura, triggered by the sun, the precursor to a migraine that more often than not fails to arrive. These shifts in vision, which sometimes manifest as falling petals or schools of swimming stars, have the odd side effect of making the world seem unstable, an illusion flung up out of walls of light.

One of the symptoms of Woolf's mental illness was migraines, accompanied at the worst of times by hallucinations both auditory and visual. No doubt the experience of finding the evidence of her senses unreliable contributed to her impression of the world as insubstantial and in constant flux, composed of an 'incessant shower of innumerable atoms', an insight that permeates almost all of her books. Some of her characters, now I came to think of it, also suffered from disturbed or heightened vision, like poor Septimus Smith in *Mrs Dalloway*, who walks reeling through Regent's Park and sees a dog morph into a man, trees quicken into life and the dead approach him from between the park benches.

I didn't see dogs change into men, but for the rest of the day my vision seemed untrustworthy, as if I'd been subject unwittingly to the same sort of visual enchantment that afflicts the cast of *A Midsummer Night's Dream*. Some of the mischief there is caused by the juice of love-in-idleness, *Viola tricolor*, which when painted on sleeping eyelids causes the recipient to fall in love with whatever they next see, be it lion, ape, or a buffoon with an ass's head. But even those who escape anointing lose faith in the reliability of their sight. 'Methinks I see these things with parted eye,' cries a shaken Hermia, 'When every thing seems double,' and in reply Demetrius answers: 'Are you sure that we are awake? It seems to me that yet we sleep, we dream.' Perhaps it was the gift of the date, or the synaptic upheaval brought on by the sun, but all day long I felt periodically uncertain of the solidity of what I saw, as if I too walked through the slipping landscapes of a dream.

I escaped into Henfield Wood, though to reach it I had to walk through a hamlet of houses unstitched from the village and set back behind their own arcing drives. I kept seeing notices on telegraph posts offering a 'substantial reward' for a lost Siamese cat. It wasn't until I passed the third that I realised the date was 8 September, almost a full year back. They added, those signs, to the sense of stopped or stoppered time that is anyway the knack of midsummer, the fulcrum of the year, when everything seems to brake for a moment before swinging through ripeness and into decay.

Oh, cheer *up*, I said to myself, but the lost cat bothered me. A wren in the wood kept calling *chink chink chink? chink chink chink?*, the final syllable given a querulous upward lift. The light was softer here, draining through ferns and hazel leaves in an overlapping fretwork of greenish scales. There's something unnerving about a wood. It's the entrance to a different world, subterranean or set aside. Henfield Wood wasn't wild. It was intensely managed, the paths clearly marked, the wide ride carrying a swooping run of telegraph poles. I could hear children shrieking, and in the field at its border glossy mares and foals munched companionably on bales of hay delivered by a girl on a quad bike. The fences were in fine repair; the paddocks electrified. This was the south-east, parcelled and divided, immaculately tidy, every square yard accounted for. And yet, no matter how prettified it becomes, a wood retains in its shadows a glint of something less than tame.

I left the path and pushed my way into a grove of ash and scrubby oak. Something was walking about in the bracken, cracking twigs and stirring leaves. Yesterday, in Rivers Wood, I felt eyes upon me and spun around, expecting to startle a blackbird. A man was standing on the path. When I turned he ducked, and hunched into the ferns. There were two pheasant pens ahead, and the road just past them. Who had scared whom, I wondered now? I'm often frightened in a wood, in a way I'm not anywhere else in the world, except perhaps a multi-storey car park. It's the fear of what might happen when there's no one to see, when you're caught in a maze no less entrapping for being built of trees than concrete.

I'd been thinking that morning of *The Wind in the Willows*, and it struck me then that if it had nurtured my love of rivers it might also be responsible for this faint mistrust of woods, for I came to it in such a way that it was impressed indelibly upon my mind. My father left when I was four, and every other weekend he drove up from London to take us to his house. The soundtracks to these journeys were story tapes – *The Ghost Stories of M.R. James*, *Three Men in a Boat*, *A Tale of Two Cities* – and of them all our favourite was *The Wind in the Willows*. We lived then in the Thames Valley, not far from where Kenneth Grahame himself grew up, and the locations, though unnamed, were instantly recognisable. My sister and I listened to that tape so often it became part of our code, turning up in birthday cards and long-standing family jokes. We liked to recite the mantra *cold chicken cold tongue cold ham cold beef pickled gherkins salad french rolls cress sandwiches potted meat ginger beer lemonade soda water*, and to replicate it as greedily as possible in our own Thames-side picnics.

One autumn in the early 1980s we were coming home in a storm, and somewhere along the way the car ran out of petrol. It was raining hard and I suppose my father felt he had no choice but to lock the doors and leave us there, with the keys in the ignition and the tape still whirring on. It wasn't dark but rain was blotting out the windows, and through the streamy glass the world seemed very distant. When we broke down the Toad had just encountered his first motor car, and after his wild raptures the story shifted key. *It was a cold still afternoon*, the narrator said, and the Mole had gone out walking. The winter air must have intoxicated him, for in one of those moods of recklessness to which he was prone he decided to visit the Wild Wood, though he'd been warned about it long ago.

My sister and I looked at each other uneasily. At first the wood seemed pleasurably spooky, and it was only when the light began to drain away that the Mole noticed something peering at him from a hole. Could it be a face? He looked hard. No. But then there was another, and another, and suddenly there were hundreds of them, evil wedge-shaped faces with hard staring eyes. Then to the faces was added a flurry of whistles, and then a patter of feet that increased in time to an almighty hail, as if something – someone? – was being relentlessly pursued. The Mole began to run too, pell-mell, his breath ragged, his legs pounding, until at last he almost fell into the hollow of a great beech tree and there took refuge beneath a pile of dead leaves.

My father returned at that moment, fortuitously enough, driven by a stranger and clutching a billycan of petrol. The Mole – we waited breathlessly – was also safe. Rat had come to find him, armed with a cudgel, and the pair of them had stumbled across Badger's den as the woods subsided into snow. No harm was done. No one had been bludgeoned to death by a weasel; we were still intact in the back seat. And yet this incident confirmed in me a creeping sense that the world was not always as pleasant as it seemed, so that when I heard the story of Kenneth Grahame himself, I cannot say I was wholly surprised at how dark it turned out to be.

* * *

Kenneth was born in Edinburgh in 1859 and spent his early years in Argyll, where his father was the Sheriff-Substitute. He lost a lot of things early on – a mother, a father, his home – and though his mother's death was caused by scarlet fever the rest were the result of drink. Cunningham Grahame was an alcoholic: a secret and morbid drunk of the kind that can wreck a family, not through violence or malice but by failing to prevent it from slipping into chaos. After his wife's death Cunningham's drinking was no longer under his control, and it became apparent to the more sober members of the family that the four bereaved children would need to be transplanted into a different home.

The one chosen for them was The Mount in Cookham Dean, a little Berkshire village a mile from the Thames. The Mount belonged to Kenneth's maternal grandmother and was, according to his own account, a boundless paradise of orchards, fir woods, ponds and streams, populated by bandits, robbers and pirates *with pistols!* This period – low in adult intervention, rich in imaginative play – sustained Kenneth deeply and though it wouldn't last two years it lived on as a lost Arcadia that fed all his later work. He drew on Cookham Dean repeatedly in the dreamy, nostalgic stories that made him famous, and he returned to the river in his final book: the tale of Ratty, Mole and Mr Toad.

The Mount and its magical gardens were sold in 1866 and at around the same time Cunningham offered to take all four of his children back. A year later, he threw in the towel and bolted, abandoning his house, resigning his job and travelling to France, where he would spend the rest of his life in a cheap boarding house in Le Havre. The children returned to their grandmother, who'd by now moved to a cottage not far from Cookham Dean, and in 1868 Kenneth was sent away to school, the fees paid by an uncle. The traumatic effects of this triad of events, so closely bound in time, can be gauged in his inability to remember *anything particularly* after the age of seven. With the loss of The Mount and his father his childhood was in all real senses at an end.

Boarding school teaches boys to conceal their feelings and hide their private selves so deeply that it's sometimes impossible to access them again. Kenneth managed the trick of self-disappearance well enough. He had, after all, long been accustomed to hiding his secret world from adults, those *Olympians* whose *stereotyped and senseless* habits he liked to mock in later stories. The problem was that this hidden self failed to mature; that Kenneth, put simply, never quite grew up. The concealed boy remained undeveloped within him, and though this meant he possessed an unusually acute sense of how a child thinks and feels, it also left him peculiarly unsuited to the life he was required to lead.

What Kenneth wanted was to attend Oxford University, a place that he conflated almost with fairyland and from which he felt painfully debarred. In an essay published posthumously he wrote touchingly of this sense of exclusion:

> But those great and lofty double gates, sternly barred and never open invitingly, what could they portend? I wondered. It was only slowly and much later that I began to understand that they were strictly emblematical and intended to

> convey a lesson. Among the blend of qualities that go to make up the charm of collegiate life, there was then more of a touch of (shall I say?) exclusiveness and arrogance. No one thought the worse of it on that account: still its presence was felt, and the gates stood to typify it. Of course, one would not dream of suggesting that the arrogance may still be there. But the gates remain.

There is an unmistakable echo of these lines in the work of Virginia Woolf. She never went to school, let alone university, and in *A Room of One's Own* she writes with a mixture of longing and irony of a visit she made to Cambridge, where she was repeatedly shut out or sent away on account of her sex, for ladies may not walk on college turf and 'are only admitted to the library if accompanied by a Fellow of the College or furnished with a letter of introduction'. Her lack of formal education left her with a lifelong sense – sometimes oppressive, sometimes liberating – of being an outsider, and this in turn provoked a diary entry that I suspect Kenneth would have appreciated: 'Insiders write a colourless English. They are turned out by the University machine. I respect them . . . They do a great service like Roman roads. But they avoid the forests & the will o the wisps.'

Instead of being allowed to try for Oxford, Kenneth was ordered by one of the hated uncles who controlled the children's finances to take a job in the City. He served an apprenticeship in the family firm and on New Year's Day 1879 started as a clerk in the Bank of England. In the late nineteenth century the Bank was, by all accounts, an exceedingly eccentric place. According to Alison Prince, Grahame's most recent biographer, it wasn't unusual to come across a clerk in the lavatory butchering the carcass of a sheep bought wholesale in the local market. The lavatories were also used for dogfights, which were so much a part of Bank culture that some of the rougher clerks kept fighting dogs chained in readiness at their desks. Drunkenness was rife, hours were short, and behaviour in general seems to have been every bit as louche and riotous as that of today's hedge fund managers and currency traders.

One might have expected such a sensitive young man to flail in this environment, but Grahame had been to public school and was accustomed to roaring boys. He kept his head down, drifted up the hierarchy, and in his free time began to write. His early pieces seem sentimental now, but they appealed to the Victorian obsession with innocence and were increasingly rapturously received. He wrote about nature, about wanderers and wayfarers, about pig-headed uncles and men who abandoned the strife of the city to wander footloose through the sleepy valley of the Thames. There are altogether too many Autumns being carried forth in russet winding-sheets for contemporary tastes, but over time these affectations declined. As Grahame began to document the world of his own childhood his writing became more simple and intense. *The Golden Age*, his second collection of stories, was almost entirely autobiographical and it appealed so deeply to readers of the time that he became famous almost overnight.

As the century drew to a close, two things changed in

Grahame's life. He was appointed Secretary of the Bank of England and he met Elspeth Thomson, the woman who would become his wife. In 1897 she was thirty-five; a strangely fey orphan who despite her girlish manner ran her stepfather's house with considerable efficiency. Kenneth was frequently ill during this period, and much of the courtship was carried out by letter from the various haunts in which he was convalescing. Of what appears to have been a torrent of correspondence only one of Elspeth's letters has survived, but there are hundreds from Kenneth, almost all written in a baby language that is as difficult to decode as it is maddening to read.

'Darling Minkie,' an early specimen begins: 'Ope youre makin steddy progress beginning ter think of oppin outer your nest & facing a short fly round.' Another, unusually romantic, example ends: 'I'm agoin' ter be pashnt my pet & go on dreemin a you till youre a solid reality to the arms of im oo the world corls your luvin Dino.' Marriage proposals, wedding plans and negotiations around living arrangements were all carried out in this nursery prattle, which allowed both participants to play at being children adrift in a mystifyingly adult world. The sweet talk also served to conceal for a time the glaring differences between the two participants, for *Dino* had no real interest in intimacy, preferring boats and rivers to human company, while *Minkie* was scarcely educated and burdened with limitless romantic expectations.

Despite the violent objections of Elspeth's stepfather and the dismay of Kenneth's family, friends and even housekeeper, the marriage went ahead. The bride drifted up the aisle dressed like a self-conscious sprite in dew-damp muslin, a chain of daisies strung wiltingly around her neck. The honeymoon was spent in Cornwall, where Kenneth proved himself deeply unsuited to the *solid reality* of a wife by disappearing on solitary boating excursions at every available opportunity. Back in London, the benign neglect continued, much to Elspeth's distress. Nonetheless, she managed to become pregnant and at the turn of the century the Grahame's only child, Alistair, was born.

The tragedy of Kenneth Grahame's obsession with childhood is encapsulated in the purblind figure of his son, who he swiftly skewered with the diminutive Mouse. If Kenneth never quite grew up emotionally, Mouse would refuse the sordid business of adulthood altogether, and his story can be read as one of the more distressing examples of that strange region in literary history which deals with the real children who inspire or are otherwise caught up in classic books, from Christopher Robin to Alice Liddell and the Lost Boys of J.M. Barrie.

Mouse was born blind in one eye and with a painful-looking squint in the other. From the start he was an unusual child and his parents became convinced that he was a genius, though he was prone to wild tantrums and had an unpleasant habit of attacking servants and stray children in the street, a tendency Kenneth found amusing and did little to discourage. *The Wind in the Willows* started life as a way of entertaining Mouse, who according to the custom of the time was brought up largely by servants and spent frequent holidays away from his parents. It began, as Kenneth explained in a note to Elspeth, as a bedtime 'tory in which a mole, a beever a badjer & a water-rat was characters' – the baby talk was evidently surviving the couple's growing separation – and was developed further via letters. The *tory* was initially a very private business and it was only much later that Kenneth was persuaded it might be fattened into a book. During the writing process he inserted the more mystical elements, including 'The Piper at the Gates of Dawn', that strange and wistful chapter in which a lost otter cub is discovered, in a moment of rapturous pantheism, at the feet of the Horned God himself. The resultant blend of childish romp and distinctly pagan nature worship confused early reviewers, but the clarity and humour of Grahame's writing has proved unusually resistant to the attritions of time and his riparian world remains beguiling a century after it was first confined to print.

The character of Toad, that hapless blusterer, is said to owe a great deal to Alistair, but while Toad's wildness was given firm limits by his faithful friends Rat and Mole, Mouse was alternately spoiled and ignored. After the years of alternate coddling and solitude, public school came as a terrible shock. Mouse seems to have had a rough time of it at Rugby, leaving after only six weeks, while a brief stint at Eton precipitated a nervous breakdown. Contrary to his parents' fantasies, the boy was neither especially academic nor easy with his fellows, though his letters possess a pleasantly cocky charm and he looks attractively built in the few surviving photographs. In the end he was packed off to a private tutor, where he managed to disport himself with sufficient success that his father, after some string-pulling, won him a place at Christ Church, one of Oxford's larger and more prestigious colleges.

Oxford had been Kenneth's dream, but Mouse foundered there

from the start. He couldn't keep up with the work, botched his exams and failed to make friends among the other undergraduates. At last, in May 1920, he walked one evening from his college to Port Meadow, a pretty 400-acre area of grazing land bordered by the Isis, the young Thames, the same river his father had immortalised in his famous book. Oddly enough, another great work of children's literature, *Alice in Wonderland*, had its origins in Port Meadow. Decades before Mouse took his walk, the Reverend Charles Dodgson, who is better known as Lewis Carroll, rowed up the river there one July afternoon with the three young Liddell sisters, who persuaded him to make up a tale about a strange world beneath the ground. Mouse, whose private childhood story had also been parcelled up and sold off to the public, walked through the meadowsweet and buttercups to the railway track, lay down across it with his head over the line and at some point before dawn was decapitated by a train. The verdict at the inquest was accidental death, but the coroner's report leaves very little doubt that Mouse had taken his own life.

In the wake of Alistair's death the Grahames left the rural farmhouse they'd inhabited for years, sold off most of their possessions, including the vast collection of toys Kenneth had lovingly collected, and ran away to Rome. They spent the next decade drifting around Europe and didn't return permanently to the heartland of the Thames until 1930. Two years after his homecoming Kenneth died of a brain haemorrhage in their cottage by the river, and was buried in a grave lined with so many thousands of sweet peas that the air was steeped with their elusive scent.

Later his body was disinterred and shifted to Holywell in Oxford, where Alistair was also buried. I'd visited this place with Matthew, quite by chance, a few years back. The graveyard was half-wild, the grass uncut, and beneath a lilac bush we came across a sleeping fox curled nose to tail in the shade. Kenneth was buried there beside his son and on the front of their joint headstone was carved: *To the beautiful memory of Kenneth Grahame, husband of Elspeth and father of Alistair, who passed the river on 6th of July 1932, leaving childhood & literature through him the more blest for all time.*

That spring I'd been reading *The Children's Book* by A.S. Byatt, which is set at the beginning of the last century, during the great flowering of Edwardian culture and art. The novel is populated by all sorts of children's authors, among them J.M. Barrie and Grahame himself, and it exposes the inadvertent, almost collateral, damage they seemed compelled to cause by dint of their obsessive interest in the young. Among the cast is a fictional writer, Olive Wellwood, who spins an ongoing private story for each of her own children. All of them find their stories subtly oppressive, but one, Tom, is destroyed by his, and I thought he might stand in some way as a tribute to Alistair Grahame.

Tom is a wild boy, happiest in the woods, and he is maimed by the entrapping experience of being sent away to school. 'His' story involves a boy whose shadow is stolen and who must pass into fairyland to claim it back. When his mother later turns it into a popular play he feels unbearably exposed and sets out on a long maddened walk from London to Kent, where he reaches the sea at Dungeness, waits for the sun to go down, and then walks into the waves. 'He had sensed,' Byatt writes at some point in this troubled, troubling story, 'that the Garden of England was a garden through a looking-glass, and had resolutely stepped through the glass and refused to return. He didn't want to be a grown-up.' It is impossible to know whether this was what Mouse intended, but as an epitaph for Kenneth Grahame it seems uncannily precise.

I was recalled to the world abruptly then. I'd been walking up a long, sloping ride and as I turned a corner a golden dog and what looked like a deerhound came racing down the path. I must have jumped, for the man who followed them greeted me kindly, observing, *You were walking in a dream and then these dogs came from nowhere*, which added to the suspicion that I might have been talking out loud.

I'd come clean through the woods, and I found myself now in a snaggle of private lanes between beautiful old houses. It was a hidden world of a different sort, the spell cast this time by money. The houses – Pegden, Pilstyes, Little Grebe – were set back behind curling drives, the gardens edged by box the everlasting and rusty stands of beech. Fragments of conversation lifted over the hedges, accompanied by the sound of lawnmowers and running taps. I could see beds and borders through gates; attic rooms and gables; eaves and chimneypots.

According to the map there was a pub a mile or two further on, down in the valley where the river crossed Sloop Lane. The houses gave way to a plateau of horse pastures and fields of blue-furled wheat, the Weald spread out far beneath. It was the last high ground I'd cross, 230 feet above sea level, and I stopped at the top of the ridge to photograph my shadow pinned against the buttercups, startling four horses into a circling canter as the shutter clicked. At the bottom of the hill there was a hornbeam grove, the trunks hard and carved as bone, unbranching to the sky. Someone had been building jumps out of fallen logs, the sort of scruffy brush and bale affairs that a friend and I used to spend whole summers bodging together in Southleigh Forest, which now I stopped to think about it must also be a remnant of the Andredesleage. And then, Lord have mercy, there was the pub, and ginger beer and a plate of ham and mustard sandwiches that I wolfed right down to the crust.

The heat had not abated. *Oh, you never help*, an old woman with a dog said to her husband. The barman wouldn't fill my water bottle, but gave me complicated directions to a standpipe in the yard. Just down the lane by the old mill the Ouse was running milky in the shadows and brown as beer in the sunlight, almost silent where it used to clap and twist. I stood on the bridge and peered down into it, riffling shallowly beneath the willows. There was a line from Grahame's book that caught it. 'The river still chattered on . . . a babbling procession of the best stories in the world, sent from the heart of the earth to be told at last to the insatiable sea.'

There was one last wood to cross before I'd join it, down on the once vast estate of Sheffield Park, which Henry VIII stole from the Duke of Norfolk and Bloody Queen Mary gave back.

As soon as I entered Wapsbourne Wood, I could hear a nagging whine that I thought at first was a chainsaw, and then a choir of flies. There were signs nailed to the trees explaining the environmental benefits of coppicing, but the scene I came upon was on a far grander scale than any coppice I'd ever seen. The wood was mainly chestnut, and for an acre or more each one had been slashed a foot from the ground, aslant so they wouldn't rot. Huge spindly oaks and hollies stood like masts amid the wreckage. The brush was piled here and there into heaps, though whether to mulch or be hauled away I couldn't tell. *Coppicing produces a variety of habitats on which many plants and animals now depend*, the sign read. It was true enough. The foxgloves grew in profusion, as rosebay willowherb will grow where bombs have fallen or fires burned, rising in quick flames across the spoiled ground.

It was very still. Tyre tracks had wrenched the mud into waves, and over them the soft ripples of birdsong passed back and forth. Sometimes the lone walker feels that he is moving backwards in time, and sometimes that he stands at the threshold of a different world, though whether it is heaven or hell is anybody's guess. The landscape hasn't changed, not in any way that can be articulated, but a sense of strangeness seeps up from all around. At other times, it is what has been done to a landscape that curdles it, so it becomes a place in which one does not like to linger, for fear of something that cannot be expressed.

I had a dream as a child that I was going to hell. Judging from the bedroom in which I woke, pooled in sweat, I must have been six. We had just moved house for the fourth time and I was in my second year at the convent that had once, girls used to say, been the home of Hanging Judge Jeffries, whose bloody Assizes were notorious for their brutality. In the summer holidays the nuns used to come to our house to pick the grapes for their communion wine, and it seemed they'd picked also the lock to my dreams.

A child raised Catholic knows the world is not all it seems; knows that other realms exist above the clouds or thousands of miles beneath the floor. Though these beliefs may in their detail be discarded, the sense remains: that the earth is porous; that the eyes are not to be trusted. Flimsy, that's how I was taught the earth is, straw-walled, so that one good huff will bring it down. The books I read as a child didn't help. They were obsessed with Neverlands and Narnias, places reached by rabbit holes or wardrobes, by lingering near woods and rivers or plunging through a mirror. The notion of a world within our world, set deep, a world that can be entered only with difficulty by mortals, is not of course the sole possession of Catholicism, and nor does it belong exclusively to those escapist stories that Kenneth Grahame and his ilk used to spin in the innocent endless days before the First World War. There are older sources for these ideas, and in that spoiled wood they seemed very near.

The word *hell* comes from the Anglo-Saxon *helan*, meaning to hide; it is related to *hole* and *hollow*. Hel, the afterlife of the Norse, was a concealed place, as the land of the dead by its nature must be. Its analogy for the Greeks was Hades – which itself means unseen – and for the Romans Dis. Nor were these realms always freighted with connotations of punishment and damnation. The older hells seem closer to vast waiting rooms where the dead, unsleeping, bide their time.

Whatever names they go by, these places weren't often visited by the living. Perhaps six or seven mortals made the journey to the underworld in classical mythology. Aeneas, the founder of Rome, went to visit his dead father, descending through the entrance in the marsh of Cumea. Odysseus, slick Odysseus, went only to the brink, sailing to the edge of Persephone's realm and summoning the dead to visit him by the banks of the river Acheron. He wanted blind Tiresias to guide him home to Ithaca but the ghosts of heroes also came, drawn by the blood he poured, and he saw among them the hunter Orion driving a crowd of all the wild beasts he'd ever slain. Orpheus went down to reclaim Eurydice, who'd been bitten by a snake, and Hercules to steal the dog Cerberus, who guarded the gates to Hades. And then there was Psyche, who in order to win back her lover Eros had to carry out three tasks, the third of which was to bring home in a box some of the beauty of Proserpine, queen of the underworld.

The translation of this last story by Robert Graves offers helpful advice for finding one's way into Hades, which is linked to the mortal realm by means of all sorts of riddling tunnels and shafts:

> The famous Greek city of Lacedaemon is not far from here. Go there at once and ask to be directed to Taenarus, which is rather an out-of-the-way place to find. It's on a peninsula to the south. Once you get there you'll find one

> of the ventilation holes of the Underworld. Put your head through and you'll see a road running downhill, but there'll be no traffic on it. Climb through at once and the road will lead you straight to Pluto's palace. But don't forget to take with you two pieces of barley bread soaked in honey water, one in each hand, and two coins in your mouth.

The two pieces of barley bread soaked in honey water are sops for the dog Cerberus. Psyche is also told to refuse all offers of food except a piece of common bread, for eating in the underworld means you must never leave. It was this taboo that entrapped Prosperpine, whom the Greeks called Persephone or Kore. After being abducted by Hades – for the king is named after his realm – she ate three pomegranate seeds – but some say it was four and some five or six – and though she was allowed to return to the earth's surface for the summer months, in winter she had to return as Hades's consort. The high goddess Persephone, Odysseus called her, the Iron Queen.

These were stories from far away and very long ago. But our native folklore is full of odd echoes that suggest familiarity with the maps and mores of Hades, as if those ventilation shafts reached up through the caves and barrows of these damper islands too. There are thousands upon thousands of local ballads and tales that tell of the fair folk that lived under the hills, in the cold stone palaces they'd hived away like bees.

One such is Cherry of Zennor, which I first came across in a collection of essays by the poet Edward Thomas, who'd found it in *Popular Romances of the West of England*, a book of folktales collected by Robert Hunt in the mid-nineteenth century. Cherry of Zennor grew up in Cornwall, and at the age of sixteen she left her family to go into service and see something of life. After a day's walking she reached the crossroads on the Lady Downs, which marked the limits of the world she knew. She plumped herself down on a stone by the roadside and, putting her head into her hands, began to sob with homesickness. When she dried her eyes she was surprised to see a gentleman coming towards her, for no one had been on the Downs before.

When he heard what she was about the gentleman told Cherry all sorts of things. He said he'd been recently widowed, and that he had one dear little boy. He lived but a short way off, down in the low countries, and if she went with him she'd have nothing to do but milk the cow and look after the baby. Cherry didn't understand everything he said, for he spoke in a flowery way, but she decided to take the job.

They went together down a long sloping lane shaded with trees, so that the sun was barely visible. At length they came to a stream of clear dark water that ran across the road. Cherry didn't know how she'd ford this brook, but the gentleman slipped an arm about her waist and scooped her up, so she wouldn't wet her feet. After descending a little further, they reached his garden gate. A boy came running to meet them. He seemed about two or three, but there was a singular look about him and his eyes were very bright.

Her job was to rise at dawn and take the boy to a spring in the garden, wash him, and anoint his eyes with ointment. She was not, on any account, to touch her own eyes with it. Then

Cherry was to call the cow and, having filled the bucket with milk, to draw a bowlful for the boy's breakfast. After her ordinary work was done, the gentleman required Cherry to help him in the garden, picking the apples and pears and weeding the leeks and onions. Cherry and her master got on famously, and whenever she finished weeding a bed, her master would kiss her to show her how pleased he was. Cherry had everything the heart could desire, yet she wasn't entirely happy. She'd decided it was the ointment that made the little boy's eyes so bright, and she often thought he saw more than she did.

One morning she sent the boy to gather flowers in the garden, and taking a crumb of ointment, she put it in her eye. How it burned! She ran to the stream to wash away the smarting and there she saw at the bottom of the water hundreds of little people dancing, and there was her master, as small as the others, dancing with them and kissing the ladies as they passed. The master never showed himself above the water all day but at night he rode up to the house like the handsome gentleman she'd seen before.

The next day, he remained at home to pick fruit. Cherry was to help him, and when, as usual, he looked to kiss her, she slapped his face, and told him to kiss the little people with whom he'd danced under the stream. So he knew she'd taken the ointment. With much sorrow he told her she'd have to leave. He made her a bundle of fine clothes and then led her for miles on miles, all the time uphill, going through lanes and passageways. When they came at last to level ground, it was near daybreak. The gentleman kissed Cherry and said that if she behaved well, he would come sometimes to the Lady Downs to see her. Saying that, he turned away. The sun rose, and there was Cherry alone on a granite stone, without a soul to be seen for miles. She cried until she was tired, and then she went home to Trereen, where they thought she was her own ghost returned.

I didn't know how old this story was, but some of its elements – the fairy ointment, the land beneath the ground – seemed familiar. The development of folk tales is much like that of roses; stories may be hybridised or grafted or pop up as sports far from their native place. Cherry's ointment is a distant cousin of the juice Puck smears across the sleepers' eyelids in *A Midsummer Night's Dream*, and I thought the story's topology might have sprung from *Tom the Rhymer*, the classic underworld story, which goes back at least as far as the thirteenth century and is probably far older.

Tom the Rhymer, who is sometimes called True Thomas or elsewhere Tam Lin, met the Queen of Elfland on Huntlie Banks and was taken by her to her own land far beneath the soil, from where he returned many years later with the gift of second sight. There are many versions of True Thomas's tale and they bleed into one another and overlap, but the world he entered would be as recognisable to Odysseus as it would be to Cherry of Zennor. There's that stream she crossed on her way to the lowlands, though here it has grown more fearsome by far than the river Styx: 'For forty days and forty nights he wade thro red blade to the knee, and he saw neither sun nor moon, but heard the roaring of the sea.' Further on there's a garden green, where fruit grows that must not be picked 'for a' the plagues that are in hell light on the fruit of this countrie'. And can Thomas leave?

Not of his own free will he can't, and nor may he open his mouth, 'for gin ae word you should chance to speak, you will neer get back to your ain countrie'.

The day hung open on its hinge. The sound I had heard was neither chainsaws nor flies; it was a pair of red tractors out cutting the hay. I could see them now through the trees. One cut and one gathered; one built the windrows and the other bobbed them dry. A whole village would once have cut these fields, and now there were two men, their faces turned from one another, the cut grass shooting out, the cut grass raking in. As I crossed where they worked I caught the sweet, sickening smell of coumarins lifting from the hay. It struck me that I had not spoken more than a couple of sentences all day. *Gin ae word you should chance to speak, you will neer get back to your ain countrie.*

What country was I walking in, what age? Across the hedge there was a perfect Tudor manor, three storeys high, with two great brick chimneys standing as tall as a man above the stone roof. As I got closer I saw the house was hemmed in by caravans and that the road was thick with dust. There were no people, just the empty vans, ranks of them, and the house that stood as silently as if it were circled by snow.

The light was falling unimpeded now, in sheets and glancing blows. I wanted, like Laurie Lee, to stagger into a village and be revived by a flagon of wine. Instead, I tramped through the dust, dodging blue-black dragonflies, and crossed the A275 by the temporary lights. Just before Sheffield Park Bridge the path ducked through a hedge into a spreading meadow of thigh-high grasses. And there was the Ouse, all of a tumble, the sun skating off it in panes of light. It was a proper river now, passing between banks made impassable by a wild profusion of mugwort, nettles and Himalayan balsam. On the far side a dog rose had scrambled its way along the branches of an elder, and the little faded roses grew intertwined with flat creamy umbels that smelled precisely of June. The water was opaque and so full of sediment it looked like liquid mud. Its surface caught and distorted the shadows of the plants and beneath them the castellated reflections of clouds slowly shuddered by.

I dropped down beneath an ash tree. My hair was wet at the nape, and my back was soaked with sweat. What a multitude of mirrors there are in the world! Each blade of grass seemed to catch the sun and toss it back to the sky. Big white clouds were pressing overhead and beneath them crossed electric blue damselflies, always in pairs and sometimes glued into a wincing knot. After a while, my brain cooled down. I sat up and drank some water and ate a slice of cheese. As I chewed, a movement at the field's edge caught my eye. A wave of golden air was working its way down the meadow, wheeling as it went. It moved like smoke, a persistent, particulate cloud made up of flakes of tumbled gold. Pollen. It was June; too late for alder and hazel, too late for willow. I weighed up the options: nettle or dock, plantain, oilseed rape or – but it was less likely – pine. A pollen grain is identified by its architecture and ornamentation; it can be porous or furrowed, smooth or spiked. Plantain pollen is covered in verrucas; the pollen of golden rod bristles all over like a miniaturised pineapple. Echinate is the technical term for this latter design, meaning prickly, from *echinos*, the Greek for hedgehog.

Pollen is designed to drift. The tiny grains – hundreds of thousands in a single pinch – often have air sacs to help them float, as waterwings buoy a swimmer. These grains can travel great distances. In 2006 residents in East Anglia and Lincolnshire reported a pollen that covered cars and could be tasted on the air. It had come across the North Sea from Scandinavia and was seen on satellite pictures as a vast cloud: *a yellow-green plume sweeping the coast*, as the BBC report put it. Scientists identified it as birch pollen, the product of a wet April and sunny May in Denmark, though crop fires in western Russia may have contributed to the dust.

I leaned back and watched the cloud come. It could have crossed oceans, though it seemed more likely that it had risen from the neighbouring field, where coppery dock and nettle grew tangled amid the grasses. Didn't Plato think there was a wind that could impregnate horses? It couldn't have been more fertile than this generative swarm, twelve feet long and a yard wide, that rolled towards the waiting flowers.

That night I stayed at The Griffin in Fletching, a village that once specialised in the making of arrowheads; indeed, it was where almost all the English arrows in the Battle of Agincourt were cut. In the thirteenth century the manor belonged to Simon de Montfort, though he visited it rarely, and in 1264 his soldiers stopped here on their journey from London to Lewes, where the first great battle of the Barons' War was fought. Local legend has it that the barons spent the preceding night in vigil in the little church, though as with many stories handed down in villages it does not quite align with the historical record.

The Griffin was old too, and prided itself on its food. I arrived too early for dinner, and so drowsed for an hour in a tiny, sloping bedroom, the light seeping in through ill-fitting blinds. I got up at seven and went to the garden with a gin in my hand. It was Midsummer Night, and the whole country was basking, the sun streaming through the oaks and turning the grasses to flames. Near where I sat, a woman was talking and her voice carried across the lawn.

That fucking cunt, she said. *Is that the fucking cunt, is that the fucking cunt that gave that girl the acid*?

I looked over. She was sitting a few tables away, a tall deeply tanned woman with an elegant neck and long, slender legs. She was drunk. The alcohol had loosened her, though her voice must always have been loud. Her friend was smaller and chubbier, with a child's messy hair and frilly skirt. There was a dog with them, a pug in a diamante harness.

I hate Brighton, the first woman said. *No one ever forgets anything*.

Her friend was preoccupied with the dog. *Smuggles! Smuggles!* she shouted. And then they began to talk together, their voices overlapping. There was no one in the garden who could not hear them. One by one the other tables fell silent, as they might in the presence of royalty or death.

I took the morning-after pill three times last year. You might have triplets! I might have quadruplets! He slammed me up against the bar – girls can always look after themselves – he slammed me up against the bar and he said – Smuggles! Smuggles! – he said if you ever talk to me about coke – he was going out with that girl – but I wouldn't have! He said if you ever, but I never, I wouldn't have. I said I've never asked you for coke. That fucking cunt, that fucking cunt. No one forgets, no one ever forgets what you've done.

Two men joined them and then they were four. They moved tables and upturned ashtrays, mislaid dog leads and sunglasses. 'The Church has decided nothing on this subject,' says the Catholic Encyclopaedia; 'hence we may say hell is a definite place; but where it is, we do not know.' *Other people*, answered Sartre. And three centuries earlier, Shakespeare: 'Hell is empty, and all the devils are here.' You can't escape, however far you travel. After supper I walked out into the churchyard where Edward Gibbon was buried, who wrote *The Decline and Fall of the Roman Empire* and died nearby of peritonitis after an operation to drain the massive inflammation of his testicles went wrong and poisoned his blood. In my head the woman's voice translated: *he had fucking big bollocks*. It was an English voice and it had been going on forever: parochial and incensed, intent on cutting everything down to size. Meanwhile, the swallows were screaming the sky into tatters. I sat on a bench and watched them drop, wings akimbo, shrieking as they fell. How strangely we spend our lives: mapping the architecture of Hades or the ornamentation of a pollen grain. *No one ever forgets anything.* It's all piled up here somewhere, on the surface or under the ground. It never stops, that's the trouble. It keeps on coming, like that golden wind, breeding from out of its own ruin.

I lay awake for a long time that night, almost stifling. It was Midsummer Eve, bang on, when the wall between worlds is said to grow thin. Hell and Hades, Dis, the courts and palaces of the *sidhe* that exist beneath barrows: all these places seemed very close, perhaps just outside the hot little room.

I have somewhere a map of hell that, in the manner of an anatomical drawing, shows its subject in both a transverse and a sagittal plane. In the first, hell is a labyrinth wound about with rivers: first Acheron, where the ferryman crosses; then the terrible Styx, which bubbles its way through a stinking marsh; and lastly Lethe, the river of forgetfulness, which runs through the interior of the earth and up to Paradise. In the second drawing, hell is seen as a series of steps. They begin as the shallow declivities where the lesser sinners roam, and then they shelve abruptly, as a shingle beach does, into the realm that is known as the Pit. The great city of hell is situated at the edge of this pit, encircled by the Styx. Beneath it, in that vast hollow at the earth's core, is the body of Satan, encased in ice.

According to Dorothy L. Sayers, who translated the edition of the *Inferno* in which these maps are found, the centre of Dante's world coincides exactly with Satan's navel. The chasm in which Satan stands was formed when he was thrown from Paradise at the culmination of the war in heaven, plummeting at speed into our own circling planet; an event that in its horror caused a rearrangement of the world's geography. The landmass of the southern hemisphere rushed back in disgust, taking up a new station in the north; the sea flooded in to fill the gap, and Mount Purgatory was created as a small island from the displaced matter at the earth's core.

Some elements of Dante's cosmology reflect the beliefs of his time; others are a matter of his own invention. In the fourteenth century, many geographers believed that all the world's land was in the northern hemisphere, and that the rest of the globe was sunk beneath the sea. But the idea that Mount Purgatory existed as an island in the southern hemisphere: this seems unique to Dante, who placed the Garden of Eden at its peak, with the celestial state of Heaven floating above it.

Dante situated Mount Purgatory at the antipodes of Jerusalem, which would put it in the South Pacific, 1,010 miles south-west by west from the nearest inhabited land, Adamstown in the Pitcairn Islands. Curiously enough, one of the most active submarine volcanoes in the world, the Macdonald Seamount, is only a couple of hundred miles from Dante's site, a tiny distance in that vast ocean. The volcano, which was not discovered until 1967, is almost two and a half miles high, its summit rising to just beneath the water's surface. Macdonald's periodic eruptions have at least twice been witnessed: by the *RV Melville* on 11 October 1986, and by the *NO Le Suroit* and the diving saucer *Cynara* in Janaury 1989.

The findings of these two ships chart a submarine world of

lava lakes and sulphide chimneys not dissimilar to the landscape that Dante and his guide so laboriously travel through. The mountain's slopes are covered in a dense scree of lapilli, pillow lava and volcanic bombs in the shape of loaves and cauliflowers, testament to the furious upheavals that take place beneath the ocean's surface. There is a fissure on the volcano's eastern flank, and the seawater there is opaque and shimmering from the superheated gas that seeps continually free. It's not hard to see why the interior of the earth might be thought to boil, but to imagine that as our final resting place: why?

As to the location of Paradise, it's to be found on a bank on the path to Sharpsbridge in the merry month of June. I left the Griffin early, after a pain au chocolat and a bowl of prunes. It was the top of the morning, the very cream, and I skimmed it off and crouched in the cornfield, gulping it down. The clouds were coming over from the west like zeppelins, casting ballooning shadows across the metallic blue-green of the wheat. The field ended in a double ditch, and from it grew a mass of flowers in a profusion of colours and forms, such as is seen trimming the edges of medieval manuscripts. Black medick, I counted, buttercup, horsetail, ribwort plantain, hedge woundwort, musk mallow and curled dock, the clustered seeds a rusty brown. Wild rose, dandelion, the red and white deadnettle, blackberry, smooth hawksbeard and purple-crowned knapweed. Interspersed with these were smaller, more delicate flowers: cut-leaved cranesbill, birdsfoot trefoil, slender speedwell, St John's wort, heath bedstraw, tufted vetch and, weaving in and out of the rest, field bindweed, its flowers striped cups of sherbet-pink and white. The stem of the knapweed was covered in blackfly, and a spider trap shaped like a dodecahedron had annexed a few pale purple flowers of vetch inside swathes of tight-woven web.

A matter of miles, and the whole landscape had changed, the woods and pastures replaced with cattle and crops, the sandstone ridges with the smoother land that precedes the Downs. It took me a full hour to walk a few yards, so absorbing was this new world. The wheat on either side of the chalk track was at different stages of ripeness: on the west clenched and blue and on the east a fuzzy gold-green that was full of larks. I sat on a concrete block where a footpath sign had fallen and gathered an ear to chew. The grains when I cracked them were milky, though those I plucked later had the taste of risen dough.

The larks were all about me, invisible and uproarious, carolling out the untranslatable song they are said to sing at the gate to heaven. I'd found an owl pellet the size of a greengage on the block, and I turned it now on my knee. It was full of tiny fragments of bone that looked at first like husks of corn, and the carapaces of beetles, which shone blackly and powdered my fingers with a glittering dust.

It was a day of uplift. Everything was rising or poised to rise, the mating dragonflies crashing through the air, the meadow browns clipping sedately by. On the other side of the valley there was a small plane parked in a field and as I got closer I could make out the airstrip that had been built about it. White arrows were rollered onto the mown grass and flaking whitewashed tyres were stacked in threes to hold the bulbs of the landing lights. The plane was cherry-red and white, the legend G-AYYT above its wing. I imagined it looping back from Paris, crossing first the blue English Channel and then the second home sea of the wheat.

The wheat was preoccupying me. It had here reached another stage, the long greenish hairs unfurling and turning it into an ocean of grass, in which the wind moved as it will across water, folding the pile first back, now forth. The wind worked across it and so did the light, and I could not at first piece together how the trick was mastered. The stalks here, on this sloped field, were almost blue, a blue that increased from the boot upward like a flush, though later in the month they would grow gilded and then bleach daily until they were almost drained of colour, becoming the common straw that was once used to roof most of England and is still required by law for repairing the thatch of some listed buildings. The heads of the wheat were golden; the hairs that are known as the beard a watery greenish gold that became bronze towards the tip. When the wind flattened the heads – ah, that was it! – they caught the light, which rippled and rushed down the hill in little ebbs and flurries. 'The grain,' explains a Roman treatise on farming, 'is that solid interior part of the spike, the glume is its hull and the beard those long thin needles that grow out of the glume. Thus as the glume is the pontifical robe of the grain, the beard is its apex.'

The wind had risen and was turning the ash leaves white side out, so that they flashed when the sun flooded by. Between

Barkham Manor and Sharpsbridge I walked accompanied by the chink of a wren and a fleet of electric blue dragonflies the size of kitchen matches. I set about stalking one, bigger than the rest, but couldn't get within six feet of it, though I tried first to tiptoe and then to swoop. Its body was the milky blue of weathered plastic, those windblown scraps you find in hedges or caught around gateposts.

Sharpsbridge itself was stubbornly unfamiliar. I'd stayed here four years ago, in a house that was being rented by the son of a famous artist. It was another sweltering summer and we walked one night for miles, accompanied by the hum of pylons and the sound of a flute spilling from an open window and into the stubbled fields. I slept in an oast house away from the others, in an empty circular room, and above my head the sky through the cowl had been sown with fistfuls of stars. But the house, which was ugly, seemed to have disappeared. Perhaps my bearings had got askew. I kept remembering odd details: a garden full of raspberry canes, a wagon by the pond that had been left to rot beneath a swarm of tiny roses.

I was getting anyway into one of those trances that come from walking far, when the feet and the blood seem to collide and harmonise. Funnily enough, Kenneth Grahame and Virginia Woolf both wrote in praise of these uncanny states, which they thought closely allied to the inspiration writing requires. 'Nature's particular gift to the walker,' Grahame explained in a late essay, 'through the semi-mechanical act of walking – a gift no other form of exercise seems to transmit in the same high degree – is to set the mind jogging, to make it garrulous, exalted, a little mad maybe – certainly creative and supra-sensitive, until at last it really seems to be outside of you and as it were talking to you, while you are talking back to it.' As for Woolf, she wrote dreamily of *chattering* her books on the crest of the Downs, the words pouring from her as she strode, half-delirious, in the noonday sun. She compared it to swimming or 'flying through the air; the current of sensations & ideas; & the slow, but fresh change of down, of road, of colour: all this is churned up into a fine thin sheet of perfect calm happiness. Its true I often painted the brightest pictures on this sheet: & often talked out loud.'

There was a stile up ahead and as I descended into a field of dock, poppies and wheat, I saw it first as a series of colour flares: rust red, scarlet and golden brown, from which a small, pale gold bird lifted, circled and disappeared. Is the red of poppies the same red as the dye the Venerable Bede describes the Anglo-Saxons making from the shucked bodies of whelks, that 'most beautiful red which neither fades through the heat of the sun nor exposure to the rain; indeed the older it is the more beautiful it becomes'? It's so very bloody you'd think it would stain, but it never does, though if the flower is crushed it leaves a smear of bitterness against the skin. The colour is lucent, fully saturated, the red caught within the petal as if within a sheet of stained glass.

The wind was right up. A kestrel hung on the other side of the hedge, wings tilting, its head as still as if it had been pinned to the sky. There were blackfly on the dock here too, and the next field was riven by a ditch. I wandered over to take a look. It was half-full of cool greenish water, from which grew a lovely proliferation of skullcap, watermint, marsh bedstraw and ragged robin, the leaves submerged beneath the surface and the blooms a little above it. A couple of bees were puttering between the flowers, the constant sound they made as lulling as a purr. I lay down on my belly and used the ditch as a sightline, following it across the meadow to the wood beyond. The river must be a field away, I thought musingly, and Isfield two miles after that. And then, in one of those tumbling rearrangements of geography by which the Mole knew he was near his old home, I suddenly realised I'd been here before.

I leapt to my feet. Yes, there was the river, coiling across the top of the meadow, almost full and topped with streamers of weed. It came as a channel ten feet wide and about as deep; the perfect size for swimming. I thought I'd fling off my clothes and tumble in, but now all I wanted was to curl at the margins and gaze down to where the water ran like liquid coal beneath the shadows of the ash. It was pulling hard, and much clearer than I'd seen it, though when I dipped a toe the sediment lifted in clouds from the clay and sent a school of tanned little minnows skeetering for the bank.

It took me the best part of an afternoon to travel the final miles to the farmhouse in Isfield where I'd taken a room. I went station by station along the waterside, beating the bounds of a route I'd walked for years. At the weir the banks were muddy and the pool very still. Up by Henry Slater's poplar plantation there was a red cinnabar moth resting on an old tin can, wings stamped with circles of solid lampblack. Near Isfield bridge I sat under a blackthorn and watched a chaffinch moving between the hard green sloes, calling as it climbed. Two fishermen passed as I lolled in the sun. Both were shaven-headed and carrying huge rucksacks, and one was talking into his mobile phone. *It is, mate. It is signposted. You go down by that garage at Piltdown, that Paki, and it's down there on the right. It is, mate, it is! All right, see you in a bit.* It was the first human voice I'd heard all day, though I'd seen a figure walking through the corn in Fletching and a man strimming nettles by a wall on a farm near Sharpsbridge, bare-headed in the sun.

The world might have been emptied of people, but it teemed with birds. The blackthorns on the bank spilled over with song. I could hear a wren clinking away, the sound like a 10p dropped against a bottle, and a whole Greek chorus of tits exchanging apprehension and admonition. I could hear them perfectly, but apart from the chaffinch I couldn't *see* a bloody thing. After straining through binoculars for twenty minutes I became petulant. The same hot feeling came over me that I remember as a child from playing hide and seek. *Come out, come out, wherever you are!* I muttered to myself. *Come out!* – the same words Christ used to raise Lazarus to life. Perhaps the spell had become tarnished over two millennia, for I did not see so much as a blue tit. I needed the ointment that Cherry of Zennor had stolen. *If the doors of perception were cleansed, then everything would be seen as it is.*

Just then a sparrowhawk lifted across the roof of the wood, sifting the sky before dropping, light and lethal, between the trees. Oh, to see as a sparrowhawk does! My vision is 20:20; as humans go I am sharp-eyed. A hawk's vision is 20:5 and its world is correspondingly magnified. There's not a needle in a haystack that could escape its gaze. What's more, the available spectrum for a raptor's eye far exceeds that of a human. They have five types of colour-receptor to our three, meaning they can, for example, perceive ultraviolet light, thus tracking mice by the ultraviolet gleam of their urine. A hawk can also see true yellow, whereas the human eye has no way of telling whether the colour of a dandelion is the yellow of the spectrum or an equal mixture of red and green. It made me want to stamp my feet in rage, the thought of all I miss.

Perhaps I was being greedy. The vision I have is enough to overwhelm me; another two receptors and I'd be on the floor. I let go of trying to find the hidden birds and let my eyes rest on the horizon. The wood where the sparrowhawk had disappeared was in perpetual motion, the branches smashing the light to smithereens. The morning's high cloud had given way to mare's tails that streaked like fog across the glassy blue. None of it was as solid as it seemed. I remembered something Matthew had told me, a few weeks before he left. He was explaining the space occupied by matter. Most, he said – meaning 99.97 per cent – of the matter in your body occupies the volume of a mote of dust so minute as to be invisible. The reason why we're not in fact so small is due to the tiny remaining proportion of matter that is composed of electron orbitals. These almost weightless rings of charge guard their own space fiercely; more than bones it is they that can be said to form the architecture of our bodies.

This fact, astonishing in itself, can be expanded out. 99.9 per cent of the matter of all the human bodies on the planet, all 6 billion of them, takes up no more space than a single sugar cube. The rest is made up of empty space and drifts of electrons, nothing more. As for the planet: a whirling cloud of charge with a fistful of protons scattered through it. I lay back on the ground, which felt solid enough, and tilted my head to the river. It had snagged a scrap of sky and a few wavering trees that kept fanning out to reveal gaps. Is it any wonder we persist with the idea of an afterlife, from Hades where the heroes rest to the heaven and hell of the Bible. Can this really be all there is amid the darkness, this coloured and insubstantial realm?

That night, after dumping my bag in Isfield and eating a bowl of cassoulet in a pub so recently refurbished it still smelled of paint, I carried on up the river to where a wooden bridge crossed onto an island. The waterlilies were blooming, yellow and without scent, and the black water poured between the posts, rippling coldly in the setting sun. There were geese in the paddock opposite, grazing alongside horses, and beyond them a field of maize or peas. A fisherman was casting under the oak, the fourth I'd seen that evening. His dog ran to and fro beside me, watching the line as it dropped out of sight. Everything steadies at sunset, the day drifting down or closing in. Two moorhens were on the far bank, dozing on a wooden step. The dog trotted off with her master, who had caught and thrown back a single silver fish.

When I turned for bed, the sky was on fire. I couldn't keep up. It was impossible. I could barely even see. There was a lapwing in the fields by the Anchor, beating through the sky on wings like oars. In the ashes of the east a narrow moon had appeared, the same dull silver as the fish I'd glimpsed. A sunset is caused by particles of pollen, dust or soot in the atmosphere scattering the light. Though the particles themselves were invisible from where I stood, they had flooded the sky with streaks of Bede's red, in Latin *coccineus*, the word he used also to describe flames. The red gave into other colours, each of them wrung from a whelk dyer's vat: bluish grey, reddish purple, violet and indigo blue. Beneath them the river ran. It caught what it could. The last colours hung there, undissolved, in that looking-glass world that's so nearly the twin of our own. In places the water was red, like the river of blood that True Thomas crossed. If I waded out now, where would I end up? I wasn't sure. No matter how closely I looked, I wasn't sure.

IV

WAKE

I WALKED BACK THROUGH FIELDS of sleeping cows as the dusk fell down about me. I was staying that night in an old farmhouse near Isfield church, in a room at the end of a long corridor separated from the rest of the house by a velvet curtain. It smelled smoky and sweet, as if apple wood or cherry had been burning for generations. I'd been lent a torch when I went out, and now, tiptoeing back in, I was given a flask of hot milk and a homemade truffle to take up to bed. It was nice to be coddled. I wrapped the duvet round me and ate my feast while flicking through a book I'd found hidden beneath a stack of *Country Life*.

It was a local history, designed like a diary and made up of scraps culled painstakingly from Victorian newspapers. The stories weren't framed or explained. They ran one to the next, disconnected and fragmentary, suicides jostling with hare hunts, floods with village picnics. All the river episodes seemed to involve violence and death. 'In June 1886,' I read, '62-year-old John Hobbs, a carter at Colin Goodman's farm in Sheffield Forest, drowned in the Ouse between Sheffield Park and Rotherfield Wood. The farmer, Daniel Watson, found the lifeless body gruesomely floating upright, with the legs embedded in sand and mud and the swollen and disfigured head just below the water line.'

The carter had drowned right where I'd stopped and watched pollen drift the preceding day. The river there moved at the base of a channel a good eight or ten feet deep. The banks were lined with nettles, and there were only a few places where the water could be glimpsed, starred with lilies and gartered by weed. Twigs and straw were caught in the crotch of a hazel opposite: a high water mark that meant the river in spate would be quite a sight. It must have been a wet June in 1886, I thought, for a grown man to be submerged upright. I turned to the index, but there were no more mentions of John Hobbs.

What a strange way to be preserved in history, bedded knee-deep in a sandbank. There aren't many records of drownings in the Ouse, Virginia Woolf aside, and the most famous of them took place six centuries before Hobbs slipped or jumped into the summer river. The Battle of Lewes was waged in the hills above the town in 1264, and many of the soldiers fighting with Simon de Montfort against Henry III are said to have fled into the marshes between Hamsey and Lewes and become trapped there, some drowning on foot and some still astride their horses. I'd walk in their tracks in the morning, and as I gave way to sleep I saw among the fluid images that precede dreams the soldiers' bodies, mail shirts glinting, as they rolled beneath the water.

I was woken by sparrows talking in the eaves. It was sunny again, and I demolished the largest breakfast I think I've ever seen, with rounds of cereal and stewed fruit followed by a fry-up and mug after mug of perfect coffee. In the course of the morning's conversation, I found out that the house was once three cottages and that the middle one had previously belonged to a man who collected Sussex folksongs, though for the life of me afterwards I couldn't remember his name. The vicar was – but how had we got on to this? – a jazz drummer, and had recently walked to Lindisfarne; the woman next door was thinking of keeping bees. It was the kind of parochial conversation that is soothing to a stranger, full of church gossip and anxieties about what the neighbours might do or leave undone. My own plans were minutely inspected. Would it take me long to reach Lewes? Had I enough water? Did I have a flask to take a little more coffee? I was regretful about the latter, since I could think of nothing nicer than a riverbank coffee after a solitary swim.

It was another baking day. I cut across the cricket pitch and took the long stony path down to the river. I'm not sure I've ever felt as happy as I did that morning, with the fields rising like foam about me. I might even have been singing as I cut across to Barcombe Mills by way of the grazing lands of Boathouse Farm. There are often sheep in these fields, but today they'd been replaced by a herd of pretty cows the colour of milky tea. I eyed them warily from the top of the stile. I am – and I confess this in shame – afraid of cows. As I gazed down at the herd, I noticed one had raised its head and was staring back at me. It had a massive neck and a curly blond poll and – I began to feel slightly sick – enormous balls like Edward Gibbon. The bull watched steadily as I teetered on the stile, trying to decide what to do. I didn't want to cross the field, but I was damned if I was going to retrace my steps. Anyway, there were more cows on the other bank, all pied except a couple of roan and white spots like Staffordshire figurines.

I swallowed hard and climbed down. It struck me that singing might prove soothing, so I launched quaveringly into 'Jerusalem', a hymn that seemed designed to avert any number of bovine crises. The bull flicked his tail and rolled one small red eye. He wasn't interested in crushing me to death, or rolling my corpse into the river. Apparently the reason cows startle is that they have poor depth perception and can't gauge distance well. The best way to approach them is with frequent pauses to allow their vision to adjust. I was too frightened for the Grandmother's Footsteps approach, but a couple of tub-thumping choruses seemed to do the job just as well.

I hurtled the last few yards, and dropped down by the stile to recover. Last night's wash of colours had vanished, the red and violet replaced with the fragmenting green of ash and willow leaves, a design that always seemed on the verge of being pulled hopelessly apart. At the edge of the field there was a bridge that carried an abandoned railway across the river. The line had been junked in the late 1960s, and seemed to have been left untouched ever since. It ran at the top of an embankment and over the years the vegetation had grown up about it to form a green tunnel that concealed a secret garden, perhaps five feet high and shadowed by interlocking branches of ash and scrawny elder. I scrabbled up for a look, climbing over a barbed wire fence and forcing my way through the bushes. The sleepers hadn't decayed, and the flat yellow flowers of tormentil bloomed between them in mats of silver leaves. You could live here, I thought, undiscovered all summer, snaring rabbits and minnows, feeding on berries and the itchy green of nettle tips. The bridge's wooden slats had long since rotted through or been removed, and only the iron girders survived. I tried to walk across, but trees had grown up between them and getting above the river would require a saw and some sturdy gloves.

I could see the Downs through the bridge's arch, and a fisherman in mechanic's blue overalls casting by the weir. No one was around by the Anchor, though at weekends the pub hires out flat-bottomed boats like bathtubs and the river rings with shrieks as rowers crash into nettle beds or scrape beneath the stooping willows. The Ouse ran almost full through the open fields, the sky twisting uneasily within it. It was moving at a crawl, the surface a fractious blue that was broken periodically by fish and flies. How deep was it? Seven feet? Eight? There was a measure somewhere upriver; I'd have to check. It was a good twenty-five feet at its widest, I reckoned, though as it sliced through ox-bows and S-bends it sometimes narrowed to almost half that.

This was the land I loved best, planate with water, their histories conjoined. A little while back I'd come across a tithe map of this area dating from 1824. All the fields bordering the banks were called *brooks*: Hovel Brook, Ox Brook, Upper Brook, Fatten Brook. The word brook, from the Old English *broc*, more commonly means a freshwater stream, but in Kent, Sussex and some low-lying regions of Germany and Holland it is also associated with waterlogged land. I didn't know if the field names had survived, but the word remains in circulation. Fishermen in Lewes use it, and the marshes outside Rodmell are labelled *The Brooks* on even the most recent Ordnance Survey maps. These washlands and water-meadows are accustomed to inundation and the ebbing river has left the soil rich. Wheat and barley have been cultivated here since the Roman conquest, and until a century ago the river also served to drive the mills that once thronged this stretch, grinding the wheat into flour for bread.

They don't exist now, though I knew there were a couple of grindstones just past the pub, heaped at the edge of someone's driveway. But the Domesday Book makes mention of three mills in Barcombe and there was certainly a corn mill and an oil mill here in the nineteenth century, for I'd seen photographs of them. The last to survive seems to have been the corn mill, which was built of pitch pine and used briefly as a button factory before burning down in 1939, a fire that was locally rumoured to be an insurance scam aimed at raising funds for the Italian war effort. Though the breast wheels and grinding stones, the presses, stoves and rollers had all been sold off or destroyed, the landscape was still marked by the millers' work. Over centuries the river had been split into an elaborate tracery of head and tail streams, cuts and leats, creating a series of islands and miniature peninsulas. The first was just up the path, a fairytale island big enough to hold a white house and a little tangled garden full of apple trees and roses.

I used to be besotted with this house, which is across a stream from where the oil mill stood. For years it was half-falling down, the home of an old lady I'd sometimes see gardening in a housecoat, armed with secateurs or pruning shears. The island was overrun by geese, which lived among the trees in goose-green sheds and shacks. After the last big floods, the house stood empty for a time, and now it gleams, the old wooden windows replaced with uPVC, the weatherboards glossily white. The geese were out when I passed by, pottering to and fro between the fruit bushes, as smart as if they too had been dipped in paint.

A bridge led onto the largest island, a vast empty meadow marked *Primmer Brook* on the tithe map. It stood open to the sky, fifteen acres of grassland ringed distantly by trees. On autumn evenings I've often watched a barn owl here, quartering the field, and once I startled it face on. It was dusk, a moon three days before full caught just above the treeline. The owl took a rough zigzagging path up the meadow, hovered a beat or two, and came to within ten feet of where I stood. Then it paused, and the full intent stare of that tiny, ghostly face rested upon me, until it registered what it was looking at and with silent smoke-gold wings flew on.

It was too early for owls now, and too hot for anything else. The sheep were calling miserably as I sat down by the stream. The river had cleaved in two, and the navigable channel ran on the other side of the field. This was nothing more than a wallow, filled with yellow lilies and fringed with rushes and purple loosestrife. I looked around. There was no one in sight, not even a sheep. I tugged off my jeans and pulled on my old black Speedo, hauling the straps up beneath the shelter of my top.

The water looked as if it had been enamelled, in little licks of gold and blue. I took a breath and skidded down the bank, streaking my thighs with mud and panicking the minnows. Jesus, it was *freezing*. I staggered forward a couple of steps, feet sinking deep into the clay, and then cast off, chest hammering with cold. Two strokes and it switched to a pleasurable burning, as if each cell were fizzing. I paddled out to the lilies and rolled onto my back. There were damselflies skittering in circles above me, their wings a powdery blackened blue that made it seem as if they'd escaped from a fire.

It was in a wallow like this that Iris Murdoch and John Bayley began their courtship, or perhaps more accurately consummated it, for the first swim is not dissimilar to the first time a couple spends a night in bed. This swim – in a stretch of the Thames that glides unshowily through the countryside north of Oxford – is the opening scene of *Iris*, Bayley's memoir about his wife. No, that's not quite true. It opens with *two* river swims, not one, separated by a gulf of forty-five years. In the first, the couple are young. They slither in like water-rats, hop out again and dry themselves with Iris's petticoat, which he describes prettily as a *waist-slip*, before darting off for lunch. In the second, they are old. It's hot, the dog days of summer, and this time John has to undress his wife. She's wearing a two-piece swimsuit, no slip, but she won't take off her socks. No matter. They clamber in and loll contentedly enough in warm water full of lilies. Iris seems calm, but when John hauls himself out, holding his hands for her to grip, she gazes at him with unalloyed terror. Alzheimer's disease has begun to obliterate her memory and it seems entirely possible that she might forget how to swim and be drowned, though such instinctive, deeply known activities are often maintained long after the rest of the mind has unravelled. Either way, it's the last time they swim in the river.

John Bayley and Iris Murdoch were married for forty-three years, until her death in 1999, and for most of that time they lived in a sprawling and quite spectacularly filthy house near Oxford, where with a grand disregard for health and safety John dug a swimming pool in the greenhouse and heated it by dangling an electric radiator in by its flex. In *Iris* he describes the world they inhabited as a sort of kingdom of childhood, in which they communicated via a private babble quite separate from the professorial fluidities they employed elsewhere, and where the central act of intimacy seems to have been a kiss and cuddle rather than any more adult act. Martin Amis, observing both this and the dirt of Cedar Lodge, once wrote that the couple suffered collectively from *nostalgie de la boue*, literally the desire to return to the sticky mud of one's origins, the ooze and squalor of infancy.

I suppose you could see the love of swimming as part of this desire to retreat or be immersed, to enter that pre-literate continuous world that Kenneth Grahame, himself no stranger to childish prattle, also fetishised. Whether this is accurate or not, it's notable that water had a quickening effect on Iris Murdoch's imagination, for her novels brim over with rivers and pools and chilly grey seas. Her characters are forever in a frenzy of undressing, teetering on freezing beaches with a bathing suit beneath their dress. In *The Sea, The Sea*, a novel I find otherwise faintly ridiculous, there's a great deal of meticulous writing about swimming and its effect on the human heart. 'Trembling with emotion I tore my clothes off and walked into the sea. The cold shock, then the warmth, then the strong gentle lifting motion of the quiet waves reminded me terribly of happiness.' Though she also wrote of drowning, this association between water and happiness remained palpable throughout Iris's life. Her first memory was of swimming in Ireland with her father, and her last words on the subject, written in her diary as Alzheimer's disease began to erode her capacity to access the past, were: 'Indescribable. Holiness.'

A brain affected by Alzheimer's atrophies, losing its function and complexity. The Iris of Bayley's memoir is, like Alice, in the process of shrinking, the silent engine of her mind winding down, until at last she resembles a mystified and mystifying child, tagging perpetually behind her husband uttering *mouse cries*, collecting pebbles and scraps of silver foil and asking again and again *When are we going?* The house – a different house by now – is filled in addition to its usual chaos with odd objects she's gathered on her excursion: dried worms, twigs, bits of dirt; the indiscriminate final mutation of a lifelong fondness for inanimate objects. Sometimes John leaves her watching television, only to discover her later standing on the other side of the room, motionless save for her hands, which are busily rooting through this unappetising debris.

In his book Bayley describes a fantasy in which these half-comforting, half-disturbing objects are lost. 'It is wonderfully peaceful to sit in bed with Iris reassuringly asleep and gently snoring. Half asleep again myself, I have a feeling of floating down the river, and watching all the rubbish from the house and from our lives – the good as well as the bad – sinking slowly down through the dark water until it is lost in the depths. Iris is floating or swimming quietly beside me. Weeds and larger leaves sway and stretch themselves beneath the surface. Blue dragonflies dart and hover to and fro by the riverbank. And suddenly, a kingfisher flashes past.' If this is an attempt to enter imaginatively the experience of memory loss it is decidedly consoling, even pleasurable. But then Iris also described what was happening to her in liquid terms, twice telling her friend Peter Conradi that she was 'sailing into the dark'.

This marriage, in which a clever and kindly man takes care of his more brilliant wife, bears a distinct resemblance to that of Leonard and Virginia Woolf, who also lived rather sluttily. Virginia, Leonard once wrote, was a ferocious creator of what he called *filth-packets*: 'those pockets of old nibs, bits of strings, used matches, rusty paper-clips, crumpled envelopes, broken cigarette-holders, etc., which accumulate malignantly on some people's tables and mantelpieces', while Leonard himself had a marmoset called Mitz that regularly relieved herself down his back.

Grubbiness aside, the resemblance goes deeper than the superficial similarity of trajectory, for all marriages must end in bereavement of some kind. Instead, it's something about the mechanics of the two relationships, for they each resemble delicate instruments that rely on careful weighting and a judicious use of space. Both women were pulled in two opposing directions throughout their lives: inward, towards the intense, almost febrile life of the mind; and outward, towards a mélange of external love affairs and passions. Despite this both felt their husbands to be the steady centre of their lives, something I think Amis had in mind when he wrote that Iris *settled,* in all senses of the word, for Bayley.

These two couples nurtured a kind of fertile separateness, a *solitude à deux* that seems wholly at odds with our modern conception of marriage. It is striking how frequently Virginia Woolf and John Bayley in particular write of the pleasure of writing alone in a room, knowing that somewhere else in the house, in their own private sphere, their spouse is also happily at work. Illness collapses these divisions, particularly illness of the mind; either, in Virginia's case, by making public and exposed what was hitherto secret, or, in the case of Iris, by obliterating the mind's hidden world altogether.

Either way, the sense of the spouse as co-traveller is destroyed. All that remains, when the beloved at last departs, is a clutter of objects and a sink of memories. In an interview after Iris's death, Bayley caught at the painful ambivalence of the latter when he described it as both 'a cool river into which he could plunge' and 'a cancer eating away at the present'. I don't doubt that Leonard Woolf would have known exactly what he meant.

⋆ ⋆ ⋆

I was getting cold in the wallow and to my intense annoyance I realised I hadn't brought a towel. In the absence of a handy waist-slip I lay in the grass to dry and as I basked there a buzzard came up from behind the trees and worked its way overhead in a series of linking circles. The clouds were tightening up into cotton wool balls, the precursor to a mackerel sky. A pheasant was coughing in the hedge, and the omnipresent wood pigeon slurred sleepily from the bridge. The present, the present. It never stops, no matter how weary you get. It comes unstintingly, as a river does, and if you aren't careful, you'll be swept off your feet. I should have warned the wood pigeon. It skimmed down to the bank, got tangled in a nettle, and toppled comically into the water, a masterclass in how not to fly.

Voices were coming from downstream, and at Barcombe Mills I found a crowd so strange it took a while to separate them out. Three men were playing with a rubber dinghy. One had a twisted face, and the speech of all three sounded distorted, their mouths moving exaggeratedly as they towed the little boat back and forth. Further on, a white-haired woman and a girl with dreadlocks were sitting on the bank in swimsuits, their legs invisible beneath the cloudy water. As I approached they slipped in together, as seals do when startled. Under the big willow, a boy was sitting full-lotus in a nest of sheepskins, naked except for his trunks. He was tanned and very beautiful, his back straight, his eyes closed. The air was heavy with meadowsweet, that funereal, sneeze-inducing scent.

I plopped in too, undressing more discreetly this time. *Isn't it wonderful*, the old lady sang out. It was. The river seemed warmer here and I trod water in the wide pool by the rushes, leaning my head back till the silt soaked into my scalp. The boy jumped in too, and disappeared towards the weir. As I dried off he returned, and stood on the bank for a long time, enfolded in a tight embrace with the younger of the women. When she turned to go he called after her: *Hey Jen? Something else we should do while we're on this summertime nature thing? It's a practice Jesus taught for healing? To go down to the river and cover ourselves with the clay where it's warmed in the sun?* There was something about his voice that made me uneasy. He had that singsong intonation I knew from festivals and retreats, high on its own visions: the antithesis of the joyous splash with which he'd launched himself into the river.

I'd been visiting this patch of ground consistently for over a decade, alone or with friends. I'd last come – it seemed astonishing that I'd forgotten this – with Matthew the weekend that we split up. It was the only time the river failed to work its spell. I felt I was walking somewhere I'd never seen before, that I was not connected to in any way. The sun was shining, there were the usual swimmers and cavorting dogs, the horses grazed by the Bevern, and I walked and breathed and wept without even really feeling any pain. It was the localised numbness that follows immediately upon upheaval, the consequence of a benevolent tincture of endorphins and adrenalin. The world seemed enormously far away, and at moments its unfamiliarity was terrifying, as if the sky hung yellow or the sun set in the east.

How long ago was that? Two months, I thought, for it had been a few days after my thirty-second birthday. We'd courted here too. I remembered kissing in the rain by the weir, and lying together in Primmer Brook one August years ago, the pinkish grasses grown over our heads so that we were hidden in a cavern away from the world, the river running north to south a few yards beyond our feet. I felt as if I were shuffling memories like cards in a deck. They fell onto the bank: a king and a jack, a four of clubs. This is, I suppose, why people go abroad after a change of some troubling sort, to walk on ground untenanted by ghosts.

Memory is a funny business. Sometimes, moving through water, I feel I'm washed of all thoughts, all desires: content to luxuriate like a starfish, rocking on my own pulse, sensate to no more than the wavering light as it sinks through space to reach my eyes. I might as well have never been born; I'm not sure I know even my name. And then, on other days, the opposite occurs. There have been times when, sunk in a river or a chalky sea, I have felt the past rise up upon me like a wave. The water has loosened something; has dissolved what once was dry; weighted as if with lead, it filters now through my own veins. The present is obliterated, but what the eye sees, what the ear hears, it is not possible to share.

The river was clotting with sodden lumps of poplar fluff. It was falling from the female trees, drifting like an artificial Christmas across the track and into the nettles. It was tempting to gather it up to plug my ears, to drown out the voices of the dead and gone. When Odysseus sailed past the island of the sirens, he used beeswax to shield the ears of his sailors, so that they wouldn't be tempted by that clear-voiced, insinuating song. But he left his own ears open, and so he heard what they offer men, which is neither material wealth nor sexual pleasure. The sirens promised Odysseus knowledge: both of what had been and what was yet to come. Bound to the mast he begged to go closer but the oarsmen ignored his pleas, rowing on until the lovely voices were lost beneath the waves.

The sirens, Homer says, lived on a meadow starred with flowers. Their father was the river god Achelous, and though in the Hellenic period they were as much birds as women, bearing both wings and claws, by the eighth century they had acquired the tails of fish, had become indeed the mermaids that sing sailors to their doom. And their song: was it like the sea moving through caverns, or like air playing across hidden holes in the cliffs as a flautist plays on a flute? I don't know if I could have resisted it, the lure of perfect knowledge. It was the mess of the past that troubled me, the attrition, the impossibility of telling whose memory was right and whose was corrupted or incomplete.

But those who did listen to the sirens didn't profit from it. When Circe first warned Odysseus about the island, she told him that the sirens sat in their pretty meadow surrounded by a great heap of bones belonging to rotting men, their skins tanned by the wind until they resembled hides. Perhaps their knowledge paralysed them, for how could you act if you knew everything that had occurred or would occur? Maybe it's better to go on as we do: half-blind, half-deaf, trailing the litter of the past behind us like a comet's tail, now flashing, now flailing through the infinite dark.

* * *

At the weir, the river got into a tangle. Andrew's Cut flowed roughly east, down to the hidden reservoir and the water treatment works. The main river sloshed under Pike's Bridge, while two little channels sheered west through a pair of sluice gates, toppling down into the millpool where fishermen cast for pike in winter and in summer sea trout and carp. The Ouse becomes tidal at Barcombe Mills, and a great deal of effort has been expended on the preservation of the sea trout, which grow unusually large here, though they are elsewhere rare in lowland rivers. The sluices and weirs had been fixed with ladders so that the fish could work their way upstream to spawn, and catches were limited to six a season.

Somewhere I'd come across a copy of the health and safety warnings issued by the local angling club. Dangers included catching Weil's disease (*All anglers should take sensible precautions, including not putting your hands in your mouth after immersing in river water and not touching any dead animals, especially rats*), being bitten by pike and wrapping your fishing line around a high voltage cable. Rabies was also a possibility, since it's not unknown for a fly fisherman to hook a bat as he casts at dusk. It was an image that struck me as horrifying, though I suppose it's no more so than fishing itself, since bats at least breathe air and are not simultaneously suffocating as they're reeled to the bank.

I stood for a long time on Pikes Bridge, looking down into the pool. No one was fishing today, and the water was dark as liquorice and as intolerant of light. The sea trout were swarming just beneath the surface, and on the wall of the old toll house there was a sign displaying the prices it had once cost to cross here: *one shilling for a motor car; one and six for a wagon and horse.* Barcombe Mills was the site of one of the earliest bridges across the Ouse, and Simon de Montfort's troops are thought to have come this way from Fletching to where Henry III and his army were camped at Lewes. For the rest of the day I'd be travelling in their wake, walking first through the old marshes where the London troops were routed and then climbing up into the town itself, where the king had been cornered and forced to sign away his power.

There are places where the past gathers as thickly and as insubstantially as pollen, places where it seems as oppressive as – how had John Bayley put it? – a cancer eating up the present. What had happened by the river almost eight hundred years before had left a mark on both the landscape and the nation that remains visible in certain lights, for it is one of the stories by which England herself was shaped.

The Battle of Lewes had its roots in the civil unrest that led to the signing of Magna Carta by John Lackland, the hopeless Plantagenet king. A generation on, the question of how far a king's power might extend remained unsettled. Indeed, the period between the Battle of Hastings and the first Tudor king was when the nation's identity began to be hammered out. In the thirteenth century, England was emerging from centuries of conquest. The most basic aspects of nationhood – how a country is governed, what language it speaks, where its boundaries lie – were still in flux, particularly with regard to the Channel. In 1227, the year in which Henry III began his rule, French was still the official language of court. English territories would be held in northern France until 1558, while French armies had controlled London not twelve years back.

Ironically enough, the man who would lead the Barons' rebellion was himself French. Simon de Montfort was born around 1208, the youngest son of a nobleman and crusader also called Simon de Montfort. The elder Simon had inherited from his mother a claim to an English earldom, but was prevented from taking it up by an edict from King John that forbade French nobles from holding English lands. Like his son, Simon was by all accounts a dogged fighter and brilliant strategist, though he put his skills to less noble ends. He was the military leader of the Albigensian Crusade, and was eventually killed in 1218 during the siege of Toulouse by the heretics he'd made it his life's work to eradicate.

As the youngest son, Simon de Montfort hadn't inherited lands of his own, and after his father's death he began the complicated process of regaining the English earldom. By 1230 he had the spoken agreement of Henry III, and within a year had taken possession of the Leicester lands. This sounds like something of a coup, but the new earl was only beginning his ascent. He became close to the king, who was a year his senior, and in 1238 married Henry's sister, Eleanor of England, during the Christmas court.

Eleanor was twenty-three and already a very rich widow. At the age of nine she'd married William Marshall, the second earl of Pembroke, and after he died in 1231 she'd sworn a vow of holy chastity in the presence of the Archbishop of Canterbury. Although Henry had given his consent, the wedding was secret, and when it was discovered caused uproar among both the nobility and priests. Henry's brother Richard of Cornwall was particularly incensed and for a few days civil war seemed a distinct possibility. Simon – courteous, cunning Simon – smoothed matters over, showering Richard with gifts before dashing off to Rome to have his marriage validated by the Pope.

The king took Simon's side, but cracks in their relationship soon started to develop. The first occurred when Simon named Henry as the assurance on a debt without first asking his permission, an act of catastrophic rudeness that enraged the king. Henry III was a generous man; he liked to give gifts, from tuns of wine to castles, and his habit of spoiling new and often French favourites, in particular his wife's relations and his own half-brothers, infuriated his barons. A generous man: what an understatement. Henry was incapable of realising limitation. He was lavish in his responsibilities to the Church of Rome, and profligate when it came to his own comforts and entertainments. When Dante called him *il re della semplice vita*, king of the simple life, and seated him alone in purgatory, we might take it as read that he was being ironic.

He kept a menagerie at the Tower of London: two leopards, a bear, the first elephant England had ever seen. He was obsessively interested in art and architecture, and his palaces were intricately embellished. The walls – what odd details survive – he liked painted green, picked out with silver stars and the heraldic roses that were the favourite flowers of his wife. The Gothic abbey at Westminster was his grandest project, and he laid the first stone when he was only twelve. 'I want to think of it in its first fairness,' the architectural historian William Lethaby wrote centuries later: 'when Henry III ordered pear trees to be planted in the herbary between the King's Chamber and the Church, evidently so that he might see it over a bank of blossom.'

And the money for that bank of blossom, not to mention the ill-planned wars on France, or the scheme to buy the kingdom of Sicily from the Pope: where was it to be found? From wherever it could be bribed, borrowed or stolen. Raising money for crusades that never took place was a favourite trick, for who would refuse their pious king, bent on the work of Rome? When his son Edward was born, Henry had turned back presents that weren't suitably lavish, and now, as he travelled round the country, he demanded extravagant gifts as well as bed and board. Nor was he averse to crueller methods. When a bad harvest in 1257 led to famine in London, he seized the corn imported from Germany and tried to sell it at a profit to his starving people. This latter scheme, following as it did upon the absurd attempt to make his son king of Sicily, led directly to the first serious conflict with the barons: the so-called Mad Parliament of the summer of 1258.

In the two decades since his wedding to Eleanor, Simon's relationship with the king had cooled. During one violent row, the monk, diarist and legendary gossip Matthew Paris reported that Simon de Montfort 'openly declared that the King was a manifest liar', to which the king replied: 'I never repented of ought so much as I now repent me that I ever allowed thee to enter England, or to hold any land or honour in that country where thou hast fattened so as to kick against me.' Nonetheless, the earl of Leicester remained unshakeably loyal to his adopted country, refusing an offer from the French nobility to return as High Steward while Louis IX was on crusade. But loyalty to the country was not the same as loyalty to the king, and in the months before the Mad Parliament Simon de Montfort became a central figure in the drive for reform.

The document the barons produced, the Provisions of Oxford, was the first real attempt to establish a national constitution. It set out rules for a council of barons and for fair and regular courts, as well as attempting to reduce corruption among the nobility and clergy. More importantly, it tried to limit the spending and legislative powers of the king, and to banish the foreign advisers on whose influence he depended. The barons presented the Provisions to Henry in full armour. The message was unequivocal: swear to uphold them or risk civil war. And the king, coward that he was, took up the quill and signed.

This sounds like a place to end a story, and so it might have proved had the king been either honest or wise. Since he was neither, dissent rumbled on. The business of establishing the Provisions across the country foundered, and for the next few years the majority of the barons drifted uneasily between the goal of reform and loyalty to the king, while Simon himself spent much of the time in France. Matters came to a head in 1263. The armies of both sides roamed the country, seizing land and raising funds by extortion and violence. According to the royalist chronicler William of Rishanger, the savagery of the rebels was such that the year:

> . . . trembled with the horrors of war; and as every one strove to defend his castles, they ravaged the whole neighbourhood, laying waste the fields, carrying off the cattle, and sparing neither churches nor cemeteries. Moreover, the houses of the poor rustics were rummaged and plundered, even to the straw of the beds.

As for the royals, Prince Edward gained entrance to the treasury at Temple one day at dusk and under the pretext of wishing to view his mother's jewels stole up to £1,000 from the coffers there, using crowbars to crack the chests. A few weeks later, the Londoners pelted Queen Eleanor with eggs and stones as she attempted to flee for Windsor by boat, an incident that would have significant consequences the following summer.

At the end of the year, there was a last-ditch attempt at peace. The two sides agreed to turn for arbitration to Louis IX, king of France, and both swore to uphold his verdict. The Mise of Amiens was announced in January 1264, and turned out to be almost entirely in favour of the king. It was not what the barons expected. Despite their promises, they refused to commit to a document that in the name of the Father, the Son and the Holy Ghost swore to *annul and make void the Oxford Statutes*. The only avenue left was to make war upon the king.

It is at this point that the story begins to approach the Ouse. On 6 May 1264, the Montfortian army left London for Fletching, the village where I'd spent Midsummer Eve. If they hoped to defeat the royalists, it would have to be in the south, where their own support was strongest. When news of the move reached Henry, who was billeted then at Battle Abbey, he turned at once for Lewes and the castle of his ally John de Warenne, a royalist so staunch that he'd signed the Provisions of Oxford after even the king himself. Both armies came up through the woods of the Weald, Henry from the east and Simon from the north, and the king lost his cook Thomas to the canny forest-bred archers, who made travel so dangerous for the royalist troops that they were forced to ride in full armour. At Lewes they were billeted in the great Cluniac priory on the edge of the town, separated from the castle by a tribu-tary of the Ouse called the Winterbourne. Behind the priory lands was the marsh that only a long time later became the fertile grazing land of the Brooks; in the thirteenth century it must have a sinister, shifting place, the province of waterfowl and eels rather than rabbits and sheep.

There was one final round of bargaining before the battle began. On 12 May, Simon and his troops, who'd by now passed through the woods to a valley beneath Mount Harry, a few miles shy of Lewes, sent two parties of bishops to negotiate with the king. The first asked for the Provisions to be reaffirmed; the second promised what amounted to a sweetener of some £30,000 to compensate for damage suffered during the preceding months. This was particularly aimed at the king's irascible brother, Richard of Cornwall, whose manor at Isleworth had been destroyed, his orchards chopped down and his expensive new fishpond drained by a mob of London rebels. The proposals were rejected, and Prince Edward – later Longshanks, Hammer of the Scots, who would brutalise the north and father Edward II, the doomed homosexual king – sent back the message that the Montfortians 'shall have no peace whatsoever, unless they put halters round their necks and surrender themselves for us to hang them up or drag them down, as we please'.

A last rush of letters, equally defiant, was exchanged the following day, by which time de Montfort had crept a little further south, to what's been calculated by the historian David Carpenter to be the land between Offham and Hamsey. I could see the hills above their camp from where I stood, furred with trees, a white scar showing the place where some of the soldiers' corpses were later buried. Before dawn on 14 May the rebel army rose and climbed into the Downs, slogging up Blackcap and working their way south until they reached the high point of land that overlooked Lewes. There they made their confessions and donned the white crosses that crusaders wore above their soldiers' mail. Then the troops assembled into three blocks, a left, a right and a centre, with a reserve wing under the command of de Montfort set a little higher up, where the progress of the battle could be observed.

In the town below, the king and his troops were woken by a returning foraging party out hunting for hay, who'd seen the baronial army massing on the hill. The story most often told is that they came in great disorder, after a night of women and wine, with Edward ahead and the king and his brother Richard lagging behind, though the fact that a document was signed by all three that morning makes this tale seem unlikely. Either way, Edward didn't ride with the main army, who came out under the famous red dragon standard that was supposed to put fear into men, perhaps because, by some contrivance, its tongue was perpetually in motion. Instead, his division came up from the castle in the company of de Warenne, climbing up through what's now the Wallands estate to come face to face with the third division of the baronial army. Though this wing was fronted by knights on horses, it was made up largely of untrained London foot soldiers: 'bran-dealers, soap boilers, and clowns', as one royalist chronicler dismissively described them.

It was a rout. Edward's men smashed straight into the enemy, taking several nobles prisoner and putting the Londoners – poorly armed and in at best haphazard armour – to flight. The matter of his mother's undignified egging was evidently still embittering him, for here he made a great tactical error. Having scattered the Londoners, he gave chase, and so it is that we come to the first bodies in the Ouse, for the chronicle of Guisborough claims sixty knights were drowned as they tried to cross the river and escape pursuit. According to the least reliable of sources the chase went all the way to Croydon, though since it is a distance that today takes almost an hour by train it seems unlikely that a man, no matter how frightened, would have run so far.

In the absence of Edward, Henry and Richard rode up from the priory towards where the prison now stands. There they met the right and centre of the Montfortian army plunging down from the summit and there between the hours of prime and noon they were defeated, though Simon's army was smaller and the left had been scattered or fled. It's hard to know how many were killed in the fighting, by mace or sword or lance.

The estimate given in the chronicle of the monks of Lewes is two thousand, and judging by the number of skeletons that have subsequently been found in mass graves hereabouts it seems a reasonable guess. Few knights would have been among their number, for knights more commonly surrendered and were taken hostage, to be bartered back by their families. As for the royals, King Henry had two horses killed beneath him and took refuge in the priory, accompanied by his servants, while poor Richard of Cornwall, who had recently gained the right to be called King of the Romans, had to make do with barricading himself in a windmill. *Come out, you bad miller*, the people called, and at dusk he did, and was led away by his enemies, a sorry comedown for the *King of the Romans, always August*, as he liked to sign himself.

By the time Edward returned the fighting was done and the town choked with fleeing soldiers. According to the chronicle of Lanercost Abbey, which was supposedly based on an eyewitness report, the soldiers fled out of Lewes by way of the Ouse, crossing the bridge at Cliffe that was then the way out to the east. There:

> . . . the mixed crowd of fugitives and pursuers became so great, that many in their anxiety to escape, leaped into the river, whilst others fled confusedly into the adjoining marshes, then a resort for sea fowl. Numbers were drowned and others suffocated in the pits of mud, while from the swampy nature of the ground, many knights who perished there, were discovered, after the battle, still sitting on their

> horses in complete armour, and with drawn swords in their lifeless hands. Quantities of arms were found in this quarter for many years afterwards.

The coincidence of men and horses dying simultaneously in the mud, without even a moment to lower their sword-arms, has been much remarked upon by later, less credulous writers, though many accounts agree that a mass of bodies and armour was later dredged from the water.

Simon might have won the battle, but he'd yet to capture the king, who was by this time barricaded in the priory with his son. For a while he tried to burn them out, using *spryngelles of fyre* – pellets of tow dipped in bitumen, naphtha and sulphur – to set alight the wooden houses of the town. Lewes is claustrophobic even now, with narrow twittens dropping away from the high street, and it must that night have been a place of horror, strewn with the bodies of dead and dying men and horses, the church of the priory lit up in flames, so that the author of the chronicle of Oxenede was moved to write: 'It was there seen that the life of man was as the grasses of heaven; a great multitude, unknown to me, was slain.' But most of the dead would have been the common foot soldiers, the *bran-dealers, soap boilers and clowns*, who had borne the brunt of a battle that would barely change their lot.

In the end, by threatening the execution of three royalist prisoners, Simon de Montfort won the king's surrender and an agreement to uphold the Provisions, subject to whatever amendment was required. He became the *de facto* ruler of England, though support rapidly ebbed away from the baronial cause, not helped by Simon's habit of helping himself to the country's treasures. For a year Longshanks and Henry were held as hostages, though they were neither manacled nor locked in a tower. By May 1265, the inevitable had occurred. Edward escaped, an army was raised and in August, after a punishing series of sorties, the great set-piece battle of Lewes was reprised at Evesham, with entirely different results. The baronial army was by then small and exhausted; it no longer had the upper hand. On seeing Edward's troops ride towards him, Simon is said to have cried out, with characteristic arrogance: 'By the arm of St James, they come on well. They learned that order from me.' A little later, and perhaps more quietly, he added: 'God take our souls, for they will have our bodies.'

The battle that followed was savage and brief, conducted on a hill near the river Avon during a sudden thunderstorm. Henry III was on the field, still a prisoner and dressed in Montfortian armour. More than one contemporary source describes him wandering between the soldiers in the pouring rain, crying out at intervals, 'I am Henry of Winchester your king, do not kill me,' and 'I am too old to fight,' until he was recognised and removed by royalists from the fray. As for Simon, his horse was killed beneath him and his armour dragged from his body. Then he was stabbed to death, and his body mutilated, though a knight was never usually killed in cold blood.

There is a strange drawing now in the British Museum that shows some of what took place. Simon's head, his hands, his feet and his genitals were lopped off. In the drawing they lie by his side, his head topped with curls, his neck gushing blood. His balls – but this the picture doesn't show – were draped across the bridge of his nose and stuffed into his mouth, and this desecrated relic was wrapped in a cloth and sent to the wife of Roger Mortimore, a royalist knight, who is said to have received it as she prayed in church.

The sea trout were no longer visible. The water was unpitted now; it caught the sky lightly and tossed it back. I'd begun to feel sick as I stood by the pool, and for the rest of the day I felt that I'd taken in some poison, though whether it had seeped from the dark water or fallen with the sun I couldn't tell. It was time to get going. I crossed the road by Pikes Cottage and ducked through a gap in the hedge. My skin had dried as if it had been varnished, and all the cuts on my legs and wrists were smarting. It had been very hot, this proto-summer; perhaps the concentration of phosphates in that little stream had been too strong.

From the road the path climbed up above the river, curving through dusty fields and across the dry, chalk-crusted beds of streams. I passed through a field of maize and one of wheat. Mayweed grew between the stones, and as I walked I kicked up circlets of dust from the dead ground. There was not a soul in sight, and in the distance I could make out Mount Harry and beside it the glaring white mark of the chalkpit at Offham, where skeletons of the fleeing Londoners had been found buried in groups of four or five.

The past seemed to have fallen across the landscape like a body that though voiceless somehow still leaked or bled its language without pause. The horror of what had happened here had seeped into the soil as rain will do, waiting in the hidden interstitial spaces like groundwater before a flood. 'The past only comes back,' wrote Virginia Woolf in her unfinished memoir, 'when the present runs so smoothly that it is like the sliding surface of a deep river. Then one sees through the surface to the depths.' I wondered if the river itself was holding it, for some things are drawn to water and behave differently when they are near it. I've watched mist gather on the surface of a stream where there is none elsewhere, and seen those little circling courts of flies that dance all evening above a single kink in a current. Voices travel further by water too, as if the air's been pulled so taut it carries impressions that would elsewhere be too subtle to perceive.

'Is it not possible,' Woolf asks earlier in the same piece, 'that things we have felt with great intensity have an existence independent of our minds; are in fact still in existence?' It's the same argument ghost hunters tender: that events are locked into the ground just as surely as gold coins lie buried there, invisible to the eye but emitting their own small disruptions to the magnetic field. There's a hill outside Halland, a few miles east of where I stood, that's still called Terrible Down, for the blood that was spilled there by Prince Edward's men. By the Rainbow in Cooksbridge, maybe a mile or so the other way, bodies are said to have been hung from the trees till they rotted, to warn of the cost of fighting a king. The brutality of it reminded me of one of the beliefs of the Albigensians, the heretical sect that Simon de Montfort's father spent his life eradicating. They thought, among other strange things, that the God of the Old Testament was in fact the Devil, and that no punishment awaits us, for this world, where man is wolf to man, is hell already and shall not be repeated.

Simon de Montfort, though he favoured the russet clothes of the poor over the baronial red and wore anyway beneath them a close-fitting hair shirt to chafe away the sins of the flesh, was by no means a saint, for all that he was later proclaimed one. But if greed drove him, or the desire to elevate his own family, so too did a sense of basic justice. Listen, he speaks for himself: 'The great men of the land bear me such ill-will because I uphold rights . . . of the poor against them.' The picture of his end had imprinted itself on my mind. The blood came from his neck in flames, whelk-red, and also from his legs; when his son heard what had been done it is written that he could neither eat nor drink for days.

I weighed it up, his death, against a story Matthew Paris tells, that dates from just before the war took hold. The king was caught in a storm and forced to take shelter at the palace of the Bishop of Durham, where Simon was coincidentally also staying. Simon, knowing the king was afraid of storms, came to the steps to greet him and seeing his face blanched white asked why he was scared now the danger had passed. The king, Paris claims, answered: 'The thunder and lightning I fear beyond measure, but by the Head of God, I fear thee more than all the thunder and lightning in the world.' It was the earl's reply that had stayed with me. 'My lord it is unjust and incredible that you should fear me your firm friend, who am ever faithful to you and yours, and to the kingdom of England; it is your enemies, your destroyers, and false flatterers that you ought to fear.'

What drove him? Avarice? Arrogance? An unwillingness to break the vow he'd sworn in 1258, to uphold the Provisions *whatever others might do*? A case may be made for all of these things. Montfort did have a tendency – echoed three centuries on by Thomas Cromwell, the commoner who guided Henry Tudor through his break with Rome – to feather his nest, giving choice appointments to his family members and bringing domestic matters into what should perhaps have been purely political affairs. And yet he was also loyal and dogged, his word was his bond, and he possessed a clarity and independence of mind that would be rare in any time.

What is it about these men who check the king, that they must be torn into so many parts? When Thomas Cromwell, who resembled de Montfort in his vision, his arrogance and his acumen, fell out of favour with Henry VIII, he also suffered a bloody death. His head was cut off and boiled, and what remained of it was placed on a spike on London Bridge, turned emphatically away from the city he loved. And though Oliver Cromwell, who went to war against King Charles and won, died in his bed of what seems to have been septicaemia, his body was three years later disinterred and subjected to a posthumous execution. For months afterwards the stinking head was displayed on a pole outside Westminster Hall, that building so loved by Henry III. No one need pity old Ironsides, but there is a peculiar savagery in this need to take a man to such pieces that all the king's horses and all the king's men couldn't put back together what was broken again.

The light was getting to me. There was nothing to stop it. It came bowling down in strips and sheets and lifted in waves from the ground. At length I came to a farm that seemed to have been deserted in the centre of a great furrowed field. The barn stood open, and on the ground before it were ranked trays of rotting bedding plants, marigolds and begonias, their leaves as dry and discoloured as paper salvaged from a fire. The morning, which had started so well, had curdled and begun to sour. I felt I couldn't walk another step, and yet I couldn't bring myself to stop in that horrible, poisoned place. A harrow had drawn the flints to the surface, so that the field seemed bleached or drained. I began to count to a hundred over and again, and the green tips of the woodland stayed just out of reach until all of a sudden I was plunged within them, breathing the reek of dog shit and elder-blossom, the contaminated summer air.

The path crossed the village of Hamsey and then I was flung out again, onto the banks where the sun beat down. The river was tidal now, and the tide was on the ebb, stinking of salt and carrying clotted creamish foam and a waste of rotten thistles. It was running far faster than I'd seen it. You'd be a fool, I thought, to swim in these teeming waters. At Hamsey Island it churned the colour of molten chocolate and as I rounded the corner and saw Lewes a cormorant winged by. There were two boys fishing on the island, both with shaved heads and shell suit jackets. They had a net and as I passed by one called out in fury *I fucking nearly caught it.*

I was walking at the top of a grassy bank built to stop the river from flooding. The meadows below were edged by ditches that sprouted scrubby, waterlogged willows, their branches tipped with gold. It was here that the Londoners are said to have drowned, rushing from the heights onto ground that grew steadily quicker, shifting beneath their feet until it had them by the knee, the waist, until it had swallowed them up and marked where they lay with weeds, if it bothered to mark them at all. Much of this land was once underwater or on the verge of it, and even now it's hard to track the little streams that dither hereabouts. Some have broken through where they're not supposed to go, and a fisherman I once met claimed there are pike in even the narrowest ditches, though whether these are refugees from the last flood or proof that some channels are linked by underground waterways he'd not yet determined. He also told me about a bottomless pool in a wood he called the Pells, though that's not the name it goes by on maps. Matthew and I went to find it last winter, with some friends who live nearby, and for a whole still afternoon we clattered through woods so deep and damp and sunk in upon themselves that though we were only feet from each other it seemed we might at any minute become hopelessly lost.

I went on in the sick heat up through the Landport estate, where England flags bloomed from car aerials and the windowsills of council houses. The children were still at school, and no one was out on the baking streets but a couple of ginger cats sprawled like corpses beneath a car. I slogged all the way to the edge of the Wallands, where the body of the battle had taken place. The roads here commemorate those who had fought, though the royalists seem to have come out best in the deal. Prince Edward's Road and King Henry's Road were lavishly lined with cherry and service trees. The houses were gabled Edwardian villas, their gingerbread porches swagged with heaps of coloured roses. Queen Eleanor hadn't done so well as one might expect from a woman who once smuggled the Crown Jewels to France. Eleanor Close was a dead end full of stubby purpose-built flats that looked out from small windows to the river beneath. As for De Montfort Road, it swooped from the Paddock to Lewes Prison, where the fiercest fighting probably took place. This theory was first advanced by the historian William Blaauw, who heard from a road-maker that when the Brighton turnpike was being lowered in 1810 three great pits of bones were found in the vicinity of the prison, each holding *quite five hundred bodies*.

By the time I reached the High Street tiny flares were going off in the corners of my vision and all I wanted was to stand for a year beneath a cold shower and wash the river from my skin. The White Hart was a broad, sprawling building opposite the castle, with pretty carriage lamps and a neat wrought-iron balcony, a façade that can't have changed much since the Woolfs bought Monks House at auction here in 1919. The lobby was even hotter than it had been outdoors, and smelled powerfully of boiled beef. My room was up in the eaves and from each of the high windows I could see martins lifting and falling like sifted flour. There was an odd hall or vestibule just inside the doorway, empty except for a locked chest that looked big enough to hide a body. The carpet was the colour of stewed damsons and so too were the curtains and chair, which was upholstered in a fabric that looked like velvet and emitted little ripples of static each time I brushed against it. Someone had stubbed a cigarette out on one of the arms. I was amazed it hadn't burned the place down. Someone else – or perhaps it was the same person – seemed to have kicked a great chunk of plaster from the wall, exposing a crumble of flint and concrete that was festooned in cobwebs.

It felt as if my blood had turned to mercury. I lay on the bed almost weeping, suddenly overwhelmed by the past few months. I hadn't thought I was running away, but now all I wanted was to turn tail and fly, back into the woods, the dense, enchanted Andredesleage where no one could find me or knew my name. Why does the past do this? Why does it linger instead of receding? Why does it return with such a force sometimes that the real place in which one stands or sits or lies, the place in which one's corporeal body most undeniably exists, dissolves as if it were nothing more than a mirage? The past cannot be grasped; it is not possible to return in time, to regather what was lost or carelessly shrugged off, so why these sudden ambushes, these flourishes of memory?

I'd been here before. Not the room, but the restaurant downstairs. We'd come almost a decade ago, Matthew and I, in midwinter, those dead weeks at the beginning of the year. It had snowed, or was just about to – see, already memory lets me down – and we drank house red in a room that smelled, then as now, of boiled beef, the warm air billowing from a concealed kitchen. I don't remember what we ate. I know that I, half-consciously, kept laying my hands on the table, wrists upturned. We hadn't yet touched, and as we left I caught the smell of chlorine from a pool concealed in the basement. We were entirely blind. We didn't know what lay ahead. So yes, I understand why the island of the sirens is piled high with bodies. If any one of us knew what the future held, I think we too would sit there, petrified, until the hide rotted from our bones.

In her unfinished memoir, *A Sketch of the Past*, Virginia Woolf turns again and again to the question of how one can make sense of what has gone before. This document – part diary, part autobiography – was begun on 18 April 1939 and added to spasmodically over the next year and a half, the last entry written on 15 November 1940, four months before she died. It eddies musingly through her early life, beginning with the gleeful free-range summers at St Ives and bowling on into the claustrophobic years of mourning that followed the deaths of her mother, Julia, and her half-sister Stella, when her father's grief made him a tyrant prone to periodic and horribly childish rages. As he grew more deaf and isolated, greedy, chubby George Duckworth, Stella's brother, rose to take his place, bullying Virginia and her sister Vanessa through a round of balls and parties as humiliating as they were dull.

Towards the end of this long, fragmentary, intensely vivid skein of writing – in fact a series of faintly different and contradictory drafts, one of which tumbled into a wastepaper basket and was rescued only by chance – the figure of Thoby, her elder brother, drifts into view. He is tilling a boat, his eyes blue with concentration. He is standing upright in a Norfolk jacket too short in the arm and too narrow across the shoulders. He is drawing a bird, holding the paper easily and starting at some unexpected corner of the page. He is . . . but here the well of memories runs dry. Thoby died of typhoid in 1906, an event Woolf alludes to but never quite arrives at chronicling.

Instead, she turns to imagining how Thoby might have turned out, concluding: 'He would have been more of a character than a success, I suppose; had he been put on.' The words seem to jolt her. She goes on cautiously; her pen is, as she once put it, on the scent. 'The knell of those words affect my memory of a time when in fact they were not heard at all. We had no foreboding that he was to die when he was twenty-six and I was twenty-four. This is one of the falsifications – that knell I always find myself hearing and transmitting – that one cannot guard against, save by noting it.' Earlier, she observed that 'the past is much affected by the present moment'. Now, for a brief instant, grasping it at all seems an impossibility, since it is irrevocably altered by the present, the platform of time from which it's glimpsed.

This piece of writing is, as I have said, fragmentary. It was written when bombs were falling on Sussex: at one point Woolf begins a section by noting 'London battered last night.' Her childhood world and the ghosts that populate it seem very distant, and yet what she discovers as she delves gropingly backward in time is surprising:

> In those moments I find one of my greatest satisfactions, not that I am thinking of the past; but that it is then that I am living most fully in the present. For the present when backed by the past is a thousand times deeper than the present when it presses so close that you can feel nothing else . . . I write this partly in order to recover my sense of the present by getting the past to shadow this broken surface. Let me then, like a child advancing with bare feet into a cold river, descend again into that stream.

It echoes what she concluded in *Between the Acts*, which was written contemporaneously and also to the accompaniment of falling bombs: that one can only make sense of the violent – the violating – present by looking back, to what has disappeared from view.

After the sun had dropped and I'd soaped myself thoroughly beneath a lukewarm shower I began to revive. I ate a curry in an empty restaurant and drank a beer down with it. The bill came with a bowl of fennel seeds coated in coloured sugar, pink and white and yellow, and for the rest of the evening the ghost of aniseed lay on the tip of my tongue like a word I knew but could not speak. While the light lasted I went down to the railway lands that lay between the town and the A27, bordered by the river to the east and the train tracks to the south-west. The railway lands had once been the station's goods yard, and after years of neglect were turned quite recently into a nature reserve. Despite some attempts at landscaping the place had not lost its haphazard feel, and the tangled hedges were full of the last punch-drunk elderflowers and the first green nubs of blackberries. I sat by the water there, watching the jackdaws wheel overhead. Once or twice a kestrel came by, pale-winged, its rusty tail splayed into a wedge, circling the Brooks in search of mice. I could hear traffic on the dual carriageway, and with it the periodic wail of a train crossing the river from Lewes to Hastings and back.

Most of this land, and much more besides, had once belonged to the Cluniac priory, where Henry took refuge before he signed away his kingdom. Though it continued to thrive after the battle, the priory had been plucked down in the autumn of 1537 during the dissolution of the monasteries at the orders of Thomas Cromwell, who employed an Italian military engineer to oversee its destruction, selling off even the lead from the roof and the bells before building the largest house in Lewes, Lords Place, from what had once been the Prior's lodgings. Three years later Cromwell himself was dead, and the building passed into private ownership and was later destroyed.

When the railway from Brighton to Hastings was built in 1845, it cut right through the ruins of the priory, which had, despite the labours of the Italian engineer, been only imperfectly erased. In the course of their excavations, the railway workers opened up a well filled with hundreds of bodies, which were said to emit such noxious odours that several were too overcome to work and had to return to their homes to recover. The bodies were believed to be the royalist soldiers who had been killed in the later stages of the Battle of Lewes, as the fighting reached the priory walls. So what did the railwaymen do with their find? They dredged out the bones, loaded them onto trucks and hauled them into the marshes, where according to the *Sussex Express* of 17 January 1846 'they were thrown into the mass of rubbish which forms the embankment through the brooks, midway between the river and Southerham corner'.

The embankment was still there. I could see it from where I sat, and tomorrow I would cross beneath it to reach the marshland beyond. But it took me a while to make sense of the story. The trains to Hastings and Newhaven, to Glynde and Ore and Seaford, travel each day across the compacted bones of the men who fought here in 1264? Unsurprisingly, not everyone approved of using human remains in this way. The *Sussex Express* published a leader condemning the practice, and a local doctor added sternly in his diary:

> It has been suggested, with much probability, that these bones are the relics of the persons who fell in the Battle of Lewes in 1264, in the streets and immediate vicinity of the town, and which were gathered up and afforded Christian burial within the precincts of the Priory, by the monks of St Pancras. In perfect accordance with the spirit of this railway age, this heap of skeleton of the patriots and royalists of the 13th century, which filled thirteen wagons, was taken away to form part of the embankment of the line in the adjacent brook.

And his name, this good doctor who cared so much about the relics of persons and how they were treated? It was none other than Gideon Mantell, the fossil-hunter who had found and named the first iguanodon and whose own spine had been damaged in a carriage accident and was later exhibited in the museum of the Royal College of Surgeons, surviving the bombs that rained down on London for fifty-seven consecutive nights and being at last destroyed in 1970 during a clearout.

Ossa hic sita sunt, the Romans used to write on their gravestones, or sometimes simply OHSS: the bones are buried here. It almost made me laugh to think of it: that the train line was built on a bank of compacted femurs and tibias, just as the Downs behind it were made from the accumulated bodies of single-celled algae and phytoplankton, a centimetre each thousand years. 'I see it – the past – ,' went on Woolf, 'as an avenue lying behind; a long ribbon of scenes, emotions.' She was wrong. The past is not behind us but beneath, and the ground we walk on is nothing more than a pit of bones, from which the grass unstinting grows.

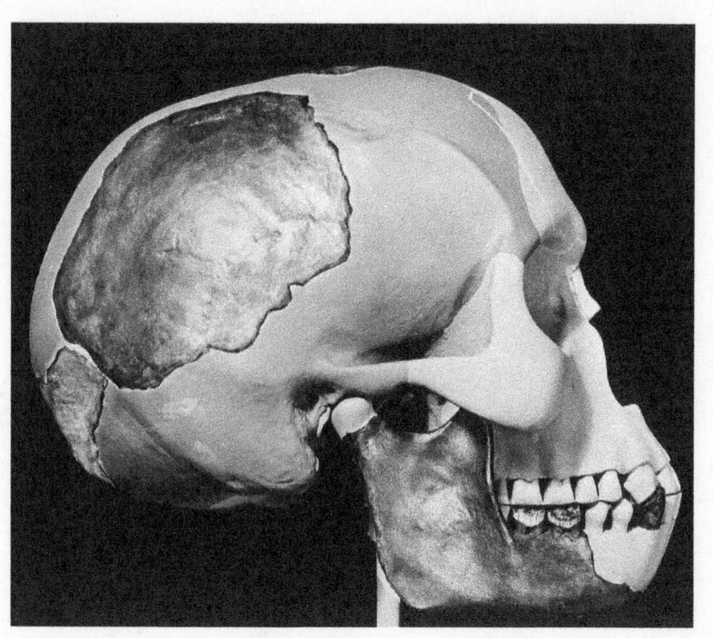

V

IN THE FLOOD

I STAYED ON THE RAILWAY LANDS for a long time. The light was draining away but the air was still warm and from where I sat Lewes looked like an island crowned with a castle, drifting above the dark sea of trees as if it were floating. It seemed to me then a town built on a fault-line or at a contested boundary: a place only imperfectly subdued, where the natural world and that which belonged to man had made no more than a precarious truce.

Perhaps a decade back, I read an article in the *Guardian* that suggested Satanists were at work here, and though it sounded like nonsense it left me with a faint unease about the place that took years to properly disperse. Then there's the matter of Guy Fawkes Night, when the residents go lavishly crazy and parade through the narrow streets with blackened faces, tossing firecrackers and hauling huge effigies of the Pope and Tony Blair, which they later set alight in recreation grounds on pyres of pallets they've been hoarding all year. This annual ritual taps into a deep seam of anti-Catholic feeling that is said to derive from the burning of seventeen Protestant martyrs in Lewes during the sixteenth century. Some were killed singly, but on 22 June 1557 ten were murdered together in a grotesque parody of the midsummer bonfires that once burned around that date. Their martyrdom is said to have been the single greatest act of violence of the Marian persecutions, which were ordered by Bloody Queen Mary in her bid to eradicate the Protestant faith.

A place of fires then; and one with an uneasy relationship to water. Lewes was built by the river for a reason. It grew rich on fishing and milling and later on the barges of Wealden iron. But the valley beneath the town is set very low, barely three feet above sea level, and at times of heavy rainfall the water swells outward into land reclaimed from what was once a stinking, sodden marsh. For centuries this tendency to inundation affected farming, but now houses and industrial estates have sprouted in the floodplain, and the last time the Ouse seriously breached its banks the outcome was very bad.

It happened in the autumn of 2000, after days of storms and rain. By Monday 9 October, pools of water had begun to form over low-lying fields and roads and people began phoning the council to order sandbags. Each time the tide ebbed out the surface water seemed to recede, but the rain didn't stop for long enough to allow the saturated ground to drain. On Wednesday night it bucketed down and at some point before the sun was up the Uck, the Ouse's largest tributary, began to flood. Things happened very fast then. At nine o'clock the town of Uckfield was six feet under water and the river had turned into a torrent that sunk parked cars and swept supermarket goods from the shelves.

Over in Lewes, the Winterbourne, that little stream that once marked the northern boundary of the Priory, was also filling rapidly. Winterbournes, as the name suggests, come to life in winter months, carrying the water stored in the great chalk aquifers of the Downs. When rainfall is acute these aquifers can behave erratically, channelling water where it hasn't been seen for decades, sometimes even centuries. To make matters more complicated, the Lewes Winterbourne coincides with the path of the A27 and the Brighton to Lewes railway line, and for much of its course is buried in culverts or diverted through concrete channels and drains. Now a culvert had become blocked with litter and the water was surging out into the new street of Tanners Brook and over the geranium beds of the Grange.

The Uck joins the Ouse at Isfield, and as the floodwater began to shift downstream the Ouse also breached its banks, gushing out into the land between Barcombe and Hamsey until all the pastures had disappeared beneath a swelling lake. By lunchtime Lewes's defences were also overwhelmed and the dirty, rain-coloured river came surging over the embankments and into town. Water rushed down the streets at the bottom of the hill and by mid-afternoon the Phoenix estate, the Pells, the new houses at Malling and the old ones at Cliffe had been submerged. Police shut down the centre of town and hundreds of people trapped in houses and offices were rescued by lifeboat crews manning inflatable boats.

The peak came with the high tide at half past nine that night, when the water reached a depth of almost twelve feet on the Malling estate, submerging the houses to the second storey. The roads and rail links had also flooded, and by evening Lewes was almost an island, cut off from the outside world by the encroaching river. Water is sly; make no bones about it. It slips in anywhere, though the doors might be barred against it, and is most equitable, favouring neither sewers nor churches. Wherever you looked it was carrying off something: prayer books, children's toys, underwear, the sodden bodies of rats. And then there were the things you couldn't see: the rumour of asbestos, farm fertiliser and pesticide; the leached-out contaminants from graves and crypts.

The evacuees passed that night in a temporary emergency shelter in the town hall, which was built, oddly enough, on the site where the Protestant martyrs had been burned. In their abandoned houses the water continued to rise, poisoning the places it seeped into with a toxic mix of sewage and heating oil, shifting furniture around and saturating everything with what looked like beer and smelled like shit.

When morning came the rain stopped and the river began to drop, but by then the water had become trapped behind the flood defences designed to keep it out. The fire brigade used mobile pumps to suck it back into the river, though 70,000 litres contaminated with oil had to be drained off and taken away in a tanker. In all, 1,033 properties were thought to have been flooded, and over 2,000 hectares of land. In their wake, the receding waters left strange cargo. One photo I'd seen showed a woman standing at her front door, a bloated cow lying dead at her feet.

Over the past few years, similar pictures have eddied in from Tewkesbury, Boscastle, Sheffield: pictures of roads swept away and cathedrals surrounded by inland seas made opaque by particles of clay. These events are meat and drink to newspaper editors, though they rarely involve the loss of life that is common in other nations. But even the overspilling of a minor river on a small archipelago carries with it a larger story, and one that stretches far back in time. There's something about a flood, something mythic and disturbing, that gets to the heart of our uncertainty about our place on the earth at all.

The Biblical flood, that primal act of destruction, took place because God – the temperamental, petulant God of the Old Testament, who the Albigensians thought was actually the Devil and who bears a decided resemblance to a Victorian patriarch of the Leslie Stephen mould – decided the world he'd created wasn't as pleasant as he'd hoped. The people had become evil and so he resolved to wipe them from the earth, along with the beasts and the creeping things and the fowls of the air, all save a breeding pair from every species. This decision is explained in a curious passage: 'The earth also was corrupt before God, and the earth was filled with violence. And God looked upon the earth, and, behold, it was corrupt; for all flesh had corrupted his way upon earth.'

Only Noah and his family were exempt from this fate, and

so they built their ark from gopher wood, and painted it with pitch, and when this was done the heavens opened and it began to rain without pause for forty days, until the whole earth was covered to the depth of fifteen cubits, even the highest mountains, and everything alive had died. Things remained like this for one hundred and fifty days and then the waters began to recede, though it took a good three months further before the tops of the highest mountains were revealed and perhaps another three before the ground was fully dry. And after that God promised never to destroy the world again, adding resignedly, 'for the imagination of man's heart is evil from his youth'.

What a horrible story. I didn't understand how a religion could be founded upon such a quixotic Creator, but I sympathised with the underlying anxiety: that we might at any moment be rubbed from the planet. There's a long lineage of these decreation stories, which arise from all corners of the globe. Some – Atlantis, Lyonesse – deal with whole civilisations that are drowned, while others are more parochial in their scope. When I was a child, my granny used to tell one about a village that was sunk beneath a lake. The villagers had done something bad – *what, Granny, what?* – and they had to be punished – *oh, probably they didn't say their prayers.* The village was in a valley that I always imagined very smooth, rollered like a bowling green, the houses huddled at the base. When the time came, a great flood of water rushed from the hills, with a noise like ten thousand horses, and the village was submerged. But the people were so wicked they didn't die! They went on about their business beneath the surface, tending the pigs and ploughing the fields, breeding away down there as if they had gills. On Sundays they all trailed off to church, wicked though they were, and if you listened carefully at the water's edge you could hear the bells pealing off the hours. Once every hundred years the spell wore off and the lake drained away. The houses dried and the people came out into their gardens and talked to one another in the unfiltered air. If you wandered through on that single, singular day the village looked like anywhere else, but if you stayed past midnight water would begin to seep up from the soil and puddle out across the streets and before you could one, two, three take a breath the lake would be drawn up over your head for another hundred years.

The story had got so tattered in the keeping that it resembled lace, more holes than thread. Where had it come from? The need to punish a wicked place by drowning must have been filched from Noah. As for the location, was it Capel Celyn, the Welsh village that was flooded to make a reservoir to provide the people of Liverpool with drinking water? The bells I thought had been borrowed from Dunwich, the medieval Suffolk town that was sunk beneath the encroaching sea, for it is often said that there were eight churches there and that their bells were sometimes heard by fishermen and sailors. Had she cobbled the story herself, or picked it up from somebody else? I hadn't asked at the time, and now it was too late.

The prohibition against staying too long was also familiar. It echoed those tales of the underworld I'd been musing on a few days back, lands that opened and shut like clams, catching the unwary in their grip. What was the line from True Thomas? *For gin ae word you should chance to speak, you will neer get back to your ain countrie.* And I had a dim memory of another mythic city: Ys, the Breton Sodom, which was sunk beneath the waves by God in punishment for the behaviour of the king's daughter, Dahut, who drank too much wine and liked to murder her lovers after a single night between the sheets.

These cities have resurfaced in the apocalyptic fiction of our own age, like the submerged London of J.G. Ballard's *The Drowned World*: ruined settlements with canals for streets where humans eke out a precarious existence if they survive at all. Water, in these fantasies, might stand for time, which also comes as a flood and has inundating qualities, or it might stand simply for itself. That winter I'd begun to pry around in the great sump of material that comprises the written history of the Ouse. The papers include newspaper articles, Acts of Parliament, coroners' reports and the diaries and documentation of the Commissioners of Sewers, who were first appointed in the sixteenth century to ensure the river's uprisings didn't overwhelm the land. The 2000 flood, it was clear, was not an isolated occurrence, but rather part of a long and painful struggle for control, in which the town and its outlying fields were periodically encroached upon by water. Sitting there, in the dark, it began to seem to me that the folktales were a way of charting the same ancient, ongoing battle, or at least of managing the fears and fantasies that water's wilfulness engendered. Either that or I'd strayed into the valley beneath the lake, and any minute now the river would rise gurgling up above my head.

* * *

It rained in the night, and I woke briefly at dawn to a changed landscape. The valley had filled with mist and only the tops of the Downs were visible above a fog the bleached pink of candyfloss. The cranes of Newhaven docks had vanished and the villages strung along the river were swallowed out of sight. I slipped back into sleep and when I woke again the false sea had receded and the valley returned, though Firle Beacon was still hung with dense white air, like those gusts of dragon's breath exhaled on cold days. The rain had stopped and a gang of jackdaws were squabbling on the roof, crying *ker-ack*, *ker-ack* and jostling for space.

The town museum was just over the road, with the castle hard above it. It seemed like a good place to get my bearings, for the castle commanded the highest views and Barbican House, which I'd visited once before, was full of the archaeological specimens that the people who'd lived in these hills had discarded over the years. Within the castle precinct there were a few fine Regency houses and a bowling green that had apparently been used consistently since the leap year 1640. Opposite it was Castle Lodge, which had once belonged to Charles Dawson, the amateur geologist who discovered the Piltdown man in a bed of ancient Ouse gravels and is now credited with its forgery.

He was good at discoveries, Dawson. He also found, let's see, the teeth of one of the earliest mammals, his own variety of iguanodon, a Saxon boat, the only known cast-iron Roman statuette, a goldfish-carp hybrid, a petrified toad preserved within a hollow flint the size of a lemon and an entire network of tunnels stuffed with miscellaneous prehistoric, Roman and medieval artefacts. The toad might possibly have been a genuine discovery, but the rest were either fakes or misattributions, as was his tale of seeing a sea serpent while travelling by ferry from Newhaven to Dieppe, its *rounded, arched loops* rising from the waves.

The story of the Piltdown man is almost the exact antithesis of that of the iguanodon, which makes it rather pleasing that Charles Dawson lived around the corner from Gideon Mantell, though nearly a century later. Like Mantell, Dawson didn't go to university and had to fit his interests in geology and archaeology around the more prosaic business of a career as a solicitor. But despite this lack of formal education, he had less trouble being accepted by the establishment. At the time of his greatest find he had built up a considerable reputation for the range and quality of his work, being made a Fellow of the Geological Society at the age of twenty-one and of the Royal Society of Antiquarians by thirty-five. The discovery of the Piltdown man came towards the end of his life, and was exactly the big, globally significant find he'd recently complained seemed always to elude him.

Oddly enough, it isn't clear *when* the first remains of the Piltdown man were found; though this is also true for Mantell's iguanodon and does not in itself imply foul play. Dawson's own accounts are vague and though they're frequently retold they never seem to settle to a particular date. In the earliest written version – a letter from February 1912 announcing the find to his friend Arthur Smith Woodward, Keeper of Geology at the Natural History Museum – he simply explained that he'd come by chance across an ancient gravel bed, which he thought was Pleistocene, and found there (the grammar is odd but this seems to be what he means) a portion of what was to all appearances a prodigiously old human skull.

In the official presentation that the two men made to the Geological Society in December of that same year, this account is much elaborated:

> Several years ago I was walking along a farm-road close to Piltdown Common, Fletching (Sussex), when I noticed the road had been mended with some peculiar brown flints not usual in the district. On inquiry I was astonished to learn that they were dug from a gravel-bed on the farm, and shortly afterwards I visited the place, where two labourers were at work digging the gravel for small repairs to the roads. As this excavation was situated about four miles north of the limit where the occurrence of flints overlying the Wealden strata is recorded, I was much interested, and made a close examination of the bed. I asked the workmen if they had found bones or other fossils there. As they did not appear to have noticed anything of the sort, I urged them to preserve anything that they might find. Upon one of my subsequent visits to the pit, one of the men handed me a small portion of unusually thick human parietal bone. I immediately made a search, but could find nothing more, nor had the men noticed anything else. The bed is full of tabular pieces of iron-stone closely resembling this piece of skull in colour and thickness; and, although I made many subsequent searches, I could not hear of any further find nor discover anything – in fact, the bed seemed quite unfossiliferous. It was not until some years later, in the autumn of 1911, on a visit to the spot, that I picked up, among the

> rain-washed spoil-heaps of the gravel-pit, another and larger piece belonging to the frontal region of the same skull.

Having alerted Woodward to his finds, the pair returned to the site when the spring floods had subsided, for it seems the gravel pit was more or less underwater for almost half the year. In the course of their excavations, they turned up more skull fragments, including a chunk of occipital bone and a broken portion of jaw complete with two molars. All were apparently from the original skull, which they decided must have been broken up by a worker's pick. In addition to this impressive haul they found a few crudely worked flints and an array of tooth fragments from a great variety of early mammals, including a Pliocene elephant, a Pleistocene beaver and horse, a mastodon and a hippo, though whether these were found in spoil heaps discarded by the builders or in the undisturbed bed itself is not clear in either man's account.

The bed itself, Dawson went on to explain, was about three to five feet deep and ran a few inches below the soil. It was formed from dark brown ironstone pebbles interspersed with angular brownish flints of a variety of sizes, ranging from half a foot to grains as small as sand. The bed was finely stratified, and the deepest layer, lying just above the yellow sandstone bedrock, was darker and more gummy than the rest due to the presence of so much iron oxide that a pick was often needed to prise free the stones. It was in this lower stratum that all the *in situ* elements were said to be discovered. The pit was situated in a field on the Barkham Manor estate, on a plateau estimated to be about eighty feet above the Ouse, which had worn through the earth over the course of hundreds of thousands of years until it reached its present depth, leaving trails and drifts of river gravels to mark its passage through time.

After Dawson had dealt with the circumstances of the find, Woodward took up the story, turning to the matter of its implications. He performed an elaborate anatomical analysis of the skull before drawing his triumphant conclusion: that the Piltdown man 'was already in existence in Western Europe long before Mousterian man' – the old term for a Neanderthal – 'spread widely in this region'. His announcement was rapturously received. The hunt for the missing link in man's origins had been quickened when Darwin published *The Descent of Man* in 1871, and for some time now the British had been lagging in the search. Satisfyingly, the Piltdown Man – officially named *Eoanthropus dawsoni*, Dawson's dawn man – was pretty much exactly what the anthropologists had been predicting: namely a creature who had developed man's substantial brain without yet losing the ape's prominent jaw.

That this hypothesis should be so absolutely borne out was regarded by several scientists as unlikely, though in that period no one went so far as to suggest forgery, preferring the theory that *two* fossil creatures had been found, one an early hominid and the other an ancient sort of chimpanzee. In answer to this, Woodward drew attention to the molars, which were worn flat in a way only observed with human use. It was a shame, both camps agreed, that there wasn't a canine present, since this would clarify for certain how the jawbone worked. What a stroke of luck, then, that just such a canine did turn up in the course of the following year's dig, conforming almost exactly to Woodward's predictions and clearly testifying to the creature's human status.

In 1914, the last find from the Piltdown pit appeared: a massive implement carved from elephant bone and looking a little like a cricket bat. And then, the following year, Dawson found another fragmentary skull somewhere on the Sheffield Park estate, though the circumstances and exact location of this are hopelessly unclear. On this private and poorly documented dig he also turned up another *Eoanthropus* molar as well as a rhinoceros's tooth that conveniently dated the cache as deriving from at least the early Pleistocene, which is to say the beginning of the ice ages. In some ways, this last molar was the most significant element of all, since it proved almost conclusively that the first jaw and skull must belong together: the double coincidence of their co-burial being too outlandish now to be entertained.

Dawson became ill at the end of 1915 and died on 10 August 1916 at the age of fifty-two. It is often suggested that he hoped to become a Fellow of the Royal Society or achieve a knighthood in recognition for Piltdown man, and that his early death prevented this from taking place; certainly many of the other figures associated with the find and its subsequent analysis were knighted. As for the gravel bed, though Woodward continued to supervise digs and even moved to the area after his retirement, nothing of any discernable antiquity was ever found at Piltdown again.

There was something distinctly fishy about the whole story, but though the Piltdown relics were subject to what seemed like exhaustive testing by anatomists and palaeontologists, and though the Piltdown Man became through the years increasingly anomalous, as subsequent international discoveries revealed man's evolution had proceeded not with an initial increase in brain size but with the development of a human-looking jaw and teeth, it was not until 1953 that the Piltdown riddle began to be tugged apart.

In the July of that year Joseph Weiner, an anatomist and anthropologist at Oxford, was at an academic dinner when a colleague based at the Natural History Museum mentioned to him in passing that there existed no record of the exact location of Dawson's Sheffield Park finds. This casual statement startled Weiner and by November 1953 he had, in a model of a priori reasoning and the application of the scientific method, proved conclusively that the Piltdown man was a fake. His team performed a battery of tests, many of which had been invented in the intervening years and were unavailable to the original investigators. Fluorine, nitrogen, organic carbon and iron levels were all assessed, and the radioactivity of the samples measured. The results were startling. The skull and jaw fragments were from wholly different specimens, and the jaw and teeth had been deliberately stained with a paint containing iron oxide and bitumen, in all probability Vandyke brown. This was true of both the Sheffield Park and the original Piltdown finds. Furthermore, the molars had been deliberately shaped by a file or similar instrument to give them their distinctively human shape. The Piltdown jaw in fact belonged to a modern ape, probably an orang-utan. As for the mammalian teeth that had served to date the finds, these were indeed of formidable antiquity but not indigenous. It seems they derived from a variety of global sources, perhaps including Tunisia and Malta, and had also been subject to artificial staining to match the ferruginous nature of the gravel.

In his 1955 book, *The Piltdown Forgery*, Weiner drew back from directly accusing Dawson of being responsible for this sustained act of mischief, which cost the scientific world years of wasted effort, though later he was unequivocal in his condemnation. There has subsequently been an array of lurid conspiracy theories that accuse all manner of prominent scientists. However, the slow debunking of Dawson's record, much of it carried out quite recently by the archaeologist Miles Russell, goes a long way to identifying him as the culprit. In addition to his impressive tally of false and dubious finds, he was observed by witnesses staining bones and carrying out practical jokes involving the falsification of archaeological relics. Then there's the matter of Castle Lodge itself, which was leased to the Sussex Archaeological Society on the understanding that they were to have first refusal if it was ever put up for sale. It's claimed in Lewes that Dawson bought the house by subterfuge, carrying out his correspondence on the society's headed notepaper to create the illusion that he was working on their behalf, though the first the society knew of this business is when they were served a notice to quit.

What motivated Dawson in these acts is mystifying. He's frequently said to have been driven by the desire for recognition and acclaim, but this also spurred Gideon Mantell, who never falsified a bone in his life. It struck me that many of Dawson's finds were attempts to prove a theory already in existence. He specialised in missing links: hybrids that explained the development of one form to another. One of these was the Bexhill boat, which represented an absurd mix between a coracle and a dugout canoe; another *Plagiaulax dawsoni*, the so-called first Cretaceous mammal. The Piltdown man, though considerably more ambitious, was in the same vein, being fabricated evidence for the already extant hypothesis of Darwin's transitional ape-man.

Bringing such stories to life must have had a profound appeal for Dawson, and it's perhaps his most accurate epitaph that he was known as the Sussex Wizard. But though the past is sometimes haphazard or resistant to interpretation, that's not the same as saying it can simply be made up. Dawson's work has left a stain. The debunking of the Piltdown story is relayed on the same sort of websites that provide scientific evidence for the existence of Noah's flood, where it stands as gleeful proof that the evolutionists got it wrong. Which is the sort of afterlife you deserve, I suppose, if you can't tell a lie from the truth.

I turned from Dawson's house to the new home of the Sussex Archaeological Society, to which they'd moved in 1904. From the outside Barbican House looked Georgian, though I'd been told that beneath the brick façade it was actually far older. The place was arranged over a couple of floors of what had evidently once been a sizeable townhouse. I wandered through rooms filled with the detritus of previous eras, past cases packed with Roman tweezers and Saxon jewellery; a broken rapier; a collection of porpoise bones found buried in the grounds of Lewes Priory; a tile bearing the smiling face of Edward I, his lazy eye just visible; a finger ring with a charm against fever engraved inside it; and an ice-skate made from the compressed thigh bone of a horse. The information on the displays was equally quixotic. In the medieval period they'd eaten porpoise and oysters at Lewes Priory, and drunk weak beer because the water was unsafe. Wool dealers and tanners had thrived in the town, and the traders who passed periodically through were known as *piepowders* for the dust that clung to their feet.

In one of the downstairs rooms there was a woman's skeleton in a glass case, a necklace of orange and green beads slung about her clavicle. Her knees were pulled to her chest, in the foetal position the Saxons used for burials. There were no Roman bones. A display about the afterlife explained that for the Romans:

> Spirits of the dead lived on in the underworld known as Hades. The purpose of the burial ritual was to ensure the successful transition from earthly life to the next world. Provisions to help the soul were placed in the grave alongside the urn or the body ... The body would be burnt on a funeral pyre which purified and released the soul. The ashes would then be placed in an urn in the grave which would be either a hole in the ground or a cist, an underground structure of stone or tiles. Mourning would continue for nine days after the burial. Romans never neglected to bury their dead as it was believed that the souls of the unburied were left to wander the gloomy marshland at the gates of Hades for a hundred years before gaining entry.

This last was the fate that almost befell Elpenor, the shipmate of Odysseus who died falling drunk from a roof on Circe's island. His death hadn't yet been marked when Odysseus descended to Hades, and he pleaded frantically for his body to be burned and buried in a barrow, complete with armour, with an upright oar to mark his grave. Better than the marsh, I guess, that place of desolation, weed-choked, frog-spawning, leaking dank clouds of gas that seem to burn but emit no heat. A marsh would swallow you whole and spit you out after the appointed century tanned bog-oak black and smelling of reed-mace and cat's tail. Better to be burned; better to be tucked in a tiled chamber with your tweezers and your coins; better to go up in sparks than be where water has dominion and frets away even the soil.

The story of Elpenor is translated in one of Virginia Woolf's Greek notebooks, which she kept to accompany her reading of Homer, Aristophanes, Euripides and so forth. Though she never went to school and was educated largely by her parents, Woolf's classical education was thorough and exacting. She was taught by a series of private tutors, the last of whom, the suffragist Janet Case, became a lifelong friend. The notebook that describes Odysseus's encounter with the dead was begun in the winter of 1907; a year after her brother Thoby was taken ill with typhoid and died in the wake of a family expedition to Greece. Thoby had been her fellow traveller through the classics, and it may be that she was thinking of him when she appended her description of Odysseus luring 'the weak races of the dead' out of Hades with the exulting words 'Beautiful! Beautiful!'

The study of Greek intertwines itself strangely through Woolf's life, appearing unexpectedly in the more dramatic, even mythic, scenes. It was to Janet Case that she confessed her half-brother George Duckworth's sexually predatory behaviour, which may or may not have gone beyond fumblings and gropings, and which apparently took place, among other locations, during Greek lessons at Hyde Park Gate. This revelatory conversation has been preserved – albeit second-hand – in a letter to Vanessa from 1911 that reads:

> She has a calm interest in copulation . . . and this led us to the revelation of all Georges malefactions. To my surprise, she has always had an intense dislike of him; and used to say 'Whew – you nasty creature', when he came in and began fondling me over my Greek. By the time I got to the bedroom scenes, she dropped her lace, and gasped like a benevolent gudgeon. By bedtime she said she was feeling quite sick.

Greek also took a role in Virginia's madness, which resembled manic depression and was never satisfactorily diagnosed. During the course of her life she had five major breakdowns: two in the wake of her parents' deaths; two around the time she married Leonard and published her first novel; and one at the beginning of the Second World War that ended with her death. In the interim she was often physically ill and beset by moods of anxiety and acute depression. These spells of insanity have been repeatedly written about, sometimes by people – among them Leonard, Vanessa and Virginia herself – who experienced them first hand, and sometimes by those who didn't. Such obsessive rehandling inevitably hardens and reduces a life, turning its complex, contradictory material into a story, with a story's reliance on intelligible consequences and colourful scenes.

In this manner, it's possible to boil Woolf's illness down to a series of vivid statements. From childhood she was troubled by moods of intense anxiety combined with physical symptoms like fever, headaches and a racing heart. During the madness that followed her father's death she attempted suicide by leaping from a window; later she overdosed on veronal and had her stomach pumped. Often she was very depressed and found it hard to eat, and at their worst these spells would be followed by mania so intense that she didn't recognise even her husband, heard voices, raved unintelligibly, and physically attacked her nurses. The treatment, which she loathed, was soporific: sedatives; bed rest; a restriction in reading, writing, walking and other supposed excitements; and a diet grotesquely heavy in milk and soothing, plumping foods. Indeed, it is largely because of his insistence on this fare that Leonard gained the posthumous reputation as his wife's jailer as well as her carer.

Among these lurid titbits of distress, one element is often repeated: that during her second breakdown she 'had lain in bed at the Dickinsons' house at Welwyn thinking that the birds were singing Greek choruses and that King Edward was using the foulest language possible among Ozzie Dickinson's azaleas'. This detail derives from an autobiographical essay, *Old Bloomsbury*, which was written almost twenty years after the event as a talk for the Memoir Club, a Bloomsbury collective in which members told artfully reconstructed life stories for the amusement of their friends. Its status as verifiable fact is equally artfully unpicked by

Woolf's biographer Hermione Lee, who observes in the course of an elegant rereading that Septimus Smith, the shell-shocked poet in *Mrs Dalloway* who later kills himself, is also subject to hallucinations of sparrows singing in Greek.

It's no longer possible to answer the question of whether Virginia lent Septimus her experience, or whether she invented it for him and then adopted it herself. What remains is the sparrows. They might have existed; they might not. Either way, they remain on the page, ambivalent and ecstatic, singing 'in voices prolonged and piercing in Greek words, from trees in the meadow of life beyond a river where the dead walk, how there is no death.'

I left the museum then, but on the way up the motte to the castle there was one last reference to the *Odyssey*. The steps coiled around the edge of a walled garden full of pink and white valerian, the sleep-inducing herb that the Saxons called All-Heal. These steps had recently been rebuilt, and each was carved with the name of a benefactor. Amid the family groupings and cheerful exhortations to keep on climbing, someone had chosen the single line *Keep Ithaca always in mind.* Ithaca was Odysseus's destination, but it was not until I returned home that I tracked the quotation to a poem by Constantine Cavafy, the gay Greek poet who had worked for thirty-three years as a clerk in the Egyptian Irrigation Service. *And if you find her poor,* the poem ends:

> *Ithaca has not deceived you.*
> *Wise as you have become, with such experience, by now*
> *you will have come to know what Ithacas really mean.*

The bees were working away in the valerian, and though the day was hot clouds were banking up on the horizon, dark below and impossibly clean above. *Keep Ithaca always in mind.* Say your prayers, keep God in your heart, have faith, persist. But what if Ithaca is no more than the island of the sirens, a place where time stops: a static heaven at the journey's end? I'd given up faith in a destination, except to be certain that bones do not always stay buried and that I will undoubtedly be outlived by the plastic bags with which my generation has bedecked the globe, as the Romans' tweezers outlasted their mortal bodies. Forget Ithaca. This is a drowning world, and there is nothing more sobering than regarding the hopes for the future of someone who is already dead. But then perhaps that is what Cavafy means: that Ithacas exist merely to keep us moving and will dematerialise like a rainbow when the journey is complete.

The shell keep was at the top of the motte, a huge pollarded lime beside it, growing out of a circle of neatly clipped lawn. I went through the doorway and up the precipitous stairs, clinging to the rail like a drunken sailor. There were no tourists; only a couple of pursed-lipped electricians surveying the wiring on the second floor. At the top I stumbled out into the light, and there before me was the town as William Morris described it, 'lying like a box of toys under a great amphitheatre of chalky hills'. The river slipped like solder through the fields, and on the other side of the narrow valley through which it passed the Downs rose up again in what was virtually a cliff of exposed chalk, which generations of jackdaws had riddled into holes to hold their courts.

I looked seaward, propping my arms on the rail and gazing out past the roofs of the town and the flickering traffic of the A27. The Levels lay cupped between the hills, flashed with tiny streams, the river carving a snake's undulating path through lush water-meadows that barely skimmed sea level. I counted the hills I knew by name: Malling Down, Mount Caburn, Firle Beacon, Blackcap, Beddingham Hill with its two dewponds, the Red Lion and the White. The hills in the west defeated me, though dead ahead I could see the strange hump of Upper Rise, which was once an island riddled with rabbit warrens. At my back was Offham Hill with its bald chalk flank, and behind it Mount Harry. A watcher posted here could have seen Prince Edward's troops ride out at dawn across the Paddock, and caught them later plunging through the Wallands in pursuit of their poorly armed and horseless quarry.

The landscape had the look in the morning light of something permanent, but its appearance was deceptive. Since the beginning of time it had been undergoing the kind of slow-paced, inexorable change that raises hills and carves out cliffs and valleys. All the world is subject to this sort of flux, which goes on beneath our feet and is only rarely discernable to the eye. But there was, as I had dimly seen the night before, another agency working its will on the valley. Man had been fidgeting away here ever since he arrived: man with his picks and his shovels; his restless mind.

Thousands, perhaps tens of thousands of years before the birth of Christ, the first early humans wandered in from what is now Europe, travelling by foot across the land bridge that would later be obliterated by the rising seas of the English Channel. At first these humans left no lasting traces on the landscape, but by something like 4000 BC a change in the valley's pollen record shows that the wildwood was beginning to be cleared. Pollen is a remarkable record of man's activity. In addition to exhibiting a great variety in architecture and ornamentation, it is unusually resistant to decay and can be preserved for millennia if trapped in acidic or waterlogged soil. Samples retrieved from peat at the base of Mount Caburn suggest the Downs were covered then by a dense lime forest that was gradually being coppiced or cut down by early pastoralists and farmers. Pollen from the cereals they cultivated has also been preserved, invisible to the naked eye, within the dark lenses of peat deposited by the river.

Time inched on. The wildwood disappeared, tree by tree, as forests have a tendency to do. The Romans came and went, leaving their urns of ash, their rational roads. Lewes was built in the Saxon era, on a grid pattern with narrow flint-walled twittens dropping away from the high street. A market was held there, and two mints; sometimes the skeletons of its inhabitants are found by metal detectorists in the hills nearby, curled like cats with their swords at their sides. Most of the villages I could see strung out along the river like beads on a rosary – Iford, Beddingham, Rodmell, Southease and Tarring Neville – were named in the Domesday Book and had been established long before the Normans came and built their castles, and filled them, as the Anglo-Saxon Chronicle has it, *with devils and evil men*.

In this dark, almost ungraspable period the lower Ouse was in all probability a vast tidal estuary, much wider than it is today and edged with vagrant, half-illusory channels that riddled through the mudflats. The river passed on its meandering way to the sea through salt marshes full of wild birds, which were themselves flanked on either side by fertile alluvial soil built up into terraces by centuries of silt deposition. The Saxons were a seafaring people and it seems from the records of Domesday that those who settled here were engaged in the herring industry, sailing to the North Sea spawning grounds to catch the teeming sea-coloured fish in drift nets, for the tithes these tiny hamlets produced equal those of some of the richest East Anglian towns.

Marshes mark the boundary between land and sea, and marsh dwellers earn their living in both directions. In Rodmell they made salt, cooking it from cakes of silty soil in coarse ceramic pans known now as briquetage, while at Iford there were two watermills, both long since tumbled down. The villages also depended on farming, but even this owed a debt to the river, for it seems that though the high downland was used for pasture, crops were grown lower down, on the alluvial slopes, while the hay to feed oxen through winter was harvested from the dank meadows that lined the water's edge.

By the end of the Saxon era the practice of reclamation known as inning was prevalent in England's marshes, and it seems likely from the abundance of meadows recorded in the valley by the Domesday scribes that it had begun in earnest here by the time

King Harold was killed on the bloody fields of Battle, not twenty miles away. With his death time snaps into focus, for if the relics of the Saxon era are fragile or have a tendency towards corrosion, those of the Normans are more solid and abiding. The tower I stood upon had been assembled by Norman hands, and if I looked south I could make out the priory they also built, which was once the size of Canterbury Cathedral and was ruined not by time or weather but as a consequence of Henry VIII's cataclysmic break with Rome.

After the Conquest marshland began to be more systematically reclaimed, and what happened in the Ouse valley is matched by work across the country, including the Somerset Levels, Romney Marsh and the Lincolnshire and Norfolk Fens. During this period ditches were dug to dry the land, and in time walls, banks and sluice gates were also built to pen the rivers in. Ironically enough, these works often had the opposite effect. The beaches of the English Channel are subject to longshore drift, the term given to the movement of shingle by the prevailing wind and tide. These shifting beaches have a tendency to close up the mouths of rivers, but before the marshes were inned their formation was countered by the fact of tidal scour. Estuaries tend to carry a considerable quantity of water, and on the ebb tide this great flux of liquid rushes through the river's mouth, scraping away the gathering glut of stones. With the drainage of the marshes this scouring power was inevitably reduced, and by the early medieval period a drifting shingle spit had forced the mouth of the Ouse from its natural exit at Newhaven three miles east to Seaford. As a result, the river began to take an increasingly tortuous course, and at the same time to slowly fill with silt.

From the beginning of the clearance of the forests, thousands of years before, the river had suffered from sedimentation, and now, as it grew progressively more shallow, so it became increasingly vulnerable to damming by reeds and waste, meaning that spring tides or heavy rains led almost inevitably to the banks being breached. With such conditions, it's not perhaps surprising that by the late Middle Ages much of the valley was underwater either permanently or when tides were high. The land was barely above sea level, and a marsh is after all a marsh not out of spite or stubbornness but because it's situated where water collects. Upper Rise and Lower Rise, the two odd tumps of greensand that stand in the centre of the Brooks, were in that period rabbit-infested islands, and most of the cow-grazed fields I could see from the castle would have been wishes, from the Old English *wisc* or marshy meadow: at best waterlogged, at worst submerged. As for the Archbishop of Canterbury, who owned 400 acres near Southerham, he shrugged his shoulders and converted his fields into a permanent fishery: bream being more amenable to submersion than corn or sheep.

Then there was the matter of the weather. In the Roman period the sea level was a good six feet lower than it is today, and the Sussex coast probably extended a mile further out. By the Middle Ages, the sea began to rise again, causing intense problems for coastal villages. With the rising tides there came upon Europe a period of terrible storms, and it was during this time that the towns of Winchelsea and Dunwich began to vanish beneath the waves. The unrest persisted in brief cycles for more than a century and a half, and can be tracked through faltering harvest records and the anxious chronicles of the monasteries.

The destruction caused by these storms could be considerable. One of the most severe took place in the spring of 1287, when Edward I had come to the throne and was working to expel the nation's Jews. By morning the sea had completely rearranged the eastern Channel coast, landlocking some towns and turning others into harbours overnight. The town of Old Winchelsea, which had been broken up piecemeal by the sea for decades, was conclusively drowned that day, and if anything remains of its two churches and fifty inns it is hidden beneath the massive sweeping expanse of Broomhill Sands, where the kite surfers like to play.

Something had to be done, and in 1422, in the wake of the infamous St Elizabeth Flood, which devastated the south coast and took perhaps five thousand lives in the Netherlands besides, the first Commission of Sewers was appointed for the Ouse. These bodies were gradually becoming prevalent in marshy regions and they functioned as a kind of water police, investigating 'the annoyances and defects of repairs of sea-banks and walls, publick streams and rivers, ditches and marsh-grounds'. In 1531 an Act of Parliament granted the commissions extensive powers as guardians, empowering them to collect a tax from landowners known as a scot, and to use these funds for the upkeep of their region's drainage. Furthermore, persistent misdemeanours could be tried in special courts, which had the right to order fines by way of punishment.

I'd seen in the county archive at the bottom of the hill some of the account books and records kept by the local commissioners of sewers, written in a multitude of hands and upon a multitude of papers. The earliest records are lost, but though the quill gives way over time to the typewriter certain words are repeated through the centuries until they take on almost the appearance of an incantation or a prayer. Over and again I read *cast, cleanse, widen, draw, raft, shoreset*: in other words dredge out weeds, dig clear the clotted bottoms of sewers and reinforce the embankments where they have begun to crumble and slip, that we may grow our crops, God willing, in the land we have wrung from the river.

But it was the Devil's own job, draining that valley. You might as well have used a sieve. Around the time that Lord Thomas Cromwell was engaged in tugging down the nation's monasteries he received a letter from Sir John Gage, one of the local commissioners, that gives a sense of how desperate local people were becoming. 'The Levell of Lewes,' he writes, 'yet be in great rewyn and continually under water in winter, and for the most parte lykwyse in somer . . . my Lord Prior of Lewes sailed to Flanders to view and see things there . . . also we sent for him that inned the Marshe beneathe Saynte Katherins, and had his advise.'

By 1539 the needs of shipping as well as farming had become pressing, and so the commission decided that a channel should be cut through the shingle spit to force the river back out at Newhaven. This allowed the barges hauling Wealden iron and wool to reach the sea without running aground, but it didn't take long for the shingle to build up again, for though a pier was put up it was unaccountably set on the eastern side of the river and so did nothing to prevent the shingle, which drove in from the south-west.

It took the Georgians, those rational thinkers, to puzzle out what needed to be done. In the mid-eighteenth century, after another series of floods and an abortive experiment with lock gates near the river's mouth, which were rapidly pulled down for want of repair, a civil engineer was invited to view the valley. John Smeaton came from Yorkshire, began as an instrument maker and shifted by degrees into becoming the foremost engineer of the Industrial Age. Over the decades he designed bridges, harbours, watermills, lighthouses and canals; even a diving bell. His very first engineering contract had been to drain the boggy reaches of Lochar Moss, and the problem of turning fens and marshes into profitable land would occupy him throughout his life. As a young man he'd travelled to the Low Countries to research hydraulic drainage, applying the tricks he learnt there years later to the three great fens of his native county: Potteric Carr, Adlingfleet Level and Hatfield Chase. By the latter part of the eighteenth century Smeaton was much in demand as a drainage expert and during the damp June of 1767 he was asked by the commissioners to survey the Ouse.

His proposals were ambitious. One plan was to build a canal alongside and sometimes underneath the Ouse that would conduct excess water directly to the sea: a prohibitively expensive scheme. The other, cheaper, suggestion was to straighten the river by a series of cuts, dredging it clear and building up the banks until it resembled and functioned like a canal, with a gated outfall sluice at the river's mouth that would prevent the tide from rushing in. It was this latter plan that found favour, but in keeping with the air of hesitation and haphazardness that seemed to attend all work on the river, the work proceeded only haltingly for the next twenty years.

Another engineer, William Cubitt, took a brief look at the project, but it was William Jessop, the son of a shipwright, who finished the job, as he was often to do with Smeaton's schemes. In 1787 Jessop was asked to re-survey the river, and armed with his plans a group of local traders and landowners took the matter to parliament. The ins and outs of what followed are excessively complicated, but by 1791 the Lower Ouse Navigation Act was passed and a little later Jessop submitted his final scheme – closely resembling Smeaton's – for draining the Levels and making the river navigable for trade. A few hundred workers were employed and, steadily, steadily over the next ten years the river's more tortuous curves were sliced away, the banks rebuilt, a breakwater flung up at Newhaven and the channel widened and dredged so that it ran both swift and clear. Barges no longer ran aground at Piddinghoe, unable to ship their cargoes of coal, salt, fruit and slate upstream. Instead, it was the river that was imprisoned, compelled to remain within the reinforced banks that the navvies built: at a cost, by the century's end, of nearly £20,000.

Did matters end there? Of course not. The lower river may have been canalised, but it still remained at risk of fluvial flooding when rain or surge tides overtopped the banks. One of the worst came in 1852, when the rains were so great sheep drowned in the fields, train lines were impassable, and harvests of hay and corn were beaten to the ground and rotted where they lay. There was another in 1960, of comparative severity to the 2000 flood, though it caused less damage, for in that period the floodplain hadn't yet filled with the housing estates and supermarkets that clutter it today. As for the defensive work, though the duties of the commissioners have long since been absorbed by the Environment Agency the old techniques of casting and shoresetting have not yet been abandoned. The banks are still raised and braced, the vegetation dragged away, work that in 2008 was estimated to cost £410,000 a year, for labour is dearer now than it was two centuries ago.

I leaned my chin on the wall and gazed down at the network of ditches, glinting in the light like fishing lines. The river turned its curves, for though its crookedness had been corrected, it was never made entirely straight. For the last ten years, I'd laboured under the impression that this view was almost natural, and now I felt a fool. Landscapes, we all agree these days, are palimpsests, laid down in layers over the centuries. While this is undoubtedly correct, it's also true that some eras work in pencil and others in indelible ink. The river bore the signature of the Industrial Age; its previous character might be discernible but it cannot be retrieved.

The first time I was shown the map that Smeaton used I couldn't make sense of what I was seeing. The Ouse looked intricate and tricky, plunging through deeps, meanders, shoals and shallows with names I'd never heard. *Iron Hole*, I traced, *Bramble Shallow, Ranscombe Pool*. Had there really been a fording point near Stock House, where the river now runs at a gallop through banks that rise a good six feet above the outlying land?

And where was Sleeper's Hole? Swallowed up by the marina at Newhaven, I guessed, while the Washing Place at Malling had been dredged clean away.

The clouds had been banking up behind Mount Harry while my back was turned. Now they started to spill south, following the river towards the Channel. I watched them slip overhead, rudderless in the fretting breeze. The river's transformations bothered me because they seemed to highlight the wrongheaded rapaciousness of my own species, carving the world up with no thought to its consequences: behaviour, ironically enough, that seems doomed to bring an apocalypse of floods and droughts upon us all. I thought of the sewage treatment works trickling their poisoned outfalls into the Bevern; of the water companies that abstracted groundwater from its secret hoards in the Downs. And then I thought ahead, a century or two. Would the river have dried up? Would its snaking passage through the valley be marked by cracked earth, nothing more? Or would the sea have inched an advance until it took the town and returned it to a salty swamp, contaminated with the bodies of cattle and the bright bobbing plastic toys with which we've filled our world? Would a watcher stand here one day and see a desert, or would they look out upon a toxic sea?

Lewes's periodic and continuing floods are a reminder that all actions store up consequences. Building on a floodplain, no matter how many sewers have been contrived, remains a risky venture – until, of course, we find a way to make it rain at will. And like those forest fires that are necessary for the germination of certain seeds, a flood is not entirely a destructive event, though I wouldn't perhaps think that if my own house had been filled with sewage, my books crimped and mildewed, my clothes washed away. But even the Environment Agency is agreed that too much of the Ouse's catchment has been reclaimed and that if Lewes is to survive the travails of climate change some land must be relinquished to the river.

I'd come, somewhere in my delvings, across a project to re-establish washlands on the banks of the Ouse. Washlands are meadows that can tolerate flooding of short duration, acting as holding bays for the excess water that would otherwise force its way through culverts and sewers and into shops and homes. As farming has grown ever more intensive these habitats have become progressively imperilled, though they once grew so richly that they could be used three times in a year, bringing forth first a harvest of hay at midsummer and then an aftermath crop that cows could graze into autumn and sheep right through to the winter storms.

The idea, cooked up by ecologists and historians at the University of Sussex, was to re-establish these wildflower meadows, reducing the risk of flooding downstream and returning to the river those fugitive grasses that I'd seen near Sheffield Park: bent and black knapweed, cock-foot, crested dog's-tail, fescue and Yorkshire fog. The scheme was a tiny one, and yet there was an elegance to it that was deeply pleasing: it was both economical and lavish and made me hopeful for the future. Perhaps we will be able to accommodate ourselves to this world after all, instead of chipping away at it until the foundations collapse and the whole thing comes tumbling down.

* * *

I swung down the stairs in a rush, suddenly full of beans and ravenously hungry. I bought a slab of pizza and a can of fizzy sugar, faintly flavoured with elderflower, in a strange sort of grocer's that had heaped in its window bread, a bicycle, potted geraniums and a spinning wheel. I took my lunch down to the railway lands and built myself a picnic in the sun. Jackdaws were flying together over the builders' yard, one calling *Ka Ka Ka* and another answering *Clack Clack Clack*. I lay back, swigging the counterfeit cordial and counting the flowers that grew entwined beneath the brambles. White clover, ribbed melilot, black medick, plantain which is good for sore throats, mugwort, curled dock, hedge woundwort with its protruding lower lip, like a currency trader with whom I once went on a blind and unrepeated date. The ground ivy was no longer in flower but I rubbed a few leaves in my hand all the same, hoping for that brisk aromatic hit.

After I'd eaten I walked on along the bank to the Rowing Club, which is on an island formed by the cut that severed Cliffe Shallow. The river had turned molten again. It was the colour of milk chocolate and just as glutinous. The surface was no longer glassy, but scored rather with lines and pockmarks, as if a struggle was going on far beneath, the stays of current cleaving together and wrenching away. The little boats swung grimly to and fro. I leant right over the river to make out their names: *Star One*, *Deejay*, *Osprey*, the tarp-covered *Triton*. A man on the far bank was lifting a kayak out of the water. The grasses here were the same metallic blue-green as unripe wheat. It was high tide, and the river had filled to just below the brim, so that some stems were reflected on the surface and others drowned beneath it.

There was another story about a submerged valley that I'd forgotten, and it came back to me then, striking a different note to those dreamy tales my granny used to spin. Floods and droughts are both predicted to increase with climate change, and the worries about insufficient water, as well as its excess, have begun to preoccupy the water companies. South East Water already manages two reservoirs supplied by the Ouse, but for years has been angling to build a third at Clay Hill, obliterating a valley just east of here to supply the region's ever-increasing water needs.

Matthew and I once looked at a house on the edge of that valley, a slate-tiled house in the shadow of Plashett Wood with a huge neglected garden out the back. The kitchen floor was rotting and there was no cooker or fridge. One of the bedrooms had been painted a bright, unhealthy pink, with a frieze on the wall that depicted a cartwheeling pig. Someone had tried to tear it down and failed, leaving it to hang in dismally fluttering strips. The rooms smelled of dogs and misery. Outside the front door mint flourished in a border full of damp clumps of discarded toilet paper. *I can't live here*, I said and so regretfully we left, for the location was pretty and we had become increasingly desperate of finding somewhere that would suit us both.

The house would survive, but the land it overlooked: that would be sunk beneath millions of litres of river water if the company's plans were approved. The valley had once been a hunting estate owned by the Archbishop of Canterbury and was now a tenanted farm, run in the old style, with crops grown in rotation in small fields that were divided by towering hedges. In the field boundaries great oaks remained, for as Thomas Browne said, *generations pass while some trees stand*. The ancient woodland that clung on in shaws was home to hordes of bats of many species: Natterer's bat, which can catch a spider from its web; Daubenton's bat, which fishes insects from the water with its feet; Brandt's bat and the rare Bechstein's; the swift noctule; the barbastelle; the brown long-eared bat; the whiskered bat and the soprano pipistrelle.

The bats rise each evening and cross the woods and glebes, hunting for beetles and midges above the remains of medieval fishponds. A reservoir will leave them with nowhere to feed or roost: no rotting trees, no woodland pools, no flowering meadows where the moths – the Oak Eggar, the Garden Tiger – circle above the pale yarrow and the glowing heads of clover. The farm and its scattered Georgian cottages will be plucked down, I guess, and there will just be water, an abundance of it, and somewhere far beneath it the ghosts of massive oaks.

I lay there in the grasses that grew at the river's edge, disinclined to get up and travel on. I lay amid the mugwort that flourished in this stretch of land, that cousin of wormwood which vanquishes parasites and which St John the Baptist is said to have worn in a girdle about his waist. The cows were grazing in the fields, wheeling away when a walker passed, and in the distance the cars crossed back and forth above the bridge where the A27 swings up to vault the river. The chalk rose white before me, carved into portals and sleeping places until it resembled nothing so much as a mouldering tower block, home to a vast family of jackdaws, a gathering so unruly that it was once accurately known as a *clattering*. I watched them come and go for a long time. There were binoculars in my pack, wedged between the sunblock and a sweating lump of cheese, and I pulled them out and set the bag behind my back, where I could rest my elbows on it.

A flotilla of nine jacks had crossed in very high, circling on the thermals that persist above Mount Caburn, when something plunged vertically out of the sky. I held my breath. It landed on a narrow ridge almost at the top of the cliff and stood there, one foot forward, shoulders hunched: part ballet dancer, part pugilist. Peregrine!

In the 1960s the peregrine population of Britain had been decimated due to relentless hunting and the increasing use of pesticides on crops. DDT was a particular problem; it accumulated in the bodies of the smaller birds that were the falcon's meat and caused the peregrines' eggshells to grow perilously thin. When DDT was banned and stricter laws regarding hunting passed, the birds recovered and came back, pair by pair, from the brink. In recent years they'd begun to return to the south, favouring city blocks as well as the cliffs of old. There was a nesting pair that lived next to my gym in Brighton, and a falconer I'd met recently told me he thought two more had settled here.

The binoculars were jammed so hard against my face that I could feel rings engraving around my eyes. The bird footed casually at the husky grass, glaring from side to side so that I could see the dark markings that gave her the appearance of wearing a helmet. I couldn't see if there was a nest beside her or if the ledge was simply somewhere to pause. And then, before I'd quite taken her in, she shifted her weight and rose sheer to the sky, up beyond the rook roads, until she was just a dark anchor among many dark shapes, all wheeling, a centrifugal surge of motion above the collapsing cliff.

I rose then too, and hoisted the bag onto my back. As I turned I could hear the water lapping almost at my heels, a flood tide rushing to glut the river. It rises and it falls, that flood, and in time it will have the barbastrelle and the brown-eared bat; it will have the Oak Eggar and the Garden Tiger; it will have the peregrine and the clattering jacks. In time I too will lie beneath the water, and here I differ from my granny, for I do not think that in a hundred years or in a thousand any one of us will be returned to the quick and ready air, any more than I think the iguanodon might rise and stalk the railway lands, or the soldiers that perished here climb to their feet and draw their swords. Right now, though, it is we who have the tenancy of this shared realm. I would like to think that we might pass it on, this small blue planet, cauled in water. Till a' the seas gang dry, I guess, and it is blue no more.

VI

THE LADY VANISHES

TO LEAVE LEWES I HAD to pass under two bridges, one carrying the road and the other the railway. The concrete was irresistible to graffiti artists and among the tags and scribbled insults someone had sketched a woman's face in quick blue lines, her cheekbones aslant, her hair sleeked back. She looked out through empty eyes at the water as it rushed between the girders, vacant and lovely, oblivious to the traffic that screeched above her.

The face struck an echo, and for once I could remember what it was. In *Birthday Letters*, Ted Hughes's last collection, there's a poem about a clay head that is abandoned by the side of a river. The book was published in 1998, a month or two before Hughes died, and all the poems in it, written over decades, concern his relationship with Sylvia Plath. In the one I was thinking of, Plath is given a terracotta bust modelled in her likeness by an American friend. The head disturbs her. The likeness is off-kilter – the lips too swollen perhaps, the eyes too close together. She doesn't want it in her room but nor does she want to toss it away, and so the two of them, Ted and Sylvia, carry it along the towpath towards Grantchester and deposit it in the branches of a willow, where it can watch the yellow leaves as they flicker down into the water.

What were they hoping to do? Avert the bad luck they both felt gathering; strike it away with a single resonant act? If so, they failed. It didn't take long for disquiet to flare: the primitive fear that harm done to a model will by sympathetic magic cause harm to the original too. What happened to the head, Hughes asks. Did boys with sticks smash it apart? Did it crumble over decades into the Granta? Or is it still there, in the bole of the willow, owl-eyed, the river's daughter, watching and not speaking: the one that got away?

We navigate by omens such as these. You don't have to be a poet to be prone to apophenia, to seeking meaningful patterns in the scattered, senseless data of the everyday. In a certain mood, the earth itself can seem a ouija board, calling out its advice, discharging symbol after symbol, relentless and malevolent, though to ordinary eyes nothing more has happened than a single black and white bird winging down the sky. I once dated – in fact loved – a man who left me as we walked together through a field. As we had been talking, he told me, he couldn't help but notice that we walked in separate furrows that ran parallel but did not conjoin. This, it seemed to him, was the essence of our relationship, though whether the path had clarified our fate or actually authored it I didn't ask.

Martin. Christ, why was I thinking about him? I shook myself physically, like a cat caught in the rain. These were marsh thoughts, uneasily buried: the doomed woman, the lost lover. They belonged to the region I was entering, the reclaimed fields of the Brooks, crisscrossed with sewers and barred with sluice gates. In the winter the ditches run like mercury but now they were brackish and dully green, home to marsh frogs, those alien interlopers that do not croak but cackle as you pass. Virginia Woolf drowned herself down here, in the lowlands that stretch between the Downs. It was hardly any wonder my mind had taken a ghoulish turn.

I came out from under the bridge then and as I stepped into the light I caught a flash of colour. At the foot of one of the pilings there was a single pyramidal orchid the flushed pink of a cat's tongue. I didn't know what it boded but it made me smile, growing there unlooked for in the trampled dirt at the base of a bypass. And then – as if I'd cried out for omens to the sibyl of the underpass – something dark shot through the space at the corner of my eye and disappeared into the river. I stepped back, stunned. What the hell had happened? Had a car shucked a hubcap as it swung across the bridge? As I craned to see a cormorant emerged from the water, lifted briefly to the air and then settled demurely on the surface. *Show off*, I muttered. *I can swim too you know.* The cormorant ignored me, as a creature that can fly through two elements no doubt has the right to do.

It was half past three. I didn't have far to go: a couple of miles of river path and then a skim over the fields to Rodmell, where Virginia Woolf had lived, off and on, from 1919 to her death in 1941. She loved walking in this marsh, and it wasn't hard to see why. God, but it was beautiful. I'd given up trying to fight through the vegetation at the top of the embankment and had climbed down to the water's edge, following a faint, yellowing path through the same blue-green grass that had earlier reminded me of wheat. Last time I'd been down here I got caught in a torrential rainstorm and had to fight my way through dripping grasses the height of my chest, until I was as conclusively drenched as if I had walked home along the riverbed.

Now I felt more like I'd fallen to the bottom of a glass dome. The Downs rose all around me and beyond them was the sky, chalky too, screened with fine cloud like the scrim that drops before a play. Behind me great white cumuli were building. A storm? It was hot enough. The air felt tense and fidgety against my fingertips and as I glanced again over my shoulder I saw the clouds above Falmer had tarnished to a spoiled grey. Something stank to high heaven too. I nosed around and turned up the corpse of a rabbit, its fur tugged into damp little tufts as if it had been suckled.

A man passed me then, moving quickly, binoculars slung about his neck. We smiled silently at one another and it struck me for the first time how safe I felt. Five days of walking, speaking hardly at all, and I seemed to have become immersed in the world, neck-deep, the panic that had shadowed me for months dissolved away. My phone had bleeped periodically but I hadn't answered it. I didn't want to rupture the buoyancy that had come so unexpectedly. At home, solitude had begun to terrify me, the threat of it, stretching endless and paper-white, though in the past I'd always loved to be alone. But here, in the fields, moving at my own pace, I did not feel islanded or isolated. There was too much occurring. Like – now! – those two oystercatchers on the far bank, still as bookends, monochrome save their tangerine beaks, crying in pitched, plaintive voices *peeppeeep peeeppeep peeppeep*.

The path stretched on before me, almost flush with the ruffled water. A train went by, calling its way to Southease, and down in the Brooks I could see a pair of tractors clearing the field, the men concealed within their cabs. There was something very strange about walking aside such brimful water, as if I could step down onto it and continue along that shifting track. The river was completely opaque now, aglint with borrowed light, its surface coloured the bluish-green of spilled petrol, teased by the wind and current into tufts and crests and little waves. Behind it I could see the bald chalkpit at Asham, where Virginia once leased a house. It was where she went to recuperate after her third breakdown, and she kept a funny sort of nature journal there, full of spare, painful accounts of moths sighted and mushrooms gathered. Her wedding night was spent at Asham, and she finished her first novel, *The Voyage Out*, whilst staying there too, in the west-facing rooms that rose out from the hill like the prow of a ship.

The house is long gone now. It was engulfed by a cement works in the 1930s and slowly wrecked by the clouds of chalk, which covered everything in a fine, wheezy dust, screening the windows and spoiling the garden and the bordering elms. It grew derelict and was pulled down entirely in 1994, when the works – now turned into a landfill site – were expanded in size. In his autobiography Leonard Woolf remembers finding the house for the first time, hidden in a hollow of the Downs amid a great field of sheep. 'The grass of the garden and field seemed almost to come to the sitting rooms and into the windows facing west,' he wrote. 'One often had a feeling as if one were living under water in the depths of the sea behind the thick rough glass of the room's long windows – a sea of green trees, green grass, green air.'

It wasn't green any more. The chalk had been quarried away, and the holes that remained gummed up with disposable nappies, household waste and the corpses of cattle infected with BSE. The pits had been cut down to below the water table and not all of them were originally lined, so that for a time the waste leached chlorine and ammonia into the long ditches that snaked down to the river. The site had reached capacity a month ago, on 16 May, the pits chock-full with rotting rubbish. And soon, or so the waste company promises, Leonard's green grass will be restored, the cap of downland smoothed back across the foxed, bedevilled earth.

Virginia thought that Asham was haunted, and wrote a short story based on her experience there. The doors, she wrote, used to open and close all night, and a couple would whisper and sigh as they tiptoed between the rooms. Had the cement works flighted them, I wondered, or had they persisted in the dust until the abandoned house was pulled apart? I liked to think that if you found the right spot amid the bin bags you would hear them, voices hushed, still patrolling a house that had long since fallen away.

I'd been reading Woolf's diaries and letters all spring, buying cheap paperbacks with ugly covers that had to be shipped from America. I coveted the beautiful Hogarth Press editions, which sold in Lewes for horrendous, heart-stopping prices. We used to have a couple of them at home, shifting bookshelves as we moved from place to place, and the last time I visited my mother I brought one back: *The Flight of the Mind*, the first volume of letters. The spine was a pale flinty grey like the breast of a pigeon, tattered at its ends and bleached a little by the sun. On the frontispiece my father had written in his tight, distinctive hand *To Denise, from Peter, with much love, 3 December 1976*. The date was her birthday, the last before I was born. I couldn't imagine my parents as a couple, though I'd seen photographs of them smiling in cut-off shorts, leaning against a bottle-green TR6 or messing about on a friend's speedboat. I wondered if she'd asked for the book. For Christmas, Matthew had given me a Hoover.

Little stories kept coming back to me now, and phrases I found so pleasurable I rolled them around within my mouth. Woolf wrote often of the river, and I remembered a story late in the diaries of a flood that had occurred just south of here. In the early years of the Second World War, a bomb was dropped near Rodmell that ruptured the banks of the Ouse, those same banks that William Jessop had contrived to fix the river to its course. The water swelled out blue across the fields and the marsh was returned to the inland sea of medieval times, the bridge cut off, the road impassable. On Guy Fawkes Night, Woolf wrote of the beauty of this *unfathomable* sea, adding: 'Oh may the flood last for ever – a virgin lip; no bungalows; as it was in the beginning.'

The pleasure of isolation quickly palled, as it always did. To read Woolf's diaries is to be tugged to and fro between the irreconcilable desires for solitude and company, the twin fears of being islanded and swamped. The experience of being marooned at Rodmell, which war and flood made literal at last, was both delicious and deadly; the waters which had risen up about Monks House were at once generative and barren.

Water, in Woolf's personal lexicon, represented a way of slipping the superficial self – the self who played bowls, or minded when a hat was criticised – and ducking down into a deeper, nameless realm. When Virginia writes about writing, which is often, the images she employs are liquid. She is *flooded* or *floated*; she *breaks the current.* When the books are going well she plunges off, happy as a swimmer, into the marine element of private thought. When the work is going poorly, however, when headaches prevail or sleeplessness sets in, her descriptions begin to acquire a nightmarish dryness.

It's hardly surprising, then, that the novels she wrote should be so flush with waterways. *The Voyage Out* begins aboard a liner bound for South America, and *To the Lighthouse* is set so close to the edge of the Atlantic that the sound of the sea is heard on almost every page. The movement of water intersperses the action of *The Waves*, and in *Orlando* two lovers are divided when the frozen Thames melts into teeming life again. As for her last book, *Between the Acts*, written as bombs undid the architecture of London and the Woolfs were once more marooned in Sussex, it revolves around a deep pond filled with lilies, in which the silvery flashes of fish – carp, were they? – are sometimes briefly glimpsed.

What is one to make of this great weight of waters? Though they are beautiful, they carry with them the risk of annihilation too. Take that fishpond with its red and white lilies, the size of dinner plates, that bloom by day and close when it grows dark. The servants won't walk near it at night because a lovesick woman drowned there once, though when men came to dredge it all they managed to salvage was the thighbone of a sheep. Or there's that strange puddle in *The Waves* which Rhoda finds herself unable to cross, a scene repeated in Woolf's own fragmentary memoir, *A Sketch of the Past*: the *grey, cadaverous* puddle that threatens identity itself.

Water is dangerous then, even – that *cadaverous* – deadly. But. I didn't want to be tugged by hindsight, to weight every word with what would take place, years later, in the Ouse. Thanatos, the death impulse, the urge towards non-being, is said to be the opposite of eros, and yet it is shot through with its own sort of sensuality. I thought of a letter Virginia had written to Nelly Cecil while she stayed in a house near Rye, amid the cornfields and sheep-pastures that had once, not so long ago, been sunk beneath the sea. 'I feel like one rolled at the bottom of a green flood,' she wrote, 'smoothed, obliterated, how should my pockets still be full of words?' Does this prefigure what was to come? *Vaticinium ex eventu*. The prophecy comes after the event. And is it not necessary to dissolve the self if one hopes to see the world unguarded?

* * *

The day was growing hotter. Big river-coloured dragonflies were lifting into the warm air and up above the pylons one or two seagulls were drifting south amid an unruly sky, the clouds torn into scraps and orts. They were bringing the hay in on Rise Farm. I could see five tractors by the hedge, though only one was mowing, the cut grass drifting behind it like smoke. The next field had already been baled in blue plastic, the exact colour of surgical scrubs. An oystercatcher cried a warning then, and as I turned a speedboat came bouncing down from Lewes. A topless man was steering and a woman and black dog sat huddled in the prow. They were flying the Jolly Roger and as they passed the wake slung out, thick and creamy, and sloshed itself against the shore.

The path had broadened and now the long grass also came to an end, giving way to pink cranesbill and clover, the little tipped yellow heads of black medick and a few of those giant dog daisies that are also known as marguerites. A wind had got up from somewhere, whipping the river into actual waves. Those clouds – I looked more closely – did not bode well. Oh *hell*. I was caught equidistant between Rodmell and Lewes, right where I'd been in the last downpour. There was nowhere to shelter out here: no trees, no bridges, not even a wall. I shoved my notebook in my pocket and glowered furiously at the sky.

Thunderheads were building above Lewes. I could see them massing behind Mount Harry, banking by the prison and the old racecourse. A haze had fallen ahead of me, dimming the fields and turning the air almost to gauze. The light fell through the altocumulus of a mackerel sky, each scale thickly whorled and pale as spun sugar. *Mackerel skies and mare's tails make tall ships carry low sails*, I muttered to myself. The sun burned through like magnesium, a distant, impeded thing. My right eye had begun to run with tears, though whether from the light or pollen I couldn't tell. White, negating white, the colour of the refiner's fire. Christ is said to have come back from the dead dressed in white, his raiment exceeding fallen snow, white as no fuller on earth could make it with their baths of chalk and urine. This sky might also have been run through a fulling mill, scoured, ground and pinned on tenterhooks to dry. I cupped a hand about my weeping eye and carried on, trying not to look at the veiled sun.

It was a strange landscape at the best of times, the Brooks, the land so flat and intermarried with water. I'd read in a history of Lewes that when the river ran high and threatened to breach the banks farmers would stake nets cattycorners between the hedges to catch the fish as they washed across the grass, and furthermore that it is from this practice that the phrase *a pretty kettle of fish* takes its origins, for the nets were known as kettles. I don't know if this is true, though. Such origin tales always strike me as dubious, like the claim that the Ouse comes as a contraction of the Waters of Lewes, which over time got rubbed down by use to the Wose and thence the Ouse.

Thinking of the marshes and their periodic immersions reminded me that there was another element to Woolf's story of the bombed river. In a letter to her friend, the irrepressible composer Ethel Smyth, she sketched the landscape again, this time inserting herself in the frame.

> Then, to my infinite delight, they bombed our river. Cascades of water roared over the marsh – All the gulls came and rode the waves at the end of the field. It was, and still is, an inland sea, of such indescribable beauty, always changing, day and night, sun and rain, that I cant take my eyes off it. Yesterday, thinking to explore, I fell headlong into a six foot hole, and came home dripping like a spaniel, or water rugg (thats Shakespeare). How odd to be swimming in a field! Mercifully I was wearing Leonard's old brown trousers. Tomorrow I buy a pair of cords for myself. Its raining, raining . . . and I've been walking, walking. The road to the Bridge was 3 foot in water, and this meant a 2 mile round; but oh dear, how I love this savage medieval water moved, all floating tree trunks and flocks of birds and a man in an old punt, and myself so eliminated of human features that you might take me for a stake walking.

Critics have tended to regard this incident in a sinister light, as a portent of what would take place on the same ground a few months on. As Hermione Lee, the most acute of Woolf's biographers, explains, 'it is an alarming conjunction of wanting to be immersed in the savage water, and wanting to become anonymous and featureless'. I'm not sure, though, that I agree. If we have any hopes at all of seeing the world, it is in those moments when the 'I' winks out, when the self empties or eddies away.

On the subject of stalking, the naturalist Annie Dillard wrote: 'For . . . forty minutes last night I was as purely sensitive and mute as a photographic plate; I received impressions but I did not print out captions. My own self-awareness disappeared; it seems now almost as though, had I been wired with electrodes, my EEG would have been flat.' This sort of dislocation with the human, identifying instead with dead or lifeless matter, seems both a natural and a necessary part of becoming absorbed in the wider realm. There's a note of ecstatic surrender in Woolf's description of the *savage medieval water*, of the fluxing world in which she has become so thoroughly dissolved, and though it is close to the desire for self-annihilation, it doesn't seem to belong entirely to someone who has lost faith with life.

But there's a larger problem here. The tendency to wring prophecy from the tide of material that Woolf left behind seems to sit uneasily with what she herself thought of the past. As she experimented with memoir, biography, and novels that contained elements of each, she noticed that the process by which events are converted into history is inevitably distorting, for the past acquires in the telling a shape and coherence that is absent from the present. It's an observation that she expressed sharply when she came to write of her brother's death, describing it, as I have already noted, as 'one of the falsifications – that knell I always find myself hearing and transmitting – that one cannot guard against, save by noting it'.

Some patterns can only be observed at great distance, it's true, but in order to view life in this way something else must be sacrificed, for when we look with hindsight, from the final outcome back, we see events inflected with a meaning that the one who lived them never grasped. I don't believe there is a single person who's not troubled sometimes in the course of their days by a sense of occlusion or tenuousness, a sense that their actions occur within such a great expanse of darkness on either side that they might prove at the last incoherent and devoid of sense. 'Yes, I was thinking,' Woolf wrote in her diary at around the same time that the Ouse was bombed; 'we live without a future. That's what's queer, with our noses pressed to a closed door.' She was speaking of the war, but I think that what she said is true of every day, whether bombs rain down or not, for the future is by its nature contingent and to read every event in terms of what is yet to occur disjoints the moment in which life is lived, divesting it of that uncertain, glancing quality that is the hallmark of the present.

Still, one can't ignore the great weight of stories about immersion and submersion, about going under and being washed away. There were two in particular that had stayed with me, one written when Woolf was very young and one in the final winter of her life. I'd read them both on a snowy day in the archive at the University of Sussex, where an assortment of Leonard and Virginia's papers and letters reside in a series of mushroom-coloured cardboard boxes that smell faintly, as indeed does much of the library, of meat stew.

The first, 'A Terrible Tragedy in a Duck Pond', was written when Woolf was seventeen, in the miserable wake of Stella's death, as a gift for her friend Emma Vaughan. It concerns a real incident in which Emma, Virginia and her younger brother Adrian capsized and sank a punt while playing aboard it late one night and with what was evidently hysterical good cheer. As the title suggests, the account is a self-conscious parody of a newspaper report, the sort of exercise one might be set at school, though Woolf of course never went, learning Greek from Janet Case and delving the rest from her father's shelves.

Woolf's gift as a mimic lends liveliness to her novels – that magpie ear for found dialogue – and her ventriloquism is an essential component of her satire. Here, the narrator employs the portentous, inadvertently bathetic tones of the provincial journalist, sloppy with facts and imaginatively unequal to the tragedy he has himself fabricated: the terrible drowning of three young people.

> The waters rose & rose, irresistible, calm. One moment dry & vigorous, then thrown from the warmth & animation of life to the cold jaws of a sudden & unthought of death – what change could be more absolute or more dreadful? Alone, untended, unwept, with no hand to soothe their last agonies, they were whelmed in the waters of the duck pond, shrouded in the green weed (we believe it to be a species of Anseria Slimatica) which we have mentioned above.

If nothing else, it stands as an effective warning to any future writer who might seek, impertinently, to reimagine Woolf's own death.

This overwrought report is followed by what purports to be 'A Note of Correction and Addition to the above, by one of the Drowned', in which the first story is undercut by the revelation of the survival of the boating party and its gleefully dripping progress back to the house. Though the humour is somewhat dependent on the squawking in-jokes that make Bloomsbury so oxygenless, there was something about the interplay of the two voices that I found intriguing, the first stitching a narrative that the second unpicks and reweaves. Then there were the final lines, which picked up on a problem that would dog Woolf throughout her life: how to capture in language the multiple impressions that the mind in a moment possesses. 'Methinks the human method of expression by sound of tongue is very elementary,' she writes, '& ought to be substituted for some ingenious invention which should be able to give vent to at least six coherent sentences at once . . . St John, happy creature, has a piano to speak for her with its variety of voices; but even that fails completely to carry forth the flood.'

Her tongue is firmly in her cheek and yet the last phrase stands out. I thought of the polyphonic voices of *The Waves*, unspooling their torrents of words that beat again and again at the limits of perception. Carrying forth the flood: it seemed to catch precisely what Woolf set out to do.

As for the other story, it was not so light-hearted. It was written a few weeks before Virginia's death, and was evidently inspired by a visit to Brighton described in the diary, when, hovering at the edge of a complete breakdown, she became disturbed by a grotesquely fat woman eating cakes in Fuller's teashop, and by the smell of fish and the embarrassment of *p-ing* in the little lavatory at the Sussex Grill while two *common little tarts* stood outside rouging and exchanging gossip. The event exercised her and she wrote it out in various incarnations. It was eventually published posthumously as 'A Watering Place', her final story.

The version I'd seen in the archive was a photocopy, full of typing errors and crossings out, tucked within its own manila folder and filed at the bottom of a box of drafts. Because of paper shortages during the war, it had been typed on the back of two corrected pages drawn from the manuscript of *Between the Acts*, though I couldn't remember now which scenes they'd held. It was set, anyway, in a little seaside town also pervaded by the smell of fish. There is a sense of unreality to this liminal, watery place. Its population – the old men that stand on the parade and watch the waves; the women with their tottering shoes and strings of pearls – have the look of shells, 'hard but frivolous . . . as if the real animal had been extracted on a pin'. At one o'clock, the action – but it is not really action – moves to a restaurant where, upstairs in the first floor lavatory, three women stand painting their faces, their talk interrupted by the flushing waters of the cubicle next door.

Much is made of the collusion of artifice and nature within this small partitioned space. Then the women begin to talk, their words borrowed in part from the Brighton tarts. They talk; the flush comes down; it drowns them out; it drains away; they are revealed. There is a horrible rhythm to the scene, which rapidly abandons all pretence at realism and turns the women back into little fish, smelling of 'some queer fishy smell that seems to permeate the whole watering place'. The story ends abruptly with a swerve of tone that seemed to me a last-ditch attempt at prettification, one of those sea changes that converts bones into coral, eyes to pearls, death to a submarine and static mirage: 'But at night the town looks quite ethereal. There is a white glow on the horizon. There are hoops and coronets in the streets. The town has sunk down into the water. And the skeleton only is picked out in fairy lamps.'

Oh, water beautifies all right. You wouldn't know at a glance that it ran quick with nitrogen; you wouldn't see the shopping trolleys or the occasional swollen body of a sheep, leaching out its gases, eyes picked away by the glinting, darting fish. Water conceals rot, smoothes edges, turns shards of glass into smooth green bullets, discards the resurrected on bank and beach, trees tumbled to stars, plastic addled into opacity.

Then there's that awful rhythm: vanquish; retreat. In an earlier version of the story a lavatory attendant is also present in the room, a woman who 'inhabits a fluctuating water world . . . constantly tossed up and down like a piece of sea weed'. I read somewhere that this thrusting up-down motion is supposed to mimic the trauma of the sexual abuse Woolf suffered as a small child at the hands of her half-brother, Gerald Duckworth, but I didn't think it needed to be skewered so neatly to retain its power: that part voluptuous, part nauseating sense of surrender to a greater force.

Let me take you: that is what the water says. Lean back, abide with me. Endow yourself and I will dandle you, though dandle, to be sure, is not so far from mangle.

* * *

The low ground by the river came then to an abrupt end and I struggled up the bank to the path that threaded along the top. But this too was almost overwhelmed by vegetation, so that with every step I had to break bodily through the entangled, chest-high grass. The wind was full in my face and my eye would not stop streaming. I continued doggedly along, head down, listening for the first break of thunder.

I'd come to where the misfit stream Glynde Reach entered the river, its muddied waters sluicing down the Levels into the greener Ouse. The railway, which ran right through to Newhaven on the eastern bank, crosses the Reach at this confluence and as I approached I counted twenty-one swans gathered by the bridge. One had black plastic caught somehow around its wing, though this did not prevent it from dipping beneath the surface in search of food, raising its head in that inelegant waggle-gulp manoeuvre as it swallowed down a root or leaf. Fish were jumping in the shadows and as I passed I could make out a ruffled line where the two rivers met, a serpentining cord of ripples that tightened almost to a crest.

Asham was dead ahead now, the white scar bared to the eye. Before the cement works closed there used to be an aerial ropeway, dismantled now, that ran down the hill to the water's edge, linking the quarry to a concrete wharf where barges delivered coal and collected cement. It was here that Virginia's body was found, on 18 April 1941, three weeks after she'd walked into the river, by two girls and two boys who'd stopped on their way to Seaford to eat their lunch and had as they sat in the field become preoccupied with flinging stones at a floating log to knock it into shore. As it drifted closer they saw that it was not a log. One of the boys waded out and, turning the body, cried out: *It's a woman – a woman in a fur coat!*

She was wearing Wellington boots and her hat remained wedged on by a string of elastic tied beneath her chin. The policeman, Collins, whom she'd recently described as rude and rasping after an altercation about blackout curtains, noted when he came to fetch the body that her watch had stopped at 11.45 a.m., which is to say a good hour and a quarter before Leonard, on 28 March, had found the letters she'd left for him in the upstairs sitting room at Monks House and run pell-mell through the Brooks to find her. Seeing her walking-stick lying upon the bank, he knew at once what had occurred, though Collins, summoned by the housekeeper Louie Mayer, had dived and dived while the blacksmith Frank Dean and his son brought ropes and dragged the river.

The cause of death, wrote the coroner, was 'immersion in the river . . . by her own act so killing herself while the balance of her mind was disturbed'. Louie added in an interview years later: 'There were heavy stones in the pockets of her jacket and she must have put them there and then walked straight down into the river. And that was terrible. It was the most terrible thing that I have ever known.'

Why does someone walk out of the world like that? When the painter Dora Carrington shot herself in 1932, two months after her beloved Lytton Strachey had died of stomach cancer, Woolf was not entirely sympathetic or endowed with fellow feeling. On the contrary, she wrote a week or so later: 'I am glad to be alive & sorry for the dead: cant think why Carrington killed herself & put an end to all this.' As for Leonard: 'it was histrionic: the real thing is that we shall never see Lytton again. This is unreal.' Time hardens such comments, calcifying them into a cruelty that was not perhaps intended, but they also form a counterweight to the sense that the river was the end Woolf plunged inevitably towards. No, even as they draw to a close gladness – *aliveness* – bubbles periodically through the diaries.

In her last winter, Woolf worked on *Between the Acts*; became treasurer of the Rodmell W.I.; played bowls. Her London house, in Mecklenburgh Square, was bombed and in October the Woolfs went down to salvage what they could from amidst the dust and rubble: diaries, Darwin, glasses, her sister's painted china. A melancholy business, but she says she likes the loss of possessions, the liberation. Glee is in ascendance, just. *Never have I been so fertile*, she writes, and binds the mouldy notebooks in coloured paper, that *they may refresh the eye*.

Then it is colder and there is less food, and little fat. The raids continue, out on the marshes. No petrol, no sugar, a slower post. Virginia's hand begins to shake. But England is good, England is firm, the wave of the Downs unbroken, *these deep hollows, where the past stand almost stagnant*. After Christmas there is a comet, snow; the sense of speaking into a void becomes tangible. James Joyce dies in Zurich. There are fires in London. More: there is a rent in the fabric. Nothing to nothing, one might say. Broken fingernails, broken windowpanes, streets lost, bricks turned to powder, so yes, dirty hands. Small beer, small beer. Then there is the day in Brighton with the tarts, the decision to cook haddock, a will towards cheerfulness. The diary ends with Leonard doing the rhododendrons, ends as any life might, which is to say on an in-breath, albeit an illusory one.

At some point the tide had begun to turn, the chalk banks revealed as the water drained away. Chalky waters are the best to swim in, almost powdery against the skin, the suspended particles delaying the light so that it seems perpetually imprisoned, dropping with infinite slowness towards the riverbed.

I was trying as I walked to recall Gertrude's speech on the death of Ophelia, in which another hellish sight is tricked out into prettiness. *Like a creature native and indued unto that element.* Was that it? I suppose we are all water's natives, swimmers first, and *indued* proclaims this while catching also, with that near-echo *endowed*, at the sense of a bride, crowned with weeds, giving herself up to the envious river. And then there was the line I thought of more than any other: *as one incapable of her own distress.*

My old Swan *Hamlet* translated the word *incapable* as *unaware*, but I suspected it was not that, or not that alone. To be incapable of one's own distress is the opposite of suffering, for the root of the word suffer, *ferre*, is to carry. In the first state, one hurtles from pain; in the second one experiences it; one bears it up. Is this when suicide occurs, when one has been so whittled by what must be borne that the undercarriage collapses and oblivion is the only solution?

A local woman drowned in the Ouse not long before Woolf.

When was it, the late 1930s? She lived up on Mount Misery, a hill between Southease and Piddinghoe that is named not by virtue of its depressing aspect but because a wayfarer is said to have prayed a Miserere there that later brought him luck. She had been a midwife, this woman, and had a son who died; her house had broken windows and one day when the tide was high she killed her dog and dropped herself into the water. Like Carrington's death this bleak little incident is not mooned over in the diary, but it is recorded, the choice not to be; it remains.

At even the most cursory glance Woolf's novels are riddled with absences like these, with what takes place when someone is lost or loses themselves. It is not perhaps surprising: if one were to take a biographical approach to criticism, one would certainly note that her mother, half-sister, father and brother were all dead by the time she was twenty-five, and that their presence echoes, say, through Mrs Ramsay in *To the Lighthouse*, or the vanquished Percival in *The Waves*. This is not to class her as a victim, for there's not a man jack among us who won't misplace someone, should we live so long.

Nonetheless, this acute sense of peril is, I wager, what drove Woolf to write throughout her life. Her take is not consoling exactly, but nor is it depressing: simply alert. I thought then, standing on the remade bank, of that chapter at the centre of *To the Lighthouse*, where over the course of years time breaks apart a house. War comes, the war that knocked down like skittles the men who walked and waltzed and talked through *Jacob's Room*; here too it brings death. The books in the house grow mouldy, the plaster falls in shovelfuls and swallows fresh from

Africa build nests in the drawing room. And then, as a pendulum slides into its opposite arc, the decay is arrested. Builders come, and housekeepers, the servants whose function it still just about is to mop and scrub and polish other people's dirt.

One senses in this chapter, which is perhaps nineteen pages long and called, appropriately enough, 'Time Passes', a great battle carried out between the forces of thanatos and eros, between the desire to destroy and the contrary impulse to order, clean and build. It is a battle, I think one can fairly say, that was carried out likewise in Woolf's own life; it is, I think one could equally add, a battle fought by everything that lives. Right at the pivot of this long scene, as the house teeters on the precipice of pitching *downwards to the depths of darkness*, Woolf begins to list the wild things that have taken refuge there. I find this passage more consoling than the mending that follows, for it seems to imply that even here, on the outer threshold of chaos, something abides; that in the untended beds that accompany human dereliction the cabbage mates with the carnation and the lavish poppy seeds itself. An unweeded garden, one might say, that grows to seed; things rank and gross in nature possess it merely. On the other hand, one might watch those windblown sports and think, as Woolf did elsewhere, *this has a holiness. This will go on after I'm dead*, and take comfort in the thought.

There is an echo of this peculiar mix of acquiescence and defiance in the matter of Virginia's memorial. Her body was cremated at Downs Crematorium, up on the Woodingdean Road in Brighton, overlooking the hated housing estates that sprang up in the wake of the First World War. Leonard attended the ceremony alone, and it was conducted, to his horror, to the accompaniment of the movement from Gluck's *Orpheus* in which the suffering Orpheus finds himself in Elysium, though not yet reunited with Eurydice's shade. Virginia had once described it as *the loveliest opera ever written*, but its hopes for the afterlife filled Leonard with rage.

He took the ashes home in a casket and buried them beneath an elm tree in the garden at Monks House, that building which seems almost to exhale damp from its greenish distempered walls. He ordered a headstone from a Lewes stonemason, and the words engraved on it were those with which *The Waves* ends: 'Against you I will fling myself, unvanquished and unyielding, O Death!' Are these the words of a lover or a soldier? They flirt; they taunt: they are steel; they dissolve with lust. Either way, they endure, as those thousands of mildewed pages have also endured, though the house that contained them was bombed; though the woman who wrote them has vanished clean away.

VII

BEDE'S SPARROW

THE THUNDER NEVER CAME. The clouds were lifting now and drifting south and as they rose the heaviness seemed to drain from the day. The scales that had covered the sun slipped or broke apart, unmaking themselves as they floated high above the valley, following the same invisible path that the birds took to the sea.

It was half past five when I reached the track that forked up to Rodmell. I'd been out on the Brooks two hours, tacking the banks in the teeth of the wind. To celebrate I sat down by the stile and ate an oatcake. My toenails were bothering me, and I carried out some rudimentary surgery with the Opinel, though it wasn't pleasant work. I thought regretfully of the small nail clippers I'd left on my desk. If only they were in my pack I could, I felt, walk on into the hills quite happily for years, though no doubt the absence of mascara would also come to bother me in time.

The Downs seemed piece by piece to have acquired dominion over the landscape. Rodmell was tucked beneath them, the poorest and richest of the houses straggling up the sides. What day was it now? I counted back on my fingers: Friday. And how near was the sea? A cormorant's flight, a crow's; twenty minutes by car, an hour by bike, a morning's walk tomorrow. As for tonight, I was staying at Navigation Cottage, the house of a friend of mine, which had been knocked up at the end of the eighteenth century to house the navvies employed to restructure the river. A father and son called Tompsett lived there once, and in addition to digging the banks their duties included opening the swing bridge to let boats pass to and fro.

I lay back in the long grass and gazed out across the Brooks. There was something subtly oppressive about these flat, dredged fields and swift, featureless river. The land should have been a model of man's ingenuity and instead the banks and ditches left me uneasy, for it seemed that the river was held back by the application of enormous force, against which it threatened momently to break through and take the valley. It was this sense of strain that bothered me, and in a way I wished it would, for I find it uncomfortable when the inevitable is postponed. I imagined it flooding every trace of fences away, imagined it flushing implacably across the fields, filling barns and houses with knots of eels. Mind you, I probably didn't have long to wait. What will it be: a hundred years before the rising sea slips in and England's edged with marsh again? Fifty? What a future we have stored up for us, when an ooze of mud replaces these false pastures, sheep-cropped and sewer-seamed, on which the wind rolls unimpeded.

I wasn't being fair. The fields yielded food, and while the sewers might not be pretty, they provided essential habitats and furthermore acted as sightlines, drawing the eye backwards through time. The one opposite, Celery Sewer, ran in a series of kinks from the Cockshut to the Ouse, providing the main drainage for the Brooks. Its outfall was barred by a sluice gate that closed with flap valves first installed in 1949 by Frank Dean, the old Rodmell blacksmith, with such skill that it was reported *you could open it with your little finger.* This was the same Frank Dean who dragged the river for Virginia's body, the same Frank Dean who waited on the bank alongside the white-faced Leonard, writing in his own memoir years later: *He was a brave man*. It was Frank who organised Virginia's cremation, and who was inadvertently implicated in the choice of music, for Leonard wanted the Cavatina from Beethoven's string quartet no. 13 in B flat major, but felt too shy to ask. No matter now. Both men are long gone, though Dean's forge in Rodmell still stands, as does the tiny garage beside it, its windows crammed with shelves of dead and dying geraniums.

Caroline texted me then. It was about the cheese, which was required for dinner and which I'd successfully procured in Lewes. God, I was starving. It felt like years had passed since the pizza on the railway lands, and centuries since I last sat down and talked with a friend. I galumphed up the path, slowing only to see if there were any dead magpies in the fields. It wasn't something I'd ever witnessed, but Caroline swore she'd seen the pied bodies stuck on sticks like scarecrows here. Grisly as this sounded, it's nothing on a story my mother recently told. She'd been walking in the fields near her house in Suffolk and had come across a tiny cage in which was crammed a dead chicken and a live and frantic magpie. Thinking the bird had made its way in by accident she opened the latch and prodded it out, only to discover later that she'd interfered unforgivably with the local method of trapping. The birds would later be killed by means of an exhaust pipe run into their chamber, and I'd read on a shooting forum that a farmer had reputedly dispatched fifty-two magpies in this manner; one, I thought grimly, for every week of the year.

Poor magpies. Hunters also use the dead as lures, propping the corpses in a field or dangling them from a fence to reel in the flock, though it's important that their wings are broken and flapping freely for this trick to work. Other techniques include placing a full size owl decoy on a post for the birds to attack, or half-filling a film canister with pellets, which if shaken in the characteristic six short, one long trill pattern can produce a rough simulacrum of the magpie's call. It is said that a human should be veiled when hunting magpies, for they are acutely sensitive to the shape of the head, and gun shops sell for this purpose a piece of cloth known as scrim.

I couldn't see any birds, either dead or alive, but there were animals grazing on either side of me: sheep to the right and cattle to the left. After a while the sheep gave way to a herd of scruffy horses and then to a smallholding filled with rubbish. There were chickens scratching about between rows of vans and horseboxes, and in one of the dank little sheds a tethered dog barked and barked in a weary, unstoppable way that suggested it had been there for a very long time and didn't hold much hope of leaving soon.

Navigation Cottage was on the corner of the village, a few doors down from Monks House. Fly saw me from her sentry post on the garden wall and raced to the gate, carolling her delight with that piercing, unlovable song with which the Jack Russell has been blessed. I delivered the cheese and then went to put my bag in the garden room. It was cool and silent in there, the half-pulled blinds filtering the light to a steady grey. I dropped down on the bed and drew the sheet over my legs. Two minutes, I thought, closing my eyes, and it was 7.30 before I woke again.

We drank beer in bottles with our dinner, sitting in the kitchen on opposite sides of the long table. There were Puy lentils to go with the cheese, those smoky earth-coloured lentils that taste sweetly of the soil. The house at its end gave into a room made of glass, which at that time had no curtains or blinds and was filled with the last of the sun. The dog bounced between our feet and then, sulking, sidled to the sofa and coiled there, a small, speckled comma turned emphatically from us. The beer had knocked me for six. I was so tired I could barely speak, despite my stolen nap. It may not even have been dark when I went back through the garden to bed, walking barefoot across the dry grass, the smell of lavender and stocks lifting in waves through the cooling air.

There was a shelf full of battered Penguins by the bed and I hesitated for a while, half-dressed, over *Childe Harold's Pilgrimage* and *Music for Chameleons*, but the need to sleep had become overwhelming. I left the window wide and as I dropped away the little room swelled with the scents of summer. The temperature plummeted in the night and at dawn I woke briefly and fumbled a second eiderdown from the cupboard. At nine o'clock I came to again, and lay for a while swaddled in my nest, listening to a blackbird calling out its trilling song in stops and starts. After a little while I drew the last of the OS maps from my pack and unfolded it across my knees.

The official path – the Ouse Way that I'd been following more or less loyally since I left Slaugham a week before – seemed to ditch the river to swoop briefly up into the Downs between Southease and Piddinghoe, passing Deans Farm at the foot of Money Burgh. I didn't mind that, but the stretch by the coast was bothering me. The Ouse gives out at Newhaven, where the ferries cross over to France, but the path sheered off just shy of the terminal, abandoning the water to follow the old medieval riverbed east as it snaked parallel to the beach along Seaford Bay to where the houses of Seaford began. There was a nature reserve down there, caught between an industrial estate and the A259, and the abandoned village of Tide Mills, which had over the years been a working mill, a sanatorium and a racing stables before crumbling into ruins on the edge of the beach.

I couldn't decide which way to go: whether to follow the river to its industrial end or to take the path's guide and veer east by the ghost bed through which it once ran. I drew a finger lightly down the page. Either way I'd be home tonight, and in a rush the feeling that had come over me in Lewes returned, the wish to slip backwards, counter to the current, as the Ouse grew by progressions narrower and more flashy, until I was at last swallowed up in the steep ghylls and woods of the Weald, the hidden land. Instead, I would be flushed out on a Saturday into the streets of Newhaven, *City of the Dead* as Woolf once called it. There were two lighthouses marked at the river's mouth, one at the tip of the long curving breakwater and the other dotted like an exclamation mark at the end of the shorter East Pier. I'll wing it, I decided: I'll leave it to my feet to choose their path, but the decision was unsatisfactory and niggled me at intervals throughout the day.

We ate eggs and toast in the kitchen and I drank down two cups of coffee before I could summon the energy to leave. The little dog followed me to the gate and howled as I walked away, a noise entirely disproportionate to her size. The air smelt of roses and the sky was very blue above Rodmell, though the valley below was once again brimful with mist. Firle Beacon was blotted out entirely, and the other hills were reduced to faint looming shadows until the sun grew hot enough to burn them free. I strolled through the churchyard, stopping beneath the rookery ash to peer over the wall at the lawn behind Monks House where Virginia and Leonard had once played their intensely competitive games of bowls. The path to the road cut up between allotments and gardens and as I passed a run of houses I could hear a woman shouting *Ella! Ella! Get back here!*, though whether to a child or a dog I couldn't tell.

The verge was bursting with poppies: red field poppies, mauve opium poppies and frilly-headed pink poppies, escapees from a garden, their elegantly crumpled petals absurdly frivolous amongst the mallow and the yarrow. The smell of roses had given way to that of warm earth, as edible as cake, and I could hear lifting over the hill the sound of bicycles and wood pigeons, a lawn-mower in the distance: that lulling summer music that makes the countryside seem sometimes as if it has been islanded in time a century back.

It was Leonard who was on my mind that morning. After Virginia died he returned to London and stayed for a time in a block of flats in Clifford's Inn. It was full of people, as a hive is full of bees, and he found the compression of lives unbearable and so returned to the bombed house in Mecklenburgh Square, and lived there like a squatter, though there were no ceilings or windows, the roof was unsound and the rooms were contaminated with a litter of soot and rubble. 'I got my loneliness and my silence all right,' he wrote years later: 'But I have experienced few things more depressing in my life than to live in a badly bombed flat, with the windows boarded up, during the great war.'

It was around this time that the bombsites of the city began to fill with flowering weeds that grew in great profusion among the mangled churches and destroyed streets: the pyrophile rosebay willowherb, which is known also as fireweed for its ability to colonise cleared ground, each single plant dispensing somewhere in the region of 80,000 almost weightless seeds; buddleia, beloved by butterflies for its honeyed scent and suffused purple; Atlas poppy; gallant soldiers; dandelion; Canadian fleabane; Oxford ragwort, which grew first on the ash-strewn slopes of Mount Etna and was introduced in the sixteenth century to Oxford Botanic Garden, from where it escaped and headed south by way of the railways. 'London is gayest where she has been the most blitzed,' a New York newspaper reported in 1944, adding that the willowherb 'sweeps across this pockmarked city and turns what might have been scars into flaming beauty'.

It wasn't the first time the city had flowered from its own ruin. London rocket, *Sisymbrium irio*, which the Bedouin smoke to cure chest infections, is said to have begun to grow in abundance in the wake of the Great Fire of 1666, when the city's core was gutted by flames, though it later became very rare, returning centuries later when the Blitz opened up the pastures of wasteground again, the weed rising up in wales of colour between the ribands of shattered walls. 'Walls, roadsides and waste places,' writes Stace, 'naturalised in a few places in Br and Ir, a more frequent casual, especially wool-alien.'

These chance recurrences: mark them. All times are not the same time, but they are all going towards the same end. The London rocket returns in our cities as a clock returns to midnight. The rosebay willowherb swells up through the ruins of law courts and cathedrals, the dandelion marches across battlefields and infiltrates the gardens of mansions. Gallant soldiers, Oxford ragwort, Atlas poppy: these weeds have come and will come again, time immemorial, time without end. It is as well to remember this, for humans believe against all evidence in stasis, though the history of the world does clearly testify that it is rot and regeneration that will be our lot.

None of this would have been news to Leonard, who had watched men hanged in Ceylon and whose motto was *Nothing matters*, later amended to *Nothing matters, and everything matters*.

He spent his life struggling against the various forms of desolation and disorder at work in this world: a humane, fiercely moral man who believed in civilisation without ever forgetting that human greed and stupidity made its existence precarious if not actively doomed.

After the grim, gruelling year that followed Virginia's death, regeneration of a sort did come for Leonard. He fell in love with a married artist, Trekkie Parsons, and she, luckily, loved him wholeheartedly back, though she never left her husband and parcelled her energy and affection between the two men until Leonard's death in 1969. *Dearest Tiger*, he called her, and bought her extravagant, coddling gifts: figs and strawberries, a Rembrandt etching, armfuls of hyacinths and lilacs from the garden at Monks House, a pretty emerald ring. It's a blessing that he found this late flowering love, for the period before she arrived was purgatorial. Hunting through the Monks House archive for something else I once came across a photocopy of a piece of paper on which he'd scrawled:

> They said: 'Come to tea and let us comfort you.' But it's no good. One must be crucified on one's own private cross. It is a strange fact that a terrible pain in the heart can be interrupted by a little pain in the fourth toe of the right foot. I know that V. will not come across the garden from the lodge, & yet I look in that direction for her. I know that she is drowned & yet I listen for her to come in at the door. I know that it is the last page & and yet I turn it over. There is no limit to one's stupidity and selfishness.

The thought of this good man left so alone is heartbreaking, though it cannot be said that Leonard was a saint. Despite his native sympathy with the underdog, he had an odd and vehement dislike of mental disability, once commenting of Virginia's half-sister Laura, who was described by the family as *mentally defective* and who had been shut away in a succession of nursing homes at the age of twenty-two or three for more than fifty years, that her death would have been preferable to that of George Duckworth, the half-brother who abused Virginia.

This harshness resurfaces in a distressing story relayed in *The Journey Not the Arrival Matters*, concerning the family of his housekeeper, Louie Mayer. Louie's mother had a severely handicapped son, Tony, whom she adored and who – or so her older son Harry told Leonard – 'was really destroying her health and all happiness by her devotion'. Harry asked Leonard to intervene and eventually, just before the war broke out, he managed to convince her to have the boy admitted to a home. Later the family became alarmed that he was losing weight and insisted he was removed amid allegations of mistreatment. Leonard helped again, but he wrote disparagingly of their *wild accusations*, before adding tersely that the child died a week or ten days later.

'There is something horrible and repulsive in the slobbering imbecility of a human being,' he observed, as he attempted to unpick why the incident had proved so disturbing. But despite these views, which no doubt seem more shocking to our age than to his own, Leonard laboured throughout his life in the service of those less privileged than himself. Nor did Louie bear any sort of a grudge. She worked for Leonard for thirty-six years, and when he became ill in his eighties fought off the ambulance men who came to take him to hospital, instead nursing him herself with the help of Trekkie so that he could stay in his own beloved house. 'Eventually we had to have the help of two nurses and then the time came when no drugs or special treatment would do anything for him,' she wrote. 'But I stayed with him every day until the end.'

I had reached by this time the steep dark lane that led to Southease. The little round-towered church was at the top of the village, sheltered by a horseshoe of magnificently shaggy elms. As I crossed to it through the graveyard I saw a couple weeding together amid a foaming sea of cow parsley. There was no one inside, and the nave had about it that particular stillness that is found only rarely, in small and rural churches, which seem by some knack of architecture or composition to have caught and held within their stones year upon year of plainsong and prayer. The building was very simple. The walls were white, the floor corroded tiles and the roof a series of vaulting beams that looked not dissimilar to the upturned keel of a boat. The traces of paintings were just visible on the plaster of the north wall: a few parallel lines in dusty ochre; the smurred outlines of human figures. The ones on the chancel arch were in better nick: a puffy cherub that looked in the late stages of jaundice and beneath it a quote from Psalm 75, the first line eroded down to *God is the judge he*, the second to *down one*, and the last to the single word *another*.

A friend of mine once sang an Ave Maria in here and it was as if the notes still held, the choirboy Latin of that old prayer lifting and shimmering amid the motes of dust. *Sancta Maria, Mater Dei, ora pro nobis peccatoribus, nunc et in hora mortis nostrae. Holy Mary, Mother of God, pray for us sinners now and at the hour of our death.* I hadn't said those words for a long time, funerals aside, and I wasn't about to start thumbing a rosary through the decades of Joyful Mysteries and Sorrowful Mysteries. But I genuflected clumsily as I slipped into a pew, for though my belief is not intact I think there's much to respect in the habits of praise. I didn't kneel, but I prayed, head bowed, the simple prayer of *thank you*, the first that I was taught.

The Lord was depicted on the stained-glass window behind the altar in his guise as a shepherd, a lamb clutched in his arms, and I remembered as I sat there a sermon I'd read by another shepherd, a Wesleyan, on the subject of grass. His name was Job, and he was quoted in M.K. Ashby's biography of her father, *Joseph Ashby of Tysoe*. 'I'm talking o' the grass,' it began:

> Of all the natural gifts of God I thought of grass to talk about. Grass is always with us. It never fails, even in the farming sense. It clothes the whole world as with a cloak. It feeds the beasts and they feed us. Permanent grass is a rest for the thoughts. 'I lay me down in green pastures.' The green colour o' grass rests the eye, the neverfailingness of it rests the anxious mind; and the feel of it is rest for the body in summer season . . . Ay, but that reminds me, grass robs death of its terrors, for who but feels soothed at the thought of the green grass waving over a body that is weary and hurt, and laden with hard and

> painful memories? When I was young my thoughts would be too much for me and I'd long to be beneath the daisies; not up in heaven. For that you want newness of spirit. But God in his mercy lets us throw off our weariness and leave it kindly buried beneath the grinsw'd.

That's faith enough, is it not? That this little life will be rounded with a sleep beneath the waving grasses, though for myself I might choose a bloom of cow parsley, the flowers arranged in white umbels tinged with green or pink, or a stand of the great masterwort, also known as melancholy gentleman, though it prefers shady places further north than this. I wondered if Leonard would have liked the sermon, for he loved the continuity of nature as deeply as he was immune to the solace of religion. He had no patience with any humbug about an afterlife, and returned from his wife's funeral in a state as much of rage as grief. 'He spoke with terrible bitterness,' wrote his friend Willie Robson, who was staying at Monks House at the time, 'of the fools who played music by Gluck . . . which promised happy reunion or survival in a future life. "She is dead and utterly destroyed" he said, and all his profound disbelief in religion and its consolations were present in those words. It was impossible to comfort him in his loneliness and sense of loss.'

The continuity he did believe in was of an earth-bound kind. In 1939, as the war approached, Virginia once called him in from the garden to listen to Hitler on the radio. He refused, shouting back: 'I shan't come. I am planting iris and they will be flowering long after he is dead.' He was right. A few of the irises were still blooming in the apple orchard in the spring of 1966, and he mentions them in the final line of *Downhill All the Way*. They smelled exquisite, Trekkie observed elsewhere: 'a very violet coloured smell' that seemed stronger than those grown by other people.

I took his point. 'Naturally,' says the Catholic Encyclopaedia on the subject of heaven, 'this place is held to exist, not within the earth, but, in accordance with the expressions of Scriptures, without and beyond its limits. All further details regarding its locality are quite uncertain. The Church has decided nothing on this subject.' Not within the earth: no, of course not. Not within this singular globe, whose evening skies are lit sometimes Mars violet or pink or mauve and filled often with flocks of birds that can in their passing bring down a plane. A plague upon your paradise, to place it *without and beyond*. I'll stick here, for my money, and when I'm dead I shall be done, meat for worms, and the tangled grasses can make free upon me, green and greenish-blue and sometimes gold.

The light, I saw then, was striking Christ's raiment, which had been coloured in shades of red: garnet red, vermilion, cherry red and cinnabar. His staff was brown and behind him the sky was pieced together from petals of Prussian blue. This window had been made in the 1850s, during the great boom in British stained glass, but something had gone wrong during the process. When the panes came to be fired the colours didn't quite fuse, perhaps because the furnaces weren't hot enough or else because there was an error in the mixing of the paint. Over the years the pigments were being shed almost imperceptibly, the glass returning stage by stage to its native translucence. Already the stylised yellow flowers had begun to erode, and a portion of Christ's beard seemed to have been shaved clean away.

The light dropped white from heaven and as it passed through the window it became instead a flood of transmitted colour intermixed with dust, so that it seemed for a moment that Newton was right: that multitudes of unimaginable small and swift corpuscles of various sizes were springing from shining bodies at great distances one after another; but yet without any sensible interval of time; and continually urged forward by a principle of motion; now indigo, now yellow, now the saturated red of wine or blood.

On the way down to the water I stopped for a minute on the green to read the notice board: the adverts for open gardens and church concerts; a request for a *mellow room-cum-studio* from a *Mature Pro Man, writer and herbalist, non-smoker, loves dogs.* The sky had cast again and the air was tipsy with the scent of roses. There was only a handful of houses in the village but each, I knew from previous open gardens, had wonders concealed behind its walls: a swimming pool reached via a tunnel of pink climbing roses; a maze of box hedges packed with delphiniums, larkspur and a riot of sweet peas. The manor house at the top of the hill sometimes sold tree peonies and just along from the church there was a nursery run by a retired notary who specialised in the breeding of hellebores, those poisonous Lenten roses that produce drooping flowers of green or pinkish-white, and sometimes plum-red and pale grey. It was too late for hellebores now. This was the month of the true rose, and the swags and stands let fall their scent as voluptuously as incense swung from a censer.

As I passed through the fields to the river the cows were lying down in the sun and the marsh frogs in the ditches called out their mocking cry, though I could not make out if what they said was *brook brook brook* or *crook crook crook*. I hunkered down to see if I could spy any little green-gold heads peeping from the slime and caught one in the act of croaking, its vocal sacs swelling massively from its cheeks like greyish bubble gum. The mist had isolated the valley, sealing Lewes and Newhaven behind walls of dense white air. The tide was running very low under Southease Bridge, and two kayakers had got caught there, poleaxed on the current. *No good mate, can't do it*, one shouted, and as I passed above them the other called back *I was absolutely flying along!* No wonder. The river was a good thirty feet wide here and the water sped beneath the bridge brown and glossy, riffled down the centre in a long swirling line of foam. Every now and then a pat broke off and drifted back along the bank on a sleepy counterflow. The high-water mark was lathered with seaweed and the wind – I sniffed hard – carried with it a juicy whiff of brine.

The sea was changing everything. The low tide had exposed ledges of silky mud, pitted here and there with puddles, that a gang of herring gulls worked over for worms. A little further on I came across a motionless flock of black-headed gulls, set down like toys on the bank, their heads all pointing north. The plants were shifting too: the mugwort and grasses replaced by lesser sea spurrey and marsh wormwood, their foliage a pale glaucous green that withstood the constant salt.

In a field beside the river a single lapwing was patrolling and I paused to watch it work. It was a very regular bird. It tottered forward six paces and then stopped dead. After a moment's contemplation it turned sharply through ninety degrees, and took another six-step run. Then it jerked to a halt and pecked briskly at the ground. Oop, it was off again: a rush of four steps, a pause, another five, like a clockwork bird that seemed always on the verge of running down. Flapwings, I call them to myself, for when they fly their chunky wings fall open like the pages of a book. Just then a heron lifted out of the reeds and turned a ponderous half-circle across the field, voided its bowels in a shower of white and glided across the river, its massive wings teetering minutely on the breeze.

The tide was still flowing out. Now there was a little egret on the bank, as skinny and delicate as a Japanese drawing, picking its way along the very rim of the water. It used its wings for balance, and its sharp head jutted forward with every muddy step. I spotted another in the air ahead, yellow feet pointed out behind it like a dancer's, so white it made the sky seem grey. It's a Johnny-come-lately, the little egret. Its traditional habitat encompasses southern Europe, Africa and Asia, but in the second half of the twentieth century it shifted its range north through France and the Netherlands, reaching the south coast of England about twenty years ago, much to the delight of ornithologists.

Not all aliens receive so warm a welcome. As the language suggests, there's a touch of xenophobia about plant and animal immigration, particularly when the species in question arrives not of its own accord but because it's been introduced by man. The fiercest opprobrium is reserved for those invasive types – grey squirrels; Japanese knotweed; American mink; Himalayan balsam with its scent of cheap perfume – that are charged with threatening the balance of indigenous flora and fauna, though I've also heard environmentalists rail against the pretty sycamore, which was introduced in the sixteenth century and has thus resided in these islands longer than many Britons. It's a controversial subject, and the rhetoric can reach pitches of outrage more commonly associated with the *Daily Mail* on the subject of asylum seekers caught renting Surrey mansions on housing benefit.

I once saw a mink in the Ouse. I was rowing down from Isfield Bridge one August with my friend Tony in a small inflatable boat the colour of custard. We were making a great deal of noise, since rubber boats that lack rowlocks are not the most efficient way to travel, when he noticed a dark head watching us from the bank. The creature was the size of a cat, with sleek, glossy fur. After a moment or two it slipped unfussily beneath the surface and reappeared on the other side, gazing up at the boat. Then it dived abruptly and crossed again, rising shallowly this time so that we could see right down its body to the tip of its broad tail. It seemed an alert and playful creature, confident without having the unnerving cockiness of a rat. But these American mink, escaped or released by activists from fur farms, have decimated populations of water voles, which are critically low in Sussex and indeed across the country.

As for Himalayan balsam, it grows abundantly all along the upper river, bringing forth in summer those pouting flowers that give it the nickname Policeman's Helmet. The nectar is intensely sweet, luring bees away from other bankside plants, while the pods disperse their cargo so aggressively that they can be flung some twenty feet. If you want to give a friend a shock, persuade them to hold one of the ripe green capsules, for the heat makes it burst in the hand with a horribly pleasurable recoil. The dense groves shade out other competitors, and hacking it back in summer is lethal as the seeds are shaken into the water to migrate downstream and start their colonies anew.

After the incident with the mink, I went to see the Otter Officer at Sussex Wildlife Trust, who in the course of our conversation described the Ouse valley as a desert. I understood what she was saying. I understood that the landscape had previously been richer and more intricate, that the roads and towns and farms with their polluting outfalls of chemicals had decimated the indigenous wildlife. I admired the work they were doing: the restoration of habitats, the tireless efforts to protect the water vole and black poplar, to encourage back the otter. Still, I was wary of her language, for there is a tendency among conservationists to devalue what is common or thriving against what is rare or on the verge of being wholly lost. I hadn't walked this week through a desert, not by any means, and I didn't see how it helped to denigrate the ten-a-penny creatures that clung on like grim death in the despoiled valley.

I wonder if this pervasive human dislike of virulent species, the pests and opportunists, is a kind of projection, if the Himalayan balsam and mink act as a dark mirror in which we catch ourselves: man the destroyer, man the weed. After all, who else is to blame for the great spate of late extinctions? It is man who grubs up habitats; man who trapped, shot or otherwise annihilated in this country the grey whale, the grey wolf, the Great Bustard, the horned dung beetle, the apple bumblebee, the Conformist, the Essex Emerald, the Flame Brocade, the Frosted Yellow, the Gypsy Moth, the Map, the Mazarine Blue, the Reed Tussock, the Swallowtail. If you destroy the habitat of a species, if you kill off the food it depends on – milk parsley, in the case of the Swallowtail – then it is done for. William Burroughs had a nice phrase for it. It no longer has *the ghost of a chance*.

Mind you, man will also go to great lengths to lure lost species back. I'd come across a story recently about efforts to reintroduce Great Bustards to Salisbury Plain. These birds were wiped out by hunting in Britain in the nineteenth century and a reintroduction attempt in the 1970s failed because the hand-reared chicks became too tame to survive in the wild, while six vagrants that appeared in Suffolk in the 1980s were shot – accidentally or otherwise – by men out hunting ducks. This time, chicks brought from Russia were being reared using a puppet shaped like the mother bird's head, while the researchers interacted with the birds clothed in shapeless reflective suits that obscured their human frame. That, right there, seems to me the outer threshold of evolution. When God commanded man to *replenish the world*, was this really what he had in mind?

Two redshanks tripped me out of this melancholy line of thought. They stood twenty feet apart and screamed at one another, beaks snapping as they shrieked their piercing *pew-pew*. I must have frightened them, for they burst simultaneously into the air, revealing a flash of white beneath each dun-coloured wing. The cranes of Newhaven had appeared in the distance behind them, silhouetted against an almighty mackerel sky, the fish's rib bones clearly delineated, the sun caught within its gut, its tail above Tarring Neville and its head at Telescombe Tye.

It was just after noon and the tide was on the turn. The surface of the river glittered slightly and on the far bank a train rushed up the valley. Stock Cottages were opposite and I figured I was pretty much exactly in line with where the old Stock Ferry used to run. According to the map a dead channel still passed by the ferryman's cottage, a vestigial blue line as functionless as an appendix. The ferry itself had apparently run twice daily, taking the farm workers to harvest and back. It was thought to have been drawn by ropes and had once sprung a leak and drowned one Oliver Symons, shepherd, and his flock of fifty-eight sheep.

The path that runs from here into the Downs is said to be prodigiously old. It felt that way today, in the silent, unpeopled landscape. An occasional fish surfaced and the sun dropped like a blow, the ground beneath it beaten very gold, the dust rising in sheaves from where it had been struck. I felt like I was saying goodbye. I wouldn't be this alone again, for once I came back from the hill I'd be rushed through Piddinghoe and into the sprawl of Newhaven. I plumped down on a bed of ground ivy and uncapped the water bottle. The river was like glass beneath me, a hawthorn wavering within it. Up above the martins were turning their cat's cradles through the sky. I could hear the road, but it was an undercurrent to the larger silence of the place. Maybe, I thought philosophically, it was something to do with the turning tide, which opened a natural pause in the day. I drew a deep breath and as I did a grasshopper leapt down my top, bounced out and whacked me smartly on the forehead.

The track to Piddinghoe led past Deans Farm before breaking uphill across the dry chalk bed of a winterbourne. I climbed past tussocky banks of wild thyme stitched with yellow crosswort and the pale flowers of heath bedstraw. Selfheal and birdsfoot trefoil, which as children we called bacon and eggs, were also growing in profusion, and between them the bees moved in their drunken drifts. The cropped turf was scattered with lumps of chalk and great knotty flints in the shape of roots or teeth. I kicked one to watch it tumble and dislodged by accident a rabbit's foot on a shard of bone like a lolly on a stick. The abundance of herbs was making me delirious. I counted as I climbed: plantain, agrimony, silverweed, cinquefoil, the evil-looking bittersweet, which is also known as woody nightshade and bears inverted heads of mauvish petals with thrusting yellow stamens. The sky above the slope was colonised by larks, rising in all directions, their voices as unbroken as the perpetual choirs of monks that are said to have worked in shifts of one hundred an hour to ensure God's glories never for a moment went unpraised.

What I couldn't see were wheatears, those plump little white-bottomed birds once so plentiful in these parts that their trapping became a kind of micro-industry. In 1743, Jeremiah Milles, a young antiquarian who would later become dean of Exeter Cathedral, went on a walking tour through Sussex and, as was then fashionable, produced an account of his journey. He was largely interested in castles and churches, but the hunting of wheatears had evidently intrigued him greatly, for he left for posterity an exceptionally detailed record of their capture.

> I ascended the downs on which I saw cast numbers of traps for wheatears. These birds are about the size of a lark with brown feathers, which have a streak of white in their wings and tails. They are a bird of passage, for they come in the month of June, and go away in September, during which time they are most prodigiously fat and are a most delicious morsel; they are supposed to be the same with the Becaficcos of Italy and Turkey. Their name of wheatears I take to be a corruption from white arse, the rumps of the birds being remarkably white and fat. There are but few parts of England where these birds come, for they frequent only the downs, and are supposed to live upon flies, because they never find anything in their stomachs, though I imagine they eat rapeseed, because I saw many of them flying about it. They are a solitary bird, appearing always single, and are foolish enough to be easily ensnared. The manner of taking them is thus. They cut up two oblong turfs out of the ground in the following shape [and here Milles drew an upturned L]; across one part of this cavity they fasten a

> small stick with two horse hair springs to it and then cover some part of the cavity with one of the turfs in this manner [and here Milles drew a horizontal line across the upturned L] but so the light may appear at each end. These birds hop about from turf to turf, and when the least cloud eclipses the other end, they make towards it and are caught in the springs. These traps are laid in rows all over the downs, at the distance of two or three yards from each other. The owner of them goes round twice a day to examine and take out what birds are caught. One man has oftentimes a hundred dozen of these traps, by which all the neighbouring country is supplied with birds. They are sold here picked and trussed for about one shilling a dozen.

At first I found this story hard to credit but a book called *Highways and Byways in Sussex* confirms it, adding that the wheatears were not killed by the traps but remained within them, caught by the neck and unable to wriggle free, until the trapper – who was usually a shepherd – returned or someone who wanted what had become known as Sussex ortolan for supper took it and left a penny in its stead. During the eighteenth century the birds were hunted in such vast numbers that in midsummer the Downs appeared to have been ploughed on account of the abundance of upturned turfs, which were restored when what was left of the flock returned to Africa each autumn. By 1904, when *Highways and Byways* was published, the practice had fallen into abeyance, but the author, Edward Verrall Lucas, who was, it might be added, the biographer of Charles Lamb and a prodigious collector of pornography besides, is at pains to explain that larks and goldfinches were still hunted in their thousands on the Downs. To this end he describes a bizarre contraption called a *lark glass*, which had apparently once been popular in France and which I can't help but suspect he might have made up.

The lark glass was apparently made from a triangular length of wood about three feet long and a few inches deep and set with little shards of mirror, which was attached to an iron spindle and rapidly spun by means of a piece of string tugged by a trapper, who sat perhaps twenty yards from the device. The reflection from these revolving mirrors possessed 'a mysterious attraction for the larks, for they descend in great numbers from a considerable height in the air, hover over the spot, and suffer themselves to be shot at repeatedly without attempting to leave the field or to continue their course'.

This spectacle would without a doubt have intrigued Leonard Woolf, who once exploded a rocket in a field so as to watch a vast flock of starlings burst into the air, blacking out the sun. Perhaps I'd come back with a disco ball and see if revolving mirrors had retained their allure. As it was they were all about me: descending larks that dropped as if lowered on a string, wings horizontal, before plunging the last storey of air in one headlong forty-five-degree dive, rolling out all the while their unstoppered phrases of exultation. *Not gone yet*, they might have been saying, or *can't catch me*, for we are more careful with our wild birds now, banning the trapping of all but the most allegedly virulent of pests: the corvids, lesser black-backed gulls, Canadian geese, parakeets and feral pigeons, which may be shot or caught in nets or those cages known as Larsen traps, though these must be provided with food, a perch and water at all times, as well as being checked at least once daily, particularly if a decoy bird is being kept inside. The Wildlife and Countryside Act 1981 is explicit on this last matter, adding that all birds must be killed in a quick and humane manner and that 'Canada geese held captive prior to being killed must be killed out of sight of other captive birds of the same species', a nicety that is not extended to the sociable crow or rook.

As I climbed on up the slope, I remembered a poem by Raymond Carver about a decoy bird, a wing-tipped goose that's kept imprisoned in a barrel by a farmer with ruined skin whose fields are filled with blighted barley. It's fed all the wheat it can eat and in return it acts as an unwitting lure for other geese, which flock so closely round that the farmer can almost touch their feathers before he guns them down. The narrator of the poem, who has wandered onto the farm while shooting with a friend, looks down into the stinking barrel and never forgets what he sees. The goose stays with him all his life; an emblem, if a living creature can ever be so reduced, of betrayal and loss and need.

There's something about this poem that makes me think the goose was real, though not everything Carver described in his tight drawl was true. It was written in the 1980s, a few years before he died, so even if it was it must also be dead by now. Perhaps it's been replaced. Or perhaps the farmer went bankrupt or died himself, in a shooting accident or from the same disease that ring-barked his hands. Either way, it sounds an echo with another bird, this one caught on the page by Hemingway: the crippled green-headed drake trapped at the end of *Across the River and into the Trees*. This mallard is brought by the dog Bobby to the duck-hunters' boat, 'intact and sound and beautiful to hold, and with his heart beating and his captured, hopeless eyes'. The Colonel places him in a burlap bag in the bows, to be kept as a caller or released in the spring, and though it's the Colonel who dies at the close of the book it's this imprisoned, helpless bird that remains in the reader's mind as the lasting symbol of any living creature's vulnerability in this world.

In the brief lives of birds man finds a parallel for his own condition, and nowhere has this been achieved with more force than by the monk Bede, who spent his days in a monastery in Northumberland praying and writing and calculating the true date of Easter, and who once compared the existence of man to that of a sparrow. The scene occurs during an account of the pagan King Edwin's conversion to Christianity in *A History of the English Church and People* and it must stand as one of the most beautiful speeches in the language, though I might add that I like its purpose not a bit.

> The present life of man upon earth, O king, seems to me in comparison with that time which is unknown to us like the swift flight of a sparrow through the mead-hall where you sit at supper in winter with your ealdormen and thanes, while the fire blazes in the midst and the hall is warmed, but the wintry storms of rain or snow are raging abroad.

> The sparrow, flying in at one door and immediately out at another, whilst he is within, is safe from the wintry tempest, but after a short space of fair weather, he immediately vanishes out of your sight, passing from winter to winter again. So this life of man appears for a little while, but of what is to follow or what went before we know nothing at all. If, therefore, this new doctrine tells us something more certain, it seems justly to be followed in our kingdom.

Passing from winter to winter again. Aye, that seems about the size of it. We're set down here with no more clue than a sparrow or a lark, arising out of darkness into light and with the knowledge that we may wink out at any time. One thousand two hundred and seventy-four years have passed since Bede died in his Northumbrian monastery, and still we are no nearer to knowing what is to follow or what went before we appeared, each one of us, on this spinning earth.

Bede used this fearful state of affairs to counsel faith in God. Throughout his life, Leonard Woolf preached the opposite creed, and it's not perhaps surprising that he has also employed animals to do so, for he loved them deeply and was rarely without at least a cat or a dog. His own philosophy – *nothing matters* – embraced the darkness that followed life, and he thought belief in the false machinery of heaven an act of cowardice. In *Growing*, he describes a menagerie he kept in Ceylon, and the memory of this fine collection of beasts, which included a pack of dogs, a baby leopard and a deer with a pronounced taste for tobacco, sparks one of his fiercest disavowals of the existence of an afterlife:

> I do not think that from the human point of view there is any sense in the universe if you face it with the gloves and the tinted spectacles off, but it is obvious that messiahs, prophets, Buddhas, Gods and Sons of Gods, philosophers, by confining their attention to man, have invented the most elaborate cosmological fantasies which have satisfied or deceived millions of people about the meaning of their universe and their own position in it. But the moment you try to fit into these fantasies my cat, my dog, my leopard, my marmoset, with their strange minds, fears, affections – their souls if there is such a thing as a soul – you see that they make nonsense of all philosophies and religions.

As for Bede and his *elaborate cosmological fantasies*, elsewhere in his *History* he takes up the story of a Northumbrian man from Cunningham, who fell sick and while lying near death in his bed was transported – or so he claimed – to the furnaces of hell and thence to the fields of heaven. After receiving this vision the man recovered, much to the amazement of his relations, and became a monk, though until then he had been married. In the remaining years allotted him he liked to retell this tale for its pedagogical value, describing to his audiences the torments and delights that awaited them after death. His hell I couldn't remember, but his heaven stayed with me, perhaps because it seemed so intensely familiar. It had the appearance, he related, of 'a very broad and pleasant meadow, so filled with the scent of spring flowers that its wonderful fragrance quickly dispelled all the stench of the gloomy furnace that had overcome me. Such was the light flooding all this place that it seemed greater than the brightness of daylight or of the sun's rays at noon.'

I'd gained a hell of a height in the last few minutes, ascending to a hedge full of wild clematis, flowering blackberry and the last few racemes of elderflower, the petals crisp and brown where they'd once been daubed with curds of pollen. In amongst the larger plants were tendrils of long-stalked cranesbill, its leaves a bloody pink, and greater stitchwort, which fell among the darker foliage in a shower of white stars. It was very warm, and I threw my pack down and walked unencumbered to where the ground fell away. There was the Weald, blue-shadowed, and from it came the river, though all I could see of it were two snatches of false blue, the colour borrowed from the sky, which is itself composed of nothing more than gas and scattered light.

There is no possibility of permanent tenancy on this circling planet. It isn't part of the deal. And though I know no more than Bede, I'll wager there aren't any sunlight fields waiting *without and beyond*, and that should one reach them one would anyway doubtless find, like the warrior Achilles, that it's better to be the meanest ploughboy on this green earth than emperor of all the dead. This is it, this brief wheeling life, and between darkness and darkness the light of noon fell on the real, withering blooms with which the chalk had been festooned, and then, as I reached the crest of the hill, it fell on the rolling breakers of the English Channel, which had been lent for that moment the blue of heaven; the colour, as Derek Jarman said in his film *Blue*, of the terrestrial paradise.

VIII

SALVAGE

THERE WAS A RAT ON THE road down to Piddinghoe, resting on its side, paws tucked primly beneath its chin. It must, I thought, stooping to examine it, have been killed very recently, though I could see no marks of injury upon it. It looked in the pink of health, coat gleaming, black eyes unveiled by the scrim that shortly follows death. A few yards on I found another, thoroughly mangled and reeking to high heaven. They were prodigiously large rats and I wondered if they might be related, if the first glossy individual had been killed while mourning at the grave of a parent or a spouse, though it seemed more likely that it had been feasting upon the corpse when a car swung round the corner and sent it voyaging through the air.

I took the low path to the river, skirting the village and coming out by Piddinghoe boatyard. An old man in a blue shirt was sitting on a deckchair there, eating a sandwich from a plastic tub. As I drew closer I heard him say *Mullet. Looks to me like they're feeding in the mud*. He was speaking to a couple standing a little back from the water and as I passed the other man laughed and said *You been catching them all before I got here.* They stood companionably in silence for a while and then began to swap fishing tips, in the slow, halting way that elderly men pass time together. I couldn't hear all that was said, but some sentences or parts of sentences lifted my way as the first man baited his hook and swung his line into the calm uprushing water. *I was after the bass. I use a little –* but this word was unintelligible – *and catch mullet with a fly. I was getting them at Beddingham, on the river there. Beddingham Reach? Yeah, I sometimes pick up tiny bass on fly. I've never picked up a really decent one on the river. Thought we'd give bread a try today. What I normally do, I use white maggot.* The woman interjected here, laughing meaninglessly, and then they took their leave, calling *Might see you again, bye now* as they lugged their own rods up the path.

Big pale clouds were riding overhead, sculpted into scoops that hardened as I watched into cumulonimbi with their threat of thunder. There was a funny riddle about Piddinghoe that I wanted to remember. Something about magpies. Yes, that was it: they shod magpies, fished for moonshine and hung their ponds out to dry. Magpies, it is supposed, were the local pied cattle and hanging the ponds out relates to the process of making whitewash from chalk. As for fishing for moonshine, it derives from one of those rustic excuses used by locals when found with smugglers' booty. The longer village version tells of a shepherd caught in the act of pulling barrels of pilfered brandy from one of the dewponds that pit the Downs hereabouts. When challenged by the Excise men he cried *The moon be drowning, I must fish her out* and with this declaration of idiocy succeeded in saving both himself and the booze.

Piddinghoe used to be an isolated little place, in which the main trade was brickmaking, but Newhaven is sweeping ever nearer and the village has long since lost the brickyard, and with it the cobbler and blacksmith, the Royal Inn and the Royal Oak, with only the boatyard to preserve it from becoming little more than a commuters' outpost. The river was changing too. Three red cranes rose behind Denton and beneath them the suburbs had come into view, the hills covered with the creep of houses that Virginia Woolf once railed against, calling them 'spot & rash & pimple & blister; with the incessant motor cars like active lice'. Discarded Coke bottles and crumbs of polystyrene were mixed in with seaweed on the shoreline, and above me a reddish kestrel held its place in the air, wings flexed; then, as the breeze turned, rowed fiercely forward for a beat or two before arcing back into its hunting stance.

What could it see among the bladder campion and knapweed, with those fine globed eyes? A mouse? A vole? A tiny and ferocious shrew, itself hard on the heels of a beetle or a slug? It is bedlam down there, in that part-visible world beneath our feet. A shrew sleeps for minutes at a time and if it doesn't eat twice its own body weight each day it will not survive the night. Imagine living with that kind of hunger: sixteen stone of meat to daily pillage and consume, your single set of teeth wearing to stumps; and when they break you're done for. *Allez-oop*. I gritted my own teeth. At least I had some oatcakes and the sweaty remains of last night's cheese.

The tide had turned while I'd been up on the hill and as I walked towards the cranes the light fell as it had all week on the tangled mirror of the grasses, to be absorbed or flung back to the sky. I could hear a grasshopper fidgeting its song and further out there was a siren testifying to some disorder in the human realm. It struck me as curious then, the idea of a whole town of people attending to their business, a whole town of people driving cars or walking the streets, their faces only partially betraying the magic lantern show that flares in utter privacy within the confines of each skull. Do animals think in these bright spools of colour, I sometimes wonder? Do they walk in their minds through landscapes known and unknown, both during waking hours and within the course of dreams? They do not replay conversations, or add great registers of numbers in their heads, but do they revisit past emotions or think on faces that have gone? It seems astonishing to me how alone man is, though he can touch and talk and gaze on others of his kind. But that picture theatre within his head: no one but he will ever see it played, and there is no medium on earth that can accurately catch its luminosity or speed.

It was the kind of thought I had frequently in the bleak months in Brighton after Matthew had left, when it began to occur to me that the whole story of love might be nothing more than a wicked lie; that simply sleeping beside another body night after night gives no express right of entry to the interior world of their thoughts or dreams; that we are separate in the end whatever contrary illusions we may cherish; and that this miserable truth might as well be faced, since it will be dinned into one, like it or not, by the attritions of time if not by the failings of those we hold dear. I wasn't so bitter now. I'd begun to emerge into a sense of satisfaction with my lot, but it would be a long time before I trusted someone, for I'd seen how essentially unknowable even the best loved might prove to be.

I'd begun to enter, as I thought these dark things, into the fringes of the port, an industrial no-man's-land where things in transport were briefly processed or broken into constituent parts. There was a wharf on the far bank and a swooping oystercatcher drew my eye to a building site populated by figures in fluorescent jackets and the red, yellow and white hardhats of Lego men. They had a radio with them but as I tried to make out the song more oystercatchers rose into the air and by the time their clear *pew pew* had passed the music was gone. A fleet of Palletline trucks was parked by the site, and beyond it a scrap-yard filled with crunched-up cars and glittering mountains of rusting metal gave off in the light the same black-gold glint as the owl's pellet I'd found in the wheat. I couldn't make head nor tail of this place, which was furnished with all manner of funnels, chutes and holding tanks. It looked as if it had been abandoned, the machinery branny with dust, but I mistrusted my perception, for I was on the wrong side of the water and gazing towards the sun. These places that are outside the human scale maintain anyway their own kind of invisibility: the eye drifts past them; their purpose is mystifying and their workings hard to name.

The path on my own side of the river had been travelling alongside a patch of wild or waste ground that the map reported was a disused refuse tip, but the land came to an abrupt end then and beyond the Yorkshire fog and the blackening skeletons of cow parsley was a broad lead-coloured side channel filled with gipsyish ranks of trawlers and barges. Many of the boats had peeling paint or were patched with sheets of blue tarpaulin slung over ruined cabins, but despite this air of decay the place was jumping. I passed a woman sprawled on the deck of a house-boat, smoking a cigarette while a black dog stretched out beside her, and further back I could see other people fiddling with painters or resting dreamily in the sun. A man in a red dinghy had got stuck in the open water between two pontoons and was turning an engine that refused to catch. After a few spluttering tugs he gave it up in disgust and began paddling in with a single oar. A boat! Why didn't I have a boat? I began to pick out my favourites, settling at last on a little white trawler with four blue portholes and a dinghy tied up at its bow. Dreaming away like this – sleeping in a cabin! Scrambled egg for breakfast! – I walked almost directly into a massively pumped-up man with two Rottweilers whose necks were almost as broad as his. *Sorry*, I mumbled, and he bowed his head magnanimously at me, like a politician or a king.

The channel must have been one of those old loops of the river that the navvies had sliced through, creating Denton Island. Boys in sports shirts were playing football on the bank, and the noise of their shouts and the barks of the dogs mixed up with the clattering stays of the boats seemed so pure a distillation of the place that I thought I would know it blindfolded. The Ouse Way, which I was still loyally following, left the water then and turned up a road lined with various river-businesses: Cantell and

Son, which proclaimed *boat repairs, moorings and ship chandlers*; Blakes Approved Osmosis Centre with its window full of red and white buoys; Newbury Engineering, *boat builders*; and among them Bridge Press, *fine lithographic printers*. Opposite these sheds and barns were the backs of council houses, and the path all of a sudden ducked between them, running up an alley between the yards.

I didn't like this alley, but it plunged out dutifully enough onto the edge of the dual carriageway, where pink valerian was growing flyblown in the verge. I'd come out at the other end of the loop, where the channel rejoined the river. There were two tanned barefoot boys in swimming trunks standing on the bridge to Denton Island, one slender and one very fat, and as I watched the first one leapt from the railing into the muddied river and swam to the bank in a speedy, splashy crawl. The fat boy hopped off too, landing with an almighty whump, and then a girl climbed up, dressed in shorts, a T-shirt and mismatched fluorescent green and pink wetsuit boots. The second boy struggled up the bank, yelling *Do you want me to stand next to you?* but his chivalry was misplaced, for she toppled as effortlessly as a marsh frog into the murkish water.

I crossed the Ouse on the wide road bridge that opens twice daily to let the boats in and out. I hardly knew it now: an industrial river, dark as oil, its surface opaque and unrevealing. There was a hideous sculpture of a cormorant on the seaward side, planted on a ramshackle jetty with its wings splayed up to the sun. The ferry from Dieppe docked just past it, and it was here that Louis Philippe, the last king of France, arrived in exile after his abdication on 6 March 1848, travelling with his wife under the name of Mr and Mrs Smith. They stayed in the Bridge Hotel, eating what *The Times* recorded to have been an enormous breakfast, and then were borne off by the local aristocracy to complete their days in genteel decline. 'The Orleans family in England are literally in poverty,' wrote Victor Hugo. 'They are twenty-two at table and drink water.' Louis Philippe had been a profligate king and his property in France was held against his debts, which, Hugo adds, included 70,000 francs to his market gardener for butter. All the court had managed to salvage were their clothes and a little jewellery, and even this was a tortuous process.

> Three long tables were placed in the theatre of the Tuileries, and on these were laid out all that the revolutionists of February had turned over to the governor of the Tuileries, M. Durand Saint-Amand. It formed a queer medley – court costumes stained and torn, grand cordons of the Legion of Honour that had been trailed through the mud, stars of foreign orders, swords, diamond crowns, pearl necklaces, a collar of the Golden Fleece, etc. Each legal representative of the princes, an aide-de-camp or secretary, took what he recognised. It appears that on the whole little was recovered. The Duke de Nemours merely asked for some linen and in particular his heavy-soled shoes.

It was hotter now, and I was becoming irritable and hungry. I wanted to get to the beach, strip off my damp clothes and swim, and after that I wanted a nice fat sandwich and a bottle of beer. There'd be cafés in Seaford, surely, or perhaps a little bar: I'd stop there at the end of the road and toast a journey done. So I didn't go into Newhaven; I set my teeth against it and turned instead east, following the Ouse Way towards the old river course that led along Seaford beach. On the map it seemed simple enough: swing down Beach Road to Newhaven Harbour station and pick up the path as it runs parallel to the sea. But Beach Road dropped through a stretch of dingy terraces with blank, unscrubbed windows into a desolate hinterland as entrapping as a bad dream. I passed a brutal-looking pub, named, presumably in honour of John Smeaton, The Engineer. There was a Parker pen factory, two car yards, and then a row of shuttered office blocks and workshops that might have been abandoned on Friday at six o'clock or decades earlier. Those empty buildings spooked me. I couldn't help feeling that I was being watched from somewhere, though I saw no one except two men in a black Subaru that twice cruised leisurely past. I went on unwillingly to the station, but faced with a chain-link fence and beyond it a holding pen of lorries I lost my nerve. There *couldn't* be a path down there. I turned round sharply and retraced my steps.

Back at the A259 I slumped beneath a dwarf hawthorn and looked seriously at the map. There seemed to be another path I could take, which joined the unfindable one by cutting through a corner of the nature reserve. Fine. I went back down Beach Road, hot and self-conscious and by now furious with myself. And sure enough I couldn't find that one either. I didn't want to look at the map again in front of these peeling houses, their front yards sprouting dense upswells of bindweed, and so as a last resort I turned despairingly through the grounds of a primary school and found behind it a path that ran through scrubby woodland in what I hoped was the right direction.

It didn't feel any safer than the street, for all that it was green. The sense of enclosure that had so unnerved me was echoed by the screening trees, and in the end I swallowed my pride and ran pell-mell under low vaults of sycamore and hazel, the trees so tightly fretted together that beneath them it was almost dusk. I burst out, sweating, onto the marsh, but my relief didn't last a minute. It wasn't the path I wanted, not *at all*. I'd come too far north, and now I was stuck, for there was half a mile of impenetrable reedbeds between me and the sea.

Damn it. I pulled off my rucksack and kicked it. Then I retrieved the water bottle and glugged down a few warm gulps. This must be the Ouse Estuary nature reserve, for it was furnished with benches, cycle tracks and gapped screens of wood that I assumed were for watching birds. It had been established a few years back in one of those compromises brokered between environment and industry, to offset the impact of an access road and a business park. The marsh, which despite ten centuries of drainage schemes remained predisposed to mud, was furthermore used as a washland when the river rose too high, reducing the risk of floods in Newhaven and pleasing the waders besides. A flood! It hadn't rained for weeks. The ground was bone dry and the reeds in their dank beds dipped and rose like a rusty ocean, the papery leaves brushing against one another and releasing a fricative hissing that also mimicked the sea. Yup, I was well and truly trapped. The only way out was to walk up to the road and follow it round to the Tide Mills car park. I looked across the reeds to where the ruins were and saw an ominous glitter. A midsummer Saturday. It was going to be hell.

The reserve was full of joggers and cyclists, a leisured drift of people moving aimlessly and at great speed. I stumped through them, cursing under my breath, then served a purgatorial sentence at the side of the A259 before turning at last up the seaward track. Both the car parks were full, and more cars were parked at random on the verge. The ground was wilder now, the brome and wild barley growing in spreading waves interspersed with bright spurs of dock and mallow. Already I could see broken walls rising to the height of a man above the tangles of vegetation, and beyond them a muddy channel surmounted by a shingle bank, a trickle of water puddling at its base. The shattered houses were made from flint, as was the custom in these parts, and here and there it was still possible to make out where doors or windows must once have been. This was all that remained of the abandoned village of Tide Mills, which was built in the eighteenth century and was once the largest of its kind in Europe, housing more than a hundred mill workers and producing at its height perhaps 1,500 sacks of flour a week.

To understand this lost place it is necessary to return for a moment to the shifting history of the Ouse, for Tide Mills was always at the mercy of water. In the medieval period, the relentless longshore drift that afflicts this coast created a shingle spit that choked the river's mouth and forced it eastward to Seaford through the marshy beach. Later, in the reign of Henry VIII, local landowners made the cut at Newhaven that transformed the little village of Meeching into today's thriving port. It didn't take long for this new channel to fail, however, largely because some fool set the pier on the eastern flank, where it was helpless to prevent the glutting flux of shingle. The land hereabouts returned to marsh and the river pried a new outfall that passed again right through the beach. Though the cut was eventually repaired and a more useful pier produced, this twisting creek persisted, and in 1761 the mill was built on its banks, powered by the waves, with the creek serving as a route for the barges that hauled in corn and lugged out flour. Under the auspices of the charismatic William Catt the place thrived, and it's said that he travelled more than once to France to advise Louis Philippe, then still in possession of his crown, on the development of similar schemes.

The decline began with the repeal of the Corn Laws in 1846. A few years later Catt died and two decades on, during a terrible storm, the sea flooded the village, devastating the houses and causing irreparable damage to the mill. In 1883 another storm finished the job, smashing the sails to pieces, and the following year the railway reached Newhaven. The Railway Company took possession of the harbour and established an immigration facility on the East Quay, right where the creek split off from the river. Sluice gates were built to let the water trickle through but there was no possibility of a barge getting by, and so the mill closed for good and began the first of its new incarnations as a home for railway workers.

Later, it was converted into a racing stables and then a hospital for boys with polio and rickets. At the start of the Second World War the families who still inhabited the place – the Jenners, Bakers, Larkins, Tubbs, Gearings, Thompsons, Watsons and Gates – were evicted and the buildings partially demolished as part of the Coastal Defence Strategy, in case German invaders should use it for shelter. During the 1940s Canadian troops practised street fighting amid the ruins and after the war was over the place was left to decay, the roofless chambers filling with shingle flung by the waves that over time spawned poppies and sports of windblown elder. I reckoned adders must have moved in by now, sunning themselves against walls where espaliered pears once grew, for one population will replace another in this world until the jig is up and the weeds cease to bloom.

In the past few years this process of decay had been arrested, if not exactly undone. Tide Mills became the subject of a research project by the Sussex Archaeological Society, and at the beginning of the millennium prisoners on probation were brought out under the auspices of English Heritage to clear the site, cutting back brambles and shifting shovelfuls of brown and blue and creamish stones to reveal the buildings' foundations. Later, local archaeologists began to assemble an archive of pictures and recollections that traced the incarnations of the village. In addition to the hospital and the mill there was a Marconi radio station here during the First World War, and a seaplane base that flew anti-submarine raids across the Channel.

A man had posted on the internet a collection of his grandfather's photographs from this latter place, melancholy pictures of planes whirring through sepia skies or coasting across dark waves. Most were backed onto paper and labelled in fountain pen and two recorded the shattered remains of a crash against a nearby breakwater, in which Lieutenants Cole and Kitchen both lost their lives. The photographer, Henry Ross Alderson, had also died young, killed in a motorcycle accident when he was thirty. There was a picture of him at the top of the page, a handsome man in a leather coat and flying goggles standing on the beach with his shadow spooling west. Some of his photos were taken from the air, and one showed a field of puffy cumulus captioned in capitals *Cloudland*: that unchartable realm man visited only in dreams until, cock-a-hoop, he contrived the balloon, the biplane and the Easyjet package.

I crossed by the blind end of the old millrace, a stagnant wallow that at high tide becomes a creek. Behind it was a shingle bank made of golden and flinty pebbles, some the colour of bread and some cracked open to reveal facets of gunmetal grey. The bank dropped sharply to reveal an army of people spread out across the stones, some furnished with fishing rods and some with those kites that can yank a man into the air. They had colonised the littoral zone, filling it with buckets and boogie boards, and they lay there calling to one another like a colony of walruses, their young skittering at their feet. The sea stretched heavenward beyond them, coloured the clarified blue-green of jelly. It was rougher than I'd expected, the waves high and sprayless. At *last*. I sat down on a railway sleeper, yanked off my trousers and jerked my swimsuit on, then abandoned the pack, shucked my sandals and darted in. The beach shelved abruptly. I was waist-deep in three steps; up to my neck in six. Then the ground fell away altogether and I floundered for a minute as the waves pummelled me, my skin stinging with cold. I pulled hard, and with every stroke the weight of water beneath me grew.

What a bay! What a day! I turned full circle, treading water, liking the way the land seemed to hold out two chalky arms to fend off or embrace the waves. I could see all the way to Seaford Head in the east, and in the west there were the two lighthouses that marked the mouth of the Ouse, gushing out into the Channel at a thousand tonnes a minute. There must have been the odd molecule drifting in these crashing waters that had travelled south beside me, working its way from the oak-shadowed source down the deep gulleys of Sheffield Park, across the gravel beds of Sharpsbridge, over the fish ladders at Barcombe Mills, past the wharves of Lewes and out through the maze-ways of the Brooks. I sniffed. Nope, not a trace of Wealden clay or rain: just salt, the pure bloom of it, and I kicked out my legs and wallowed there in joy.

The price came later, when I had to haul myself gracelessly up the pebbles and attempt to dry and dress without the aid of a towel. It wasn't a very dignified performance, but I managed not to reveal too much clammy flesh to an elderly gentleman with a panama hat who sat openly gawping from the top of the bank. There were two little girls playing by the water's edge, one screaming like a car alarm each time the waves splashed her feet.

The sea was very blue now, the colour dissolving into light

at its rim. Leonard Woolf used to swim down here during the Asham years, when he and Virginia were just beginning their married life. There was in those days a diving raft moored a little way from shore, and on 1 August 1914 he bicycled over from Asham, as was his custom that sweltering summer. It must have been a day rather like today, and Leonard swam out to the raft and dived from it far down into the sea. When he surfaced, he 'came up against a large man with a large red face who was swimming out from the beach. I apologised and he said to me, almost casually, "Do you know it's war?"' and so it was, though on account of the tremor in his hands Leonard didn't fight, but published books and worked in the service of the Labour Party, devoting himself to the cause of peace as his wife and the world unravelled. Poor Leonard. He was already convinced when he died in 1969 that the barbarians had smashed through the gate and I imagined him walking this beach in despair, his narrow shoulders stooped, for he loved mankind at large but was not so fond of their individual incarnations, sweating sunscreen with their shrieking spawn about them.

I rose then and turned away from the crowds, climbing to the top of the bank and picking my way into a shallow gully that muddled vaguely east. It was, I guessed, the remains of the Tide Mills creek, a dry riverbed that might carry a trickle when the winter seas ran high. I looked back to the shattered village, the houses subsiding into the shingle. There seemed to be something emblematic in the many fates of Tide Mills, a lesson that if I could only grasp it might stand me in good stead. But what struck me instead was a sense of foreshortening, as if my own time was already sinking out of view. If we could glimpse the people who will one day walk amidst our ruins – *Jenner, Baker, Larkin, Tubbs* – I think we would be paralysed, like the men on the island of the sirens – *Gearing, Thompson, Watson, Gates* – who sat in their flowering meadow unable to move a muscle or draw a breath until the hide rotted from their bones in strips. It's a mercy that time runs in one direction only, that we see the past but darkly and the future not at all. But we all have an inkling of what lies ahead, for against the ruins of the ages it is apparent that our time is nothing more than the passing of a shadow and that our lives – was it Derek Jarman who said this too? – run like sparks through the stubble.

The tenacity of our physical remains, their unwillingness to fully disappear, is at odds with whatever spark provides our animation, for the whereabouts of that after death is a mystery yet to be unpicked. What is this world, really? We're told we have infinite choice and yet there's so much that occurs beyond the perimeters of our command. We do not know why we're set down here and though we may choose the moment when we leave, not a single one of us can shift the position we've been assigned in time, nor bring back those we love once they have ceased to breathe. To reclaim the dead there's been invented no programme, no potion, no spell, not since Christ stood at the threshold of Lazarus's grave and ordered him *Come out*. The dead have gone to wherever they go and even now they forget our names, as Anticlea, the mother of Odysseus, is said to have done until she drank from the trench of sheep's blood that her son had poured and so recovered for a moment the semblance of a human heart.

These sound like cheerless thoughts, but they filled me with a strange exhilaration. *Nothing matters*, Leonard used to say, and then again, *everything matters*. Down in the riverbed, in this territory of vanishings, I might have been at loose in any time. The things that survived here did so against all odds, blooming into the teeth of the wind, amid the shifting beds of shingle. The plants rose from the stones like a conjurer's trick, working roots down into hidden pockets of sabulous soil: white and gold stonecrops with their flowers like stars; the spiked leaves and overblown petals of yellow horned poppy; great outcrops of sea kelp, the leaves whittled into extraordinary shapes by the relentless churnings of the air.

I crunched an apple as I strolled along. There wasn't a soul in sight, though I knew there were hordes of people beyond each ridge. I didn't want to go home, it was true, but I was nonetheless as purely happy as I've ever been right then, in that open passageway beneath the blue vault of sky, walking the measure allotted me, with winter on each side. There was a caravan park ahead, on the lee of one of the hills that rose above Seaford. The town was coming; there was no escaping it, and still I walked as if in a dream, among the larks and the valerian. I felt untethered, almost weightless, which is a consequence sometimes of swimming in the more buoyant waters of the sea. But it wasn't just that. I had the sense I'd fallen into some other world, adjacent to our own, and though I would at any moment be pitched back, I thought I might have grasped the knack of slipping to and fro. It struck me as funny then that I was walking at the grassy bottom of the old Ouse, and since no one could see me there's no one to say that I didn't turn at the last a few gay steps of a waltz, like the little people in Cherry of Zennor who danced their hearts out beneath the stream.

The path officially ended by the yacht club. An old couple were sitting on a bench there, watching the tide as it inched inexorably in. I greeted them and the man said *You're striding out faster than I could* and I wanted to say I've walked the whole river from beginning to end but I didn't, I smiled and I thought how friendly people were, when you met them as a stranger with a pack on your back. The thought of food was still propelling me and I went on up the esplanade to the edge of town. The beach was full of people swimming and fishing, a wall of pink and white bodies that ran all the way to Seaford Head. The heat was making my head spin, and my skin was crusted with salt. There were no cafés, though I walked on much further than I had planned. In the end I gave it up and bought a Mr Whippy that tasted faintly of strawberries and powerfully of vegetable fat. I hadn't eaten since breakfast, except a handful of oatcake crumbs and the apple, and I wondered as I licked it if this was the corollary to the pomegranate seeds that Hades spooned into Persephone's mouth, the food that would entrap me in the mortal realm. It had happened to Cherry, had it not, whose story ended with the words: *The sun rose, and there was Cherry seated on a granite stone, without a soul within miles of her. She cried until she was tired, and then she went home to Zennor, where they thought she was her own ghost returned.*

I climbed the steps to Bishopstone station just as the train to Brighton pulled in. There was no time to acclimatise. It was over. I was going home. I rested my head against the glass, looking out at the land I'd passed so slowly through. In the seat behind me a man with a puffy, sulky face was talking on a mobile phone. *I'll text you Parky's number*, he said. *Yes, I know Laurence, he went to Eton.* Outside the Downs had disappeared, obliterated by a swelling wall of thunderheads. The cloud was growing as I watched, banking up into headwalls and cornices and deep ice-blue gullies. It looked like the aftermath of an explosion, like the world beyond the hills had been bombed to smithereens. But that's how we go, is it not, between nothing and nothing, along this strip of life, where the ragworts nod in the repeating breeze? *Like a little strip of pavement above an abyss*, Virginia Woolf once said. And if she's right, then the only home we'll ever have is here. This is it, this spoiled earth. We crossed the river then and pulled away, and in the empty fields the lark still spilled its praise.

BIBLIOGRAPHY

THOUGH IN THE MAIN BOOKS have been organised according to the chapter in which they first appear, all background material referring to Virginia Woolf that isn't directly quoted in the text is, for the sake of coherence, listed under Chapter VI.

I CLEARING OUT

Conrad, Joseph, *Heart of Darkness* (Penguin, 1973, first published 1902)

Miłosz, Czeslaw, *New and Collected Poems 1931–2001* (Penguin, 2005)

Woolf, Virginia, *The Diary of Virginia Woolf*, eds. Anne Olivier Bell and Nigel Nicolson, 5 vols (Hogarth Press, 1978–84)

—— *The Letters of Virginia Woolf*, ed. Nigel Nicolson and Joanne Trautman, 6 vols (Hogarth Press, 1975–80)

II AT THE SOURCE

Anderson, Lorraine, ed., *Sisters of the Earth* (Vintage, 1991)

Auden, W.H., *Selected Poems* (Vintage, 1990)

Brook, Tony, 'The End of Mantell's Spine', in *Newsletter of the History of Geology Group of the Geological Society of London,* number 31, September 2007

Cadbury, Deborah, *The Dinosaur Hunters* (Fourth Estate, 2000)

Camden, William, *Camden's Britannia*, annotated and ed. Gordon J. Copley (Hutchinson, 1977, from the edition of 1789)

Cleere, Henry and Crossley, David, *The Iron Industry of the Weald* (Merton Priory Press, 1995, first published 1985)

Dealny, Mary Cecilia, *The Historical Geography of the Wealden Iron Industry* (Benn Brothers Ltd, 1921)

Edmonds, William, *The Iguanodon Mystery* (Kestrel Books, 1979)

Fitter, Richard, Fitter, Alastair and Blamey, Marjorie, *Wild Flowers of Britain and Northern Europe* (Collins, 1996, first published 1974)

Heaney, Seamus, *Selected Poems* (Faber, 1980)

Jarman, Derek, *Modern Nature* (Vintage, 1992)

—— *The Garden* (Thames & Hudson, 1995)

Jeffrey, David L., *A Dictionary of Biblical Tradition in English Literature* (Ethics & Public Policy Center, 1996)

Jenkins, Rhys, *The Rise and Fall of the Sussex Iron Industry* (transcript of a talk read at the Iron and Steel Institute, Westminster, on 27 January 1921)

Jones, David K.C., ed., *The Shaping of Southern England* (Academic Press, 1980)

Lloyd-Taylor, Arthur, *Wealden Iron and Worth* (1972, for private circulation)

Mantell, Gideon, *The Journal of Gideon Mantell*, ed. with an introduction and notes by E. Cecil Curwen (Oxford University Press, 1940)

McCarthy, Edna and 'Mac', *Sussex River: Journeys along the banks of the River Ouse: Seaford to Newhaven* (Lindel Organisation Ltd, 1975)

—— *Sussex River: Journeys along the banks of the River Ouse: Newhaven to Lewes* (Lindel Organisation Ltd, 1977)

—— *Sussex River: Upstream from Lewes to the Sources* (Lindel Organisation Ltd, 1979)

Owen, Terry and Anderson, Peter, *The Sussex Ouse Valley Way* (Per-Rambulations, 2005)

Parish, Reverend W.D., *A Dictionary of the Sussex Dialect* (Snake River Press, 2008, first published 1875)

Rose, Martial, ed., *The Wakefield Mystery Plays* (Norton, 1969)

Willard, Barbara, *Sussex* (Batsford, 1965)

Wooldridge, S.W. and Goldring, Frederick, *The Weald* (Collins, 1972, first published 1953)

Woolf, Virginia, *Between the Acts* (Penguin, 2000, first published Hogarth Press, 1941)

III GOING UNDER

Anon, 'Tom the Rhymer', in *The English and Scottish Popular Ballads Volume I*, collected by James Child (Houghton Mifflin, 1882)

Apuleius, *The Golden Ass*, trans. Robert Graves (Penguin, 1958)

Bede, *A History of the English Church and People*, trans. Leo Shirley-Price (Penguin, 1975, first published 1955)

— *Bede's Ecclesiastical History of the English People*, ed. B. Colgrave and R.A.B. Mynors (Oxford University Press, 1991)

Byatt, A.S., *The Children's Book* (Chatto & Windus, 2009)

Biggam, C.P., 'Whelk dyes and pigments in Anglo Saxon England', in *Anglo Saxon England*, vol. 35 (Cambridge University Press, 2006)

Brennan, Teresa and Jay, Martin, eds, *Vision in Context* (Routledge, 1996)

Cawley, A.C., ed., *Everyman and Medieval Miracle Plays* (Everyman, 1993, first published 1956)

Dante, *The Divine Comedy: Hell*, trans. Dorothy L. Sayers (Penguin, 1949, republished 1957)

Ehrlich, Paul, Dobkin, David and Wheye, Darryl, *The Birder's Handbook* (Simon & Schuster, 1988)

Grahame, Kenneth, *Pagan Papers* (General Books, 2009, first published 1893)

— *The Golden Age* (Aegypan Press, 2010, first published 1895)

— *The Wind in the Willows* (Egmont, 2006, first published 1908)

Graves, Robert, *Greek Myths*, 2 vols (Penguin, 1957)

Hékinian, Roger, Stoffers, Peter and Cheminée, Jean-Louis, *Oceanic Hotspots: intraplate submarine magmatism and tectonism* (Springer, 2004)

Henderson, George, *Vision and Image in Early Christian England* (Cambridge University Press, 1999)

Homer, *The Odyssey*, trans. S.H. Butcher and A. Lang (Macmillan, 1887)

Jeffries, Richard, *Landscape with Figures: An Anthology of Richard Jeffries's Prose*, ed. Richard Mabey (Penguin, 1983)

Prince, Alison, *An Innocent in the Wild Wood* (Allison & Busby, 1996)

Ramachandran, Vilayanur S. and Rogers-Ramachandran, Diane, 'How Blind Are We?' *Scientific American Mind* (June 2005)

Stace, Colin, *New Flora of the British Isles* (Cambridge University Press, 1997)

Thomas, Edward, *One Green Field* (Penguin, 2009, first published 1906 as *The Heart of England*)

Thompson, A.H., ed., *Bede: His life, times and writing* (Oxford University Press, 1935)

Virgil, *The Aeneid*, trans. Frederick Ahl (Oxford World's Classics, 2008)

Woolf, Virginia, *A Room of One's Own* (Flamingo, 1994, first published Hogarth Press, 1929)

— *The Common Reader* (Penguin, 1992, first published Hogarth Press, 1925)

IV WAKE

Adams, Tim, 'Marriage made in heaven', in the *Observer* (18 March 2001)

Amis, Martin, 'Age Will Win', in the *Guardian* (21 December 1991)

Bayley, John, *Iris: A Memoir of Iris Murdoch* (Duckworth, 1998)

Beamish, Tufton, *Battle Royal* (Frederick Muller, 1965)

Blaauw, W.H., *The Barons' War* (Nicholls & Son, 1844)

Carpenter, David, *The Battles of Lewes & Evesham 1264/65* (Mercia Publications, 1987)

Conradi, Peter J., *Iris* (HarperCollins, 2001)

Fleming, Barbara, *The Battle of Lewes 1264* (J&KH Publishing, 1999)

Labarge, Margaret Wade, *Simon de Montfort* (Cedric Chilvers, 1962)

Maddicott, J.R., *Simon de Montfort* (Cambridge University Press, 1994)

Murdoch, Iris, *The Sea, The Sea* (Vintage, 1999, first published Chatto, 1978)

Paris, Matthew, *Chronicles of Matthew Paris,* trans. Richard Vaughan (Sutton, 1984)

Powicke, Sir Maurice, Treharne, R.F. and Lemmon, Lt. Colonel Charles H., *The Battle of Lewes 1264: its place in English history* (published by the Friends of Lewes Society, 1964)

Sadler, John, *The Second Barons' War* (Pen & Sword, 2008)

Segal, J., 'Kleos and its Ironies', in *Reading the Odyssey*, ed. Seth L. Schein (Princeton University Press, 1996)

Turk, Tony, *A Victorian Diary of Newick 1875–1899* (Tony Turk, 1999)

Vaughan, Richard, *Chronicles of Matthew Paris* (Alan Sutton, 1984)

Waley, Daniel, 'Simon de Montfort and the historians', *Sussex Archaeological Collections 140* (Sussex Archaeological Society, 2002)

Woolf, Virginia, *Moments of Being*, ed. Jeanne Schulkind (Pimlico, 2002, first published Sussex University Press, 1976)

V IN THE FLOOD

Anon, *The Anglo-Saxon Chronicle*, trans. James Ingram (Echo Library, 2007, first published 1823)

Brandon, P.F., 'The Origin of Newhaven and the Drainage of the Lewes and

Laughton Levels', *Sussex Archaeological Collections CIX* (Sussex Archaeological Society, 1971)

Brandon, Peter, ed., *The South Saxons* (Phillimore 1978)

Brandon, Peter and Short, Brian, *The South East from AD 1000* (Longman, 1990)

Brook, Anthony, ed., *What on Earth is under Sussex?: A Series of Essays Exploring the History of Geology in Sussex* (*Journal of West Sussex History* 77, 2009)

Browne, Thomas, *Hydrotaphia and the Garden of Cyrus*, ed. W.A. Greenhill (Macmillan, 1929, first published 1895)

Cavafy, C.P., *The Collected Poems*, trans. Evangelos Sachperoglou (Oxford University Press, 2007)

Cracknell, Basil, *Outrageous Waves: Global Warming & Coastal Change in Britain through Two Thousand Years* (Phillimore, 2005)

Darby, H.C. and Campbell, E.M.J., eds, *The Domesday Geography of South-East England* (Cambridge University Press, 1962)

Dawson, Charles and Woodward, Arthur Smith, 'On the Discovery of a Palaeolithic Human Skull and Mandible in a Flint-bearing Gravel Overlying the Wealden (Hastings Beds) at Piltdown, Fletching (Sussex)', *Quarterly Journal of the Geological Society 1913*, vol. 69

Eddison, Jill and Green, Christopher, *Romney Marsh: Evolution, Occupation, Reclamation* (Oxford University Committee for Archaeology: Monograph 24, 1988)

Ellis, Sir H., 'Commissioners of Sewers for the Lewes Levels', *Sussex Archaeological Collections X* (Sussex Archaeological Society, 1858)

Environment Agency, *Adur and Ouse Catchment abstraction management strategy: Final strategy* (Environment Agency, 2005)

—— *Lewes Flood Report: March 2001* (Environment Agency, 2001)

Evans, Paul, 'Lost Horizons', in the *Guardian* (27 February 2008)

Fagan, Brian, *The Little Ice Age* (Basic Books, 2001)

Farrant, J.H., 'The Evolution of Newhaven Harbour and the Lower Ouse before 1800', *Sussex Archaeological Collections CX* (Sussex Archaeological Society, 1972)

Hallam, H.E., ed., *The Agrarian History of England and Wales Volume II, 1042–1350* (Cambridge University Press, 1988)

Hartley, Dorothy, *Water in England* (Macdonald, 1964)

Holford-Strevens, Leofranc, 'Sirens in Antiquity and the Middle Ages', in *Music of the Sirens*, eds. Linda Phyllis Austern and Inna Naroditskaya (Indiana University Press, 2006)

Houghton, John, *The Great River of Lewes* (printed by Parchment Ltd, 2002)
— *Unknown Lewes* (Tartarus Press, 1997)
Green, Peter, 'Finding Ithaca', in *New York Review of Books*, vol. 53, number 19 (2006)
Leslie, Kim and Short, Brian, eds., *An Historical Atlas of Sussex* (Phillimore, 1999)
Loyn, H.R., *Anglo-Saxon England and the Norman Conquest* (Longman, 1962)
Millar, Ronald, *The Piltdown Mystery* (S.B. Publications, 1998)
Rudling, David, ed., *The Archaeology of Sussex to AD 2000* (Heritage, 2003)
Russell, Miles, *Piltdown Man: The Secret Life of Charles Dawson* (Tempus, 2003)
Thomas, Andy, *The Lewes Flood* (S.B. Publications, 2001)
Thorburn, Margaret, *The Lower Ouse Valley: A History of the Brookland* (Withy Books, 2007)
Weiner, J.S., *The Piltdown Forgery* (Oxford University Press, 2003, first published 1955)
Woolf, Virginia, *Greek & Latin Notebooks, 1907–1909*, unpublished (Monks House Papers, University of Sussex Special Collections)
— *Mrs Dalloway* (Penguin, 1992, first published Hogarth Press, 1925)

VI THE LADY VANISHES

Bell, Julian, 'Monk's House and the Woolfs', in *Virginia Woolf's Rodmell*, ed. Maire McQueeney (Rodmell Village Press, 1991)
Briggs, Julia, *Virginia Woolf: An Inner Life* (Penguin, 2006)
Brosnan, Leila, *Reading Virginia Woolf's Essays and Journalism* (Edinburgh University Press, 1999)
Caramagno, Thomas C., *The Flight of the Mind: Virginia Woolf's art and manic-depressive illness* (University of California Press, 1992)
Dillard, Annie, *Pilgrim at Tinker Creek* (Harper's Magazine Press, 1974)
Einsley, Loren, *The Immense Journey* (Vintage, 1957)
Hansen, Carol, *The Life and Death of Asham: Leonard and Virginia Woolf's Haunted House* (Cecil Woolf Bloomsbury Heritage Series, 2000)
Hughes, Ted, *Birthday Letters* (Faber, 1998)
Lee, Hermione, *Virginia Woolf* (Chatto & Windus, 1996)
— *The Novels of Virginia Woolf* (Methuen, 1977)
Light, Alison, *Mrs Woolf and the Servants* (Fig Tree, 2007)
Luckhurst, Nicola and Ravache, Martine, *Virginia Woolf in Camera* (Bloomsbury Heritage Series 31, 2001)

Luke, Helen M., *The Way of Woman* (Gill & Macmillan, 1995)

Nicolson, Nigel, *Virginia Woolf* (Weidenfeld & Nicolson, 2000)

Poole, Roger, *The Unknown Virginia Woolf* (Cambridge University Press, 1995, first published 1978)

Noble, Joan Russell, *Recollections of Virginia Woolf by her contemporaries* (Cardinal, 1989, first published Peter Owen, 1972)

Spatter, George and Parsons, Ian, *A Marriage of True Minds* (Hogarth Press, 1977)

Stape, J.H., ed., *Interviews and Recollections* (Macmillan, 1995)

Woolf, Leonard, *Sowing* (Hogarth Press, 1960)

— *Growing* (Hogarth Press, 1961)

— *Beginning Again* (Hogarth Press, 1964)

— *Downhill All the Way* (Hogarth Press, 1967)

— *The Journey Not the Arrival Matters* (Hogarth Press, 1969)

Woolf, Virginia, *The Voyage Out* (Duckworth, 1915)

— *Jacob's Room* (Penguin, 1992, first published Hogarth Press, 1922)

— *To the Lighthouse* (Penguin, 2000, first published Hogarth Press, 1925)

— *Orlando* (Penguin, 1970, first published Hogarth Press, 1928)

— *The Waves* (Vintage, 2004, first published Hogarth Press, 1931)

— *The Death of the Moth and other essays* (Hogarth Press, 1942)

— *The Moment and other essays* (Hogarth Press, 1947)

— *The Captain's Death Bed and other essays* (Hogarth Press, 1950)

— *Collected Essays*, 4 vols, ed. Leonard Woolf (Chatto & Windus, 1996–7)

— *The Complete Shorter Fiction*, ed. Susan Dick (Harvest, 1989)

— *Selected Short Stories*, ed. with an introduction and notes by Sandra Kemp (Penguin, 1993)

— *A Writer's Diary*, ed. Leonard Woolf (Hogarth Press, 1953)

— *The Platform of Time: Memoirs of Family and Friends* (Hesperus 2007, republished with new material, 2008)

— 'A Terrible Tragedy in a Duck Pond' (unpublished story, Monks House Papers, Special Collections, University of Sussex Library)

— 'Greek and Latin Studies' (unpublished notebook, Monks House Papers, Special Collections, University of Sussex)

— 'The Watering Place' (unpublished draft of Woolf's last story, Monks House Papers, Special Collections, University of Sussex Library)

Zwerdling, Alex, *Virginia Woolf and the Real World* (University of California Press, 1986)

VII BEDE'S SPARROW

Adamson, Judith, ed., *Love Letters: Leonard Woolf & Trekkie Ritchie Parsons 1941–1968* (Chatto & Windus, 2001)

Farrant, John, *Sussex Depicted: Views and Descriptions 1600–1800* (Sussex Record Society, vol. 85, 2001)

Glendinning, Victoria, *Leonard Woolf* (Simon & Schuster, 2006)

Hemingway, Ernest, *Across the River and into the Trees* (Penguin, 1966)

Jarman, Derek, *Chroma* (Chatto & Windus, 1994)

Lucas, Edward Verrall, *Highways and Byways of Sussex* (Macmillan, 1904)

Philip, Neil, ed., *Between Earth and Sky* (Penguin, 1984)

VIII SALVAGE

Hugo, Victor, *The Memoirs of Victor Hugo*, trans. John W. Harding (Bastian Books, 2008, first published 1899)

PERSONAL ACKNOWLEDGEMENTS

My thanks go first to Robert Macfarlane and Robert McCrum, both of whom have been instrumental in making this project possible and who have been unstintingly kind.

One of the great pleasures of writing this book has been conversing and corresponding with people far more knowledgeable than me. I should like to thank the following: Caroline Archer for putting me up at Navigation Cottage. Julian Barker for discussions on botany and greensand. John Bleach at the Sussex Archaeological Society for patiently explaining the topography of the Battle of Lewes, as well as drawing my attention to the bodies buried beneath the railway embankments. Ian Dunford at East Sussex Archaeology and Museums Partnership for answering endless archaeological queries. Anna Fewster for her brilliant take on Woolf's books. Alison Light, for directing me to two quotations I would not otherwise have found. Helen Macdonald for her beautiful map, as well as last-minute bird aid. The staff of the Berg

Collection at New York Public Library, Brighton Library, East Sussex County Records Office, Lewes Library, and the University of Sussex Library Special Collections, where, fortunately for me, much of the Woolf archive resides. Sarah Pearson, curator at the Hunterian Collection, for revealing the real fate of Gideon Mantell's spine. Will Pilfold and Margaret Pilkington at the River Ouse Project for answering my queries about washlands. Sam St Pierre at the Sussex Ouse Conservation Society. Liz Williams at the Railway Lands for helping with bird identification. Nathan Williams for his trove of folk songs and indigenous ballads.

I've been very lucky with my publishers, and owe a great debt of gratitude in particular to Nick Davies, my editor, whose enthusiasm, sensitivity and insight I've deeply appreciated. In addition, I'd like to thank all at Canongate, especially the wonderful Norah Perkins, and Annie Lee. I'm also very grateful to my agent Jessica Woollard and the staff at the Marsh Agency.

I've been blessed with an exceptional group of early readers, among them Robert Dickinson, Denise Laing, Euan Ferguson, Peter Laing, Elizabeth Day, Helen Macdonald and William Skidelsky: thank you all. A special mention must go to Jean Hannah Edelstein, publishing guide par excellence, who went beyond the call of duty in almost every respect. I'd also like to thank Stuart Croll, Clare Davies, Tom de Grunwald, Grace Dunford, Maud Freemantle, Tony Gammidge, Barbara Howden Richards, Kitty Laing, Robin McKie, Lili Stevens, and Carole and Charles Villiers for their interest and support, as well as Mat Ash, who first took me to the river.

Sins of error and omission are of course my own.

PERMISSIONS ACKNOWLEDGEMENTS

The author and the publisher would like to thank The Society of Authors as the Literary Representative of the Estate of Virginia Woolf, and The University of Sussex and The Society of Authors as the Literary Representative of the Estate of Leonard Woolf.

Extracts from *Moments of Being*, *The Diaries of Virginia Woolf* and *The Letters of Virginia Woolf* (edited by Nigel Nicolson and Joanne Trautmann), published by Hogarth Press, are reprinted by permission of Random House.

'The Diviner' by Seamus Heaney is reprinted by permission of Faber and Faber.

'In Praise of Limestone' by W.H. Auden, copyright © 1978, is reprinted by permission of The Estate of W. H. Auden.

'Ithaca' by C.P. Cavafy translated by E. Sachperoglou in *Cavafy: Collected Poems*, is reprinted by permission of Oxford University Press

'Luminous wise and deeply compassionate . . .
a fierce and essential work'
Helen Macdonald, author of *H is for Hawk*

CANON GATE

The Canons are books without boundaries.
Some are classics already, the rest will be soon.

'Beguiling, beautifully written . . . brilliant and original'
John Carey, *The Sunday Times*

CANONGATE

‘My book of a lifetime, my book for these dark times, an antidote to stupidity, cruelty and oppression of all kinds’
Olivia Laing